Faith & Reason

The Cradle of Truth

Gerard M. Verschuuren

En Route Books and Media, LLC
5705 Rhodes Avenue
St. Louis, MO 63109

Cover credit: TJ Burdick

LCCN: 2017955136

Copyright © 2017 Gerard M. Verschuuren
All rights reserved.

ISBN-10: 0-9991143-8-7
ISBN-13: 978-0-9991143-8-4

Table of Contents

TABLE OF CONTENTS 3

PREFACE 5

1. **THE POWER OF REASON 7**
   a. Our Reasonable Nature 8
   b. Reasoning Explained 17
   c. Reasoning Overvalued 27
   d. Reasoning Undervalued 31

2. **THE POWER OF FAITH 39**
   a. Our Religious Nature 39
   b. Faith Explained 44
   c. Faith Overvalued 57
   d. Faith Undervalued 64

3. **FAITH AND REASON 73**
   a. Not Reason-Alone as in Rationalism 74
   b. Not Faith-Alone as in Fideism 81
   c. No Double Truth 88
   d. Proofs for God's Existence 102

4. **NATURAL THEOLOGY 117**
   a. God Is All-Present 123
   b. God Is All-Knowing 127
   c. God Is All-Powerful 131

5. **DOGMATIC THEOLOGY 141**
   a. Holy Trinity 143

    b. Incarnation 147
    c. Providence 151
    d. Suffering 158
    e. Salvation 170
    f. Predestination 177
    g. Dogma... 184

6. **MORALITY AND REASON** 195
    a. The Basis of Morality.................................... 196
    b. The Natural Law 205
    c. Moral Law Essentials 210

7. **MORALITY AND FAITH** 221
    a. Faith, not Science 221
    b. From Heaven 229
    c. Moral Conscience 234
    d. Moral Blindness...238

8. **SCIENCE AND REASON** 243
    a. Inductive Reasoning......................................244
    b. Deductive Reasoning....................................248
    c. The Problem of Causality 254

9. **SCIENCE AND FAITH** 263
    a. Against Scientism..263
    b. Faith as the Cradle of Science 271
    c. The Catholic Roots of Science 278

10. **INDEX** 289

ENDORSEMENTS... 295

ABOUT THE AUTHOR 297

Preface

Of course, it's a travesty, but a very widely held one. We all have heard how some people caricature religious believers. On weekdays, they are critical, want proofs, look for arguments, and believe something only if there is no further doubt. Then, on Sundays, they turn a switch, set their understanding to zero and their gaze on infinity; they need no proofs, they open their mouths and swallow revealed truths and absurd dogmas. The contrast painted in this parody is clear: Religious believers live a schizophrenic life. It is the life of *reason* on weekdays and the life of *faith* on Sundays.

The underlying assumption is also clear: Reason is objective, scientific, and verifiable, while faith is subjective, personal, and irrational, even bordering on mania or madness—they just can't go together. This perceived contrast cannot be true, though. It is based on distorted and shallow concepts of faith, reason, and the differences between the two, as we will see in this book.

On the one hand, we can't be asked to accept in faith what we can't understand, can we? God gave us brains and expects us to use them to understand even the mysteries of faith, to the extent such understanding is possible. So faith must have something to do with reason.

On the other hand, we can't be asked to put all faith aside either, can we? Reason itself depends on faith: faith in our senses, faith in our intellect, faith in our memories, and faith in what others have discovered. Besides, there is more to life than reason. Faith can cover issues that science and rationality are inherently incapable of addressing, but that are nevertheless entirely real. Seen this way, faith provides answers to questions that would otherwise be unanswerable. So reason must have something to do with faith.

This means that "weekdays" and "Sundays" cannot be disconnected from each other, as the caricature suggests. They should be in close harmony—the harmony of faith and reason. The Boston College philosopher Peter Kreeft uses the following analogy: "Walking to the beach is like reason and swimming is like faith. You have to go to the place where you can swim before you can swim. And you have to go to the place where you can believe before you can believe." In other words, reason takes us to the water so we can swim in faith. But while swimming, every once in a while, we need to go back to the beach of reason to get our footing back. That's the "back-and-forth" of faith and reason.

This reciprocal relationship between faith and reason has been a constant theme in Catholic intellectual history, and it explains why the Catholic intellectual tradition is so rich, strong and full, perhaps unlike anything else in the world. In his famous Regensburg address and elsewhere, Pope Benedict XVI stressed the perennial relevance of Pope John Paul II's encyclical *Fides et Ratio* (Faith and Reason) and the need for Faith to purify Reason, and for Reason to purify Faith. The question is how to make this happen and why it has become necessary more than ever to stress their connection and mutual relevance. Let this book be your guide in answering the many questions you might have.

1. The Power of Reason

There is not one person who doesn't reason. In everyone's life, there are numerous moments we do some kind of reasoning. We decide to go to the store in the morning because we have an appointment somewhere else in the afternoon. It may not be a sophisticated kind of reasoning, but it is based on the "reasonable" assumption that we cannot be at two different places at the same time. Sometimes, we reason in a much fancier way: each time we are exposed to someone's sneezing, we develop cold-like symptoms, so we come to the conclusion we should shun sneezers or take medication. Or take this one: individuals left to themselves cannot realize all the good things they might otherwise obtain, therefore they must live and work with others. That was the way of reasoning of a famous philosopher, Aristotle.

As a matter of fact, each time we engage in a discussion or dispute, we use reasoning to defend our position or to explain why we disagree with the position of others. Each time we look for any kind of explanation, we are in search of some form of reasoning. Aristotle once came up with the following line of reasoning: since it is the interposition of the earth that causes a lunar eclipse, the form of this line will be caused by the form of the earth's surface, which is therefore spherical—and not flat (*On the Heavens*, Book II, Chapter 14). Thanks to reasoning, he was far ahead of his time without any fancy research. That's just another simple example of what reasoning can do for us.

a. Our Reasonable Nature

Given our nature of reasoning, it makes sense then that we categorize one another as members of the species *Homo sapiens*—where "sapiens" stands for "wise" or "intelligent." More specifically, St. Thomas Aquinas calls a human being *animal rationale*—a term that more accurately defines us as animals that use reason [*ratio*]. Rationality is our hall mark. Our capacity for reasoning sets us apart from the rest of the animal world. Pope John Paul II, in his Encyclical *Fides et Ratio* ("Faith and Reason", 64), went even as far as saying, "the human being is by nature a philosopher."

Rationality is our capacity to make rational judgements and decisions (which does not mean, of course, we always think rationally!). In fact, it is rationality that gives us access to the world of truths and untruths—a world beyond our control. Rationality is our capacity for abstract thinking and having reasons for our thoughts, thus giving us access to the "unseen" world of thoughts, laws, and truths. We peer further back in time, and further into the future, than any other animal. No other species would ever think to ponder the age of the Universe, or how it will end. Weighing evidence and coming to a conclusion are rational activities par excellence. Reasoning leads us from one idea to a related idea; it is a matter of pondering realities beyond that which we experience through our physical senses, thus allowing us to transcend the current situation through the mental power of reasoning. It is our gateway to truth.

Philosophical giants such as Aristotle and St. Thomas Aquinas would put it this way: all we know about the world comes through our physical senses but is then processed by the immaterial intellect that extracts from sensory experiences that which is *intelligible*. Well, it is the rationality of our intellect that makes the world intelligible and understandable; it gives us the power to comprehend the Universe through reasoning and to discover truths about this world. It is the mind's rationality that gives us access to the laws of nature and the structure of this Universe. Without rationality, we would not even know there are laws of nature. However, laws of nature have to be discovered, they are not invented; they are not just mental creations but must be anchored in reality and truth. Reason helps us to discover them.

The power of reasoning is uniquely human. Rationality does not exist in the rest of the animal world—in spite of contrary claims made by many evolutionists who believe that rationality came to us through genes developed in the course of evolution. So from now on, I will use the word "animal" only for nonhuman animals, for there is a deep divide between the two. Animals may be intelligent to a certain degree, but they certainly are not rational, reasoning beings. True, pets sometimes outsmart their owners when they play a whole repertoire of tricks on their owner's emotions—but that is a matter of intelligence at best, not intellect. When a dog avoids another dog that it was bitten by before, it does so because a material cause—a bite—makes the dog do so. It is a result of conditioning, not reasoning.

We ourselves can do the same, of course, after a dog's bite. But we also can show the same behavior after we have seen someone else being bitten by that dog. However, in the latter case we did not experience the material cause of a bite ourselves. Instead, we used reasoning. Our argument follows from a rational inference like this: animals exhibit patterns of behavior that are likely to be repeated; this dog has exhibited aggression towards someone who approached it; therefore, there is a good chance that the dog may exhibit the same behavior towards me if I approach it. In short, there is some immaterial cause involved, some form of reasoning. Animals drink because they are thirsty—that is not a mental reason but a material cause. Human beings, on the other hand, can drink because they have various kinds of reasons other than quenching their thirst.

More in general, it could be said that, although animals do have the capacity to sense and remember things, they lack understanding in the sense of asking questions, formulating concepts, framing propositions, and drawing conclusions. They show no signs of abstract reasoning or having reasons for their "thoughts" (if they have any); they do not think in terms of true and false; they do not think in terms of cause-and-effect with "if-then" statements and "if-and-only-if" statements. Instead, they are "moved" by motives, drives, instincts, emotions, stimuli, and training—but not by reasoning. In other words, animals do not have an intellect endowed with the faculty of rationality—regardless of their intelligence.

It is important to stress the difference between intelligence and intellect. Rationality is not a matter of intelligence but of *intellect*. Whereas intelligence can be graded on an IQ scale, intellect cannot. One can be intelligent to various degrees (or even intellectual to various degrees), but one cannot have intellect to various degrees. Since intelligence works only with perception of sense-data, animals may show various forms of intelligence in their behavior, because intelligence is a brain feature and as such an important tool in survival. We find spatial intelligence in pigeons and bats, social intelligence in wolves and monkeys, formal intelligence in apes and dolphins, practical intelligence in rats and ravens, to name just a few. Intelligence is a matter of processing sense-data—something even a robot can do by "cleverly" processing sounds, images, stimuli, signals, and the like.

Intellect is very different from this. Like intelligence, intellect also uses sense-data, but unlike intelligence, it changes perception into cognition. It does so by using mental concepts, which makes sensorial experiences intelligible for the human mind. The concept of gravity, for instance, helps us understand what happens around us when objects fall to the ground and planets orbit the sun. While reasoning allows us to move from one thing we know to another, the intellect can create concepts through which we are able to understand and know the world we live in. So this raises the question what a *concept* is.

A concept is the result of abstraction from what we have experienced through the senses. For instance, we have seen several round objects and then we abstract from this the concept of "circle." This concept is highly abstract. It is very unlikely that we ever encounter a perfect circle in this world, which means we do not really "see" a circle. Besides, the concept of circle does not include any specific size, whereas the "circular" objects around us do. True, we can visualize a circle without imagining any specific size, but concepts have a universality that images can never have. Therefore, the concept "circle" can be used for any specific circular object regardless of its size and its imperfections.

In addition, a concept has an intricate web of connections with other concepts—in case of a circle, for instance, with concepts such as "radius" and "diameter." Even a "simple" concept such as "green" or "greenness" has many connections to other concepts, which explains why green objects turn gray in twilight (the rod effect) and red when receding very quickly (the Doppler effect). As a result, concepts go far beyond what the senses provide—they transform "things" of the world into "objects" of knowledge, thus enabling us to see with our "mental eyes" what no physical eyes could ever see before.

No wonder then that concepts play a crucial role in how we know the world. Thanks to concepts, we can see similarities that are not immediately evident and not directly tied to what we perceive. Everyone can see things falling, but to perceive gravity one needs the concept of gravity in order to see what no one had been able to see before Isaac Newton. The concept of gravity allows us to "see," for example, the similarity between the motion of the moon and the fall of an apple. To take another example, biologists were not able to see the similarity in building blocks between animals and plants until the concept of a "cell" had been developed; neither could they see the similarity between leprosy and tuberculosis until the concept of "bacteria" had become available. Through concepts like these we are able to see similarities that would have eluded us if we didn't have those concepts. We do not really or directly perceive gravity, bacteria, cells, genes, circles, and the like, yet these concepts make the world more understandable and intelligible to us.

Some may object to all of this that we are making too much of concepts. Although they don't have intellect, aren't animals able to do the same thing with their intelligence? True, animals are able to see similarities by mere perception; that's how they can identify and recognize and categorize food, predators, and mating partners. So they may even be able to recognize a circle when presented with a circular object, which could be considered a simple form of abstraction. However, their seeming act of abstraction is closely tied to a perceptual act. Dogs, for instance, can only recognize a circle when presented with a circular object. We could call this "perceptual abstraction," because it is closely tied to actual perception. Humans, on the other hand, can also see similarities through concepts, even apart from any perceived object. Only human beings can think about a circle or about circularity in general, apart from any specific perceived object. That's what we do in geometry, for example. We could call this "conceptual abstraction" to distinguish it from "perceptual abstraction."

Conceptual perception and abstraction are unique to human beings. Concepts are our powerful tools to see similarities even when they are not directly visible. So when animals are able to see similarities too, that doesn't mean they use concepts. Some think, though, that they do. Their reasoning goes as follows: concepts classify things; animals classify things; therefore, animals use concepts. But this is an invalid, false argument—the conclusion of which does not logically follow from its two premises (see 1.b).

The difference there is between physical entities and mental concepts explains also that words can either be used as *signals* to refer to physical entities (such as concrete objects and situations), or they can be used as *symbols* to refer to mental entities (especially abstract concepts). Take, for instance, a word such as "poison": it can be a symbol referring to a concept that explains its nature and working, or it can be a signal on a label that alerts us not to take that stuff. This difference explains once more how the world of animals differs from the world of humans. Humans can use both signals and symbols, but animals can use only signals. Animals treat everything in their surroundings as signals that call for a direct response, but they cannot use concepts and reasoning to ponder realities beyond their needs for food and sex. They act mainly by "instinct," not by reasoning. Even when they use their intelligence, they do so without intellect. Let us explain this a bit further.

Many animals are able to communicate with each other through signals—just listen to birds on an early spring morning. However, signals are not symbols; those birds are having an exchange of signals, but not an exchange of ideas. Signals refer directly to a specific thing or situation, whereas concepts usually do not. When we train a dog to associate a command such as "The boss!" with its real boss, then the dog has been conditioned to respond to such a command by looking for the real boss. The command has become a *signal*. Signals depend on the actual presence of the "real thing"—for instance, due to associative conditioning through training. The dog has a physical image of its own boss, but it has no mental concept of what a "boss"—any boss, for that matter—is like. Humans, on the other hand, can use the word "boss" also as a *symbol*—a mental concept of "any boss." They often use that word to talk about what their own boss is like, or should be like—preferably only when their physical boss is not actually present. A signal calls for direct action, whereas a symbol calls for reasoning.

Consequently, it does not matter whether you train a dog with a command like "Here!" or a command like "Hector!" Dogs react the same way, not realizing the latter command refers to themselves. For animals, both commands work through association, but only humans know they are fundamentally different. Animals cannot make this distinction, so they treat everything in their surroundings as signals that call for an immediate response. Animals are "born positivists"—they take everything as a signal at face value. Humans, on the other hand, deal with things after making a "detour" through symbols and concepts; they extrapolate from what is seen to what is unseen; they can assign various conceptual interpretations to the things they see. They move from the world of sensible singulars (things, situations, and events) to the world of immaterial universals (concepts, symbols, and facts). That is the reason why *Homo sapiens* has also been called an *animal symbolicum*.

Apparently, symbols and concepts are part of our human capacity for reasoning. Whereas reasoning is pondering realities beyond that which is experienced through the senses, animals, in contrast, seem to live their lives entirely in the present, without having any thoughts about the past or the future—perhaps memories, but not thoughts, symbols, or interpretations. If pets have a pedigree, it is thanks to their owners; if they have birthdays, wish lists, appointments, or schedules, it is because their owners create those; and if they have graves, those were dug by their owners as well. Animals need food but never use reason or intellect to make their own food. Cats or dogs have never come up with the thought of going to the pet store and buying their own food, let alone of starting their own pet store.

When we look at things, we often tend to do so either in an anthropomorphic way or in a dehumanizing way. In the field of biology, for instance, the anthropomorphic approach makes animals look like humans-in-the-making; and the dehumanizing approach makes humans look like glorified animals. Something similar can be seen in the field of artificial intelligence: the anthropomorphic approach makes computers look like machines with a human mind; and the dehumanizing approach makes the human mind look like a computer. In either way, we are actually, and intentionally, ignoring or neglecting the specific differences between both sides of the equation—which makes either approach rather deceiving.

Since we are masters of anthropomorphism, we tend to think that animals have got to be like humans, even when the differences are the most obvious. If we have language, animals must have language too; if we have rationality, animals must have something like it; if we have intellect, animals must have it too; if we have moral rights, animals must have them as well; and the list goes on and on—to think differently is considered an unwarranted feeling of superiority. Since Aesop's *Fables*, talking animals have become very popular in literature. Donald Duck is one of the more recent inventions. But it was more in particular Charles Darwin who made us see human beings as "glorified animals," and animals as "humans in the making." Our inability to let animals be animals has something to do with our inability to let human beings be human beings.

However, the warped perception of anthropomorphism cannot obliterate the fact that there is an enormous disparity between them and us. Only humans are conscious of time; they can study the past, recognize the present, and anticipate the future; they even desire to transcend time, thinking about living forever. Only humans wonder "what caused or will cause what and why?" Only human beings have inquisitive minds asking questions such as "Where do we come from?" and "Why are we here?" Only humans have the capacity to be scholars and scientists; they can even study animals, whereas animals can only watch humans but never study them. Animals may look inquisitive but never are inquisitive. Humans are inquisitive, even if they don't look it.

Human beings are always in search of some kind of worldview or explanation of life—which certainly goes far beyond their need for food and sex. In short, human beings are questioning, reasoning beings; they are driven by rationality, which gives them the capacity to make rational decisions—without any guarantee, of course, that those decisions are always rational. In short, humans could not live without reason. From early childhood on, they never seem to tire of asking "Why?"

b. Reasoning Explained

Reasoning works basically with arguments. Arguments usually lead to conclusions based on some premises. Traditionally, arguments are divided into two different types, deductive and inductive. Although every argument involves the claim that its premises provide evidence for the truth of its conclusion, only a deductive argument involves the claim that its premises provide *conclusive* evidence. In deductive reasoning, premises and conclusion are so related that it is absolutely impossible for the premises to be true unless the conclusion is true as well. In other words, if the premises are true, then the conclusion *must* be true.

Here is a simple example of a valid deduction: (1) All humans are mortal. (Premise); (2) I am a human. (Premise); (C) I am mortal. (Conclusion follows from 1 & 2). This argument seems to be valid, since the truth of the premises would guarantee the truth of the conclusion. And the conclusion also seems to be truthful, since, in addition, the premises do seem to be true too.

Deductive arguments are most common in mathematics. Let's assume the following algebraic properties of equality: If $a=b$, then $a+c=b+c$ or $a-c=b-c$ or $a*c=b*c$. Now we can deductively solve the equation $5x - 18 = 3x + 2$ as follows: subtract $3x$ on both sides: $2x - 18 = 2$; then add 18 to both sides: $2x = 20$; and finally divide both sides by 2 to solve the equation: $x = 10$. The conclusion follows with certainty from the premises.

Deductive arguments are often also used outside the domain of mathematics. An example of this would be the following: since tests proved that it took at least 2.3 seconds to operate the bolt action on Lee Oswald's rifle, Oswald could not have fired three times to hit President John Kennedy twice and Texas Governor John Connally once in 5.6 seconds or less, for that would take $3 \times 2.3 = 6.9$ seconds. This seems to be a valid conclusion of the deductive type.

However, this argument uses another, hidden, premise that can easily be overlooked, namely that in the time it takes to fire three shots, it is only necessary to operate the bolt twice. So then the conclusion is no longer necessarily true. It turns out to be an example of faulty reasoning.

Hidden premises or assumptions more often than not put the conclusion of a deductive argument in jeopardy. Columbus, for instance, reasoned in a deductive way that the earth must be round as follows: as a ship sails away from shore, the upper portions of it remain visible to a watcher on land long after its lower parts have disappeared from view—so the earth must be round. But again, there is a hidden premise involved, which states that light rays follow a rectilinear path. If they followed a curved path, concave upwards, we would still see the same happening to the ship, even on a flat earth! So this argument only qualifies as deductive, leading to a conclusive conclusion, if we specify all the necessary premises involved and accept them as true. Perhaps, some of Columbus' sailors were still afraid to fall off the edge of the world.

An inductive argument, on the other hand, involves the claim that its premises provide *some* evidence for the truth of its conclusion, but no conclusive evidence. The truth of the conclusion does not follow necessarily from the truth of its premises. In other words, if the premises are true, then the conclusion *may* be true. Thus the conclusion is only probable, or probably true. Very often an inductive argument is an argument by analogy. For instance, we infer that we will enjoy reading a book by a certain author on the basis of having read and enjoyed other books by that author. We may find, however, that our favorite author's latest book is actually a bummer.

Yet, some inductive arguments by analogy are more cogent than others. The problem is that we need to find out first which similarities, or analogies, between certain cases are *relevant*. Imagine, you love pets and have repeatedly noticed that your dog and your cat have clear urine. You might think being a pet animal is the similarity that causes their urine to be clear. But that would mean your rabbit and your hamster should also produce clear urine, until you discover they actually have cloudy urine. What causes this difference in urine? You might come up with various kinds of explanations of why their urine differs. Well, it turns out that once you know that there are carnivores and herbivores, you have found the correct explanation for a difference in their urine. This step could not have been made without two new concepts: "herbivore" and "carnivore." There are those concepts again!

Apparently, reasoning is not always as easy as it may appear. For one thing, there are many potential flaws lying in wait. Collectively, they are referred to as *fallacies*. There are many different types of fallacies, but let's focus on only a few of them. Fallacies are more than mistaken ideas or false beliefs—they are incorrect arguments, errors in reasoning. Some are so obviously incorrect as to deceive no one; others may seem to be correct but prove, upon closer scrutiny, not to be so.

Some fallacies result from mere carelessness in our reasoning. An example would be: if everyone is special then no one is special anymore. What this "argument" is meant to convey is that no one is special, but instead it should say: then no one is special anymore in being special. Other fallacies are caused by some ambiguity in the language used to formulate an argument. This ambiguity leads to a slight, or not so slight, shift of meaning. Take this case: divorce is no longer news; no news is good news; hence, divorce is good news.

Then there are fallacies that violate logical rules. So-called if-then-statements are an example of this: if Y happens *because* of X, then Y must happen *after* X. But this cannot be reversed: if Y happens after X, then we cannot validly conclude that Y is the cause of X. Or take this example: You may feel better after taking some medication, but feeling better may not be caused by the medication. What we have here is the classic rule of "after this and yet not because of this" [*post hoc sed not propter hoc*]. They call it a sign of insanity to expect different results when repeating exactly the same actions over and over again, but it is actually poor logic.

Then there is *circular reasoning*. It is often of the following form: "X is true because Y is true; Y is true because X is true." An example would be: this product is great because its label says it is great; and the label says it is great because the product is great. The premises are just as much in need of proof or evidence as the conclusion, and as a consequence, the argument fails to persuade. Here is another case: there's no greater argument for the existence of God than the truth of his existence. There is no reason to accept the premise(s) unless one already believes the conclusion. A more famous example is the following: "Why do certain individuals survive? Because they are the fittest. How do we know they are the fittest? Because they survive." If fitness is defined in terms of survival, this amounts to a tautology. In other words, fitness has to be defined first in terms of something else than survival for the argument to work.

Circular reasoning is sometimes connected with circular causation. The problem of circular causation is rather obvious. You cannot be your own parent, for instance. Or, you cannot give your own existence to yourself or receive it from yourself. In a make-believe circular series of causes, none of the causes can really be a cause at all. Michael Augros explains this with the following example: *A* is suspended six foot above the floor; it is being held there by *B*, which in turn is being held up by *C*, which in turn is being held up by *A*. Effectively, then, *A* is holding up itself, which is absurd. Although everything in the circle seems to have a cause, none of them actually does.

And then there is the fallacy of *infinite regress*. A series of statements leads to infinite regress if the truth of the first one requires the support of a "next" one in line, but there is no "last" one in line, because "next" goes on into infinity. Infinite regress is considered "vicious" when it keeps explaining a phenomenon in terms of the very phenomenon it is supposed to explain. If one continues along the same lines, the initial problem will recur infinitely and will never be solved. Something like this happens when we try to explain something we see with our eyes by assuming there is a tiny person (*homunculus*) inside our brain who processes what we are perceiving with our eyes. What we have here is a case of infinite regress: to explain how this little person sees, we must assume another little person inside his head; and this goes on and on—there is no end to it. Something similar happened when two biologists in the

17th century thought that through their primitive microscopes they could discern a tiny person inside a human sperm cell. What they thought they saw would entail that this human person in turn would also carry sperm cells with a human person inside, and so on and on into infinity.

Fallacies are pitfalls anyone may tumble into when we use reasoning. To avoid them requires constant vigilance. St. Thomas famously warned us that a small mistake at the beginning of an argument leads to a large one at the end. Therefore, we need to be aware of hidden premises. We also need to be aware that words are slippery and often have a variety of different meanings. Shifts in the meanings of terms can make arguments fallacious. To avoid such fallacies we need to keep the meanings of our terms clearly in mind—for example, by carefully defining them. Many spurious debates arise from hazy concepts. That's why philosophers are known for making "distinctions."

In other words, reasoning may have its pitfalls and deceive us. Yet, reason can also protect us from deceptions and fallacies by helping us analyze and define our arguments. When others show us faults in our arguments, we can at least grasp the validity of their reasoning and see why the arguments we originally used were flawed. That is the power of reason in spite of its imperfections in daily usage.

So in general we can use deductive or inductive arguments to make our claims. But there is another less direct way to argue for a claim, which is sometimes called *reductio ad absurdum*. In this sort of argument, we begin by assuming the opposite of the claim we want to prove, and show that from this claim something absurd follows. This shows that the opposite of the claim that we want to argue *for* is false, and so that the claim we want to argue *against* is true.

Here is an example: (1) Some computer program guarantees victory in every game of chess, no matter who the opponent is. (Premise to be reduced to absurdity); (2) If that program is put on Computer 1, then Computer 1 will win every game of chess it plays. (Follows from 1); (3) If the program is put on Computer 2, then Computer 2 will win every game of chess it plays. (Follows from 2); (4) The program could be put on both Computer 1 and Computer 2. (Premise); (5) Computer 1 and Computer 2 could be matched against each other in a game of chess (Premise); (6) There could be a game of chess in which both players win (Conclusion). This conclusion shows that the first premise—some computer program guarantees victory in every game of chess, no matter who the opponent is—is reduced to absurdity and therefore cannot be true.

The technique of a *reductio ad absurdum* has been used for many other arguments to prove that a system is deficient by demonstrating that it creates contradictions or inconsistencies. The philosopher and physicist Karl Popper, for instance, used this technique to show that the notion of complete determinism—the belief that everything is completely predetermined—is inherently wrong. He achieved this as follows: Suppose we have a huge computer that can predict the future based on data regarding all initial conditions and all the laws needed to derive effects from causes. The machine gives answers by turning a lamp on in case of "no" and off in case of "yes." Now we feed and ask the computer to predict whether the lamp will be on or off after 99 years. After going through numerous calculations, the computer predicts that the lamp will be on by actually switching the lamp off (or reversed)—which makes either prediction wrong.

Is this a "knock-down" argument that conclusively defeats determinism? It depends. There are several explanations why the argument may not work, because various assumed and sometimes hidden premises in the argument may not be correct—for instance, it may not be possible to specify all necessary data and/or laws; or prediction is inherently different from explanation; or a computer with the needed calculating power just does not exist; or prediction-before-the-fact always takes so much time to calculate that it becomes explanation-after-the-fact. If none of these premises can be questioned, only then must the conclusion be that determinism leads to contradiction and thus cannot possibly be an all-pervasive phenomenon and therefore must be rejected.

A final question is whether we can really trust logic. Isn't everything in this world based on *matter*? How could there be room for logic then, for logic is essentially immaterial? This could be seen as a serious attack on the power of logic. Attacks like these have been attempted many times. Charles Darwin, for instance, asks in an early private notebook, "Why is thought, being a secretion of brain, more wonderful than gravity as a property of matter?" The paleontologist Stephen Jay Gould was another one to claim that the mind is an illusion produced by the brain. Some have said that logical processes in the brain evolved only for survival value, so we cannot really trust their validity, only their value in survival.

However, it could be argued that such attacks actually attack themselves. First of all, they attack the power of reasoning and logic by using the power of reasoning and logic—which sounds like a case of circular reasoning. Second, if these attacks were really effective, then they would undermine their own claims. If one believes that logic is merely an evolutionary product, then we should point out that this belief provides no reason for us to believe that this belief is true. If Darwin really believes that a thought is merely a brain secretion, then we would have no reason to trust Darwin's brain secretions either. Or when Stephen Jay Gould claims that the mind is an illusion produced by the brain, we should seriously question anything Gould says, if his thoughts are just illusions by his own verdict. All these are examples of how reasoning can show us that certain beliefs lead to contradictions and thus are absurd.

In his book *Miracles*, C.S. Lewis applies this technique to naturalism—the view that only natural, material, or physical forces operate in the world. This is his line of reasoning according to Victor Reppert:

1. No belief is rationally inferred if it can be fully explained in terms of non-rational causes.
2. If naturalism is true, then all beliefs can be fully explained in terms of non-rational causes.
3. Therefore, if naturalism is true, then no belief is rationally inferred (from 1 and 2).
4. We have good reason to accept naturalism only if it can be rationally inferred from good evidence.
5. Therefore, there is not, and cannot be, good reason to accept naturalism.

In short, naturalism undercuts itself. If naturalism were true, then we cannot sensibly believe it, or virtually anything else.

Something similar can be said about materialism—the belief that "matter" is all there is. Let us conclude with one more argument that the legendary biologist J.B.S. Haldane made about materialism: "If materialism is true, it seems to me that we cannot know that it is true. If my opinions are the result of the chemical processes going on in my brain, they are determined by the laws of chemistry, not those of logic." It could very well be argued that arguments like this one save logic and rationality from complete destruction and keep the power of reasoning standing.

c. Reasoning Overvalued

Reasoning may be powerful, but how far does its power really go? Can reasoning solve all our problems? Is reasoning the only way we have in order to find out the truth? These are various questions that people, especially philosophers, have asked themselves. The answers they have come up with are very diverse, but we won't go into all the details.

The most extreme claim has come from what is called rationalism. It has several versions, but we should at least mention a few of them. One of them is that the final criterion of truth is not sensory but entirely intellectual and deductive. Whereas philosophers such as St. Thomas hold that all knowledge comes through the senses, rationalism has such a high confidence in reason that empirical proof and physical evidence are regarded as unnecessary to ascertain truth—in other words, truth can be gained independently of sense experience. Sense experience is therefore seen as a rather confused and merely tentative approach to gaining knowledge. So reason alone, unaided by experience, is supposed to be able to arrive at basic truth regarding the world. That is a rather extreme claim, which may eventually be detrimental to all we claim to know.

Another version of rationalism has it that at least some human knowledge is gained through a priori, rational insights. The term *a priori* means in this context that the insight is prior to experience. Some representatives of this view such as René Descartes speak of innate ideas (e.g. those of infinity and substance) that do not come from experience. Descartes, for instance, attempted to prove the truth of the senses from the existence of God, their Author. But that seems to turn things upside down. As Michael Augros astutely remarks, "we would have to be sure there was a god before we could be sure there were dogs and cats."

Thinkers like Descartes hold that we have some innate ideas and that we can logically deduce truths about the world from "self-evident" premises. Gottfried Leibniz is another philosopher who believes these ideas are so thoroughly innate that they enter into all our thoughts and reasoning. Others such as Immanuel Kant argue that certain truths exist and that the intellect can directly grasp these truths, for they are true because of the structure of the mind that knows them. An example would be "Every event must have a cause." Supposedly, this cannot be proven by experience, yet experience is impossible without it because it describes the way the mind must necessarily order its representations. The way we experience the world is only possible if the mind provides a systematic structuring of its representations. So, in this version of rationalism, experience is not the source of all our ideas; instead it is the mind's structuring that makes experience possible. A claim like this makes our grasp of reality rather shaky.

A third version of rationalism is that *all* truth can be discovered by unaided human reason—nothing is beyond its reach. In this view, the reason of man has become the measure of all things, thus excluding everything that is not discovered by mere reasoning. As a consequence, anything that cannot be apprehended or explained by reason must be rejected. This version of rationalism holds that truth should be determined by reason and factual analysis alone, rather than being a source of knowledge in addition to faith, dogma, tradition, or religious teaching. This is a definite shift from the more moderate position that reason has precedence over other ways of acquiring knowledge, thus leading to the more extreme position that reason is the only path to knowledge. In this view, reason is not only a supreme criterion of truth but actually the only criterion of truth.

A fourth version of rationalism is the result of scientific developments. In the popular mind, reason has been truncated to the way science operates—modern, experimental science, that is. In our society, when hearing the word "truth," most people automatically understand it to mean "scientifically verified" facts or information. Reasoning is understood to be thinking and reasoning based on experiment, critical analysis, and empirical evidence. The results of science, so it is widely thought, are verified facts and publicly accessible truths. In fact, to many contemporary minds, only the results of science are considered *bona fide* verified facts or publicly accessible truths (more on this in chapters 6.a and 6.b).

A fifth version of rationalism, similar to the previous version, is that faith and religion have become highly suspicious. Defenders of this view maintain that one cannot make an act of faith without being absolutely certain that what one is committing oneself to is truthful and trustworthy. A revealing example of this rationalistic position is the British atheist philosopher Bertrand Russell. Toward the end of his life, Russell was interviewed by the BBC and asked what he would say if, upon his death, he actually met God in person. Russell—consistent rationalist to the last—said simply, "I would say: 'Sir, why did you not give me better evidence!'"

In general it could be said that most versions of rationalism are somehow associated with a movement referred to by its followers as the *Age of Reason*, or simply the *Enlightenment*. It assumes that the "Age of Faith" has been replaced by the "Age of Reason"—as if "faith" and "reason" are utterly disparate ways of looking at the world. Especially during the 18th century, Enlightenment thinkers, particularly in Britain and France, questioned traditional authority and embraced the notion that humanity could be enormously improved through rational change. Rationalism became associated with "Free Thought" as the only possible intellectual attitude of a reasoning and reasonable person. It became current for a new philosophy of life, as opposed to supernatural Revelation and the authority of Holy Scripture. With an unbounded confidence in man's capacity to think and act in virtue of his own inner rational power, rationalism has come to reject anything associated with religion and Revelation.

The question over what counts as reason and what does not

is apparently an important one. For many, anything not related to scientific knowledge of the empirically known Universe does not qualify as reason. Whenever rationalism glorifies the power of reason, it always curtails its power at the same time by putting it in competition with faith and religion. The reasoning behind it goes as follows: if you accept faith, you can only do so by neglecting reason; if you choose reason, you must abandon faith, in spite of the fact that rationalism itself is based on faith—faith in the powe of reason (more on this in chapters 4 and 5).

In short, rationalism leads to an overestimation of reason and rationality by giving them almighty power. It causes us to believe there is nothing better than reason, thus making everything else look powerless and useless. It invites everyone to enter the "Age of Reason," and leave everything else behind, including the "Age of Faith."

d. Reasoning Undervalued

In the 19th century, the extremism of rationalism in any of the above forms often instigated a counter-movement of irrationalism. Irrationalism is a multi-faceted reaction against the dominance of rationalism. As such, it played a significant role in Western culture, especially so at the turn of the previous century. Irrationalism is not necessarily opposed to reason; it can consist of a simple awareness that the rational aspect of things tends to be overemphasized and that this needs to be compensated for by an emphasis on intuition, feeling, emotions, and the subconscious. But it can also take a more extreme form, which amounts to the view that the rational element is something contrary to life and altogether negative.

In the history of Western thought we find various positions of irrationalism. Blaise Pascal came as an early precursor of Christian existentialism and famously stated that "heart has its reasons that are unknown to reason." He also said, "It's the heart which perceives God and not the reason." More in general, Immanuel Kant came to the conclusion that reason cannot give certain and ultimate knowledge about reality. Then there is Voltaire who was very skeptical about the natural lights of human reason and the ability to find definitive answers. Soon irrationalism would expand into many other areas of culture, including psychoanalysis, with people such as Sigmund Freud and Carl-Gustav Jung.

In spite of 19th century Positivism—which appeared as the culmination of human confidence in reason based on scientific advances—the positivist belief that scientific reason would make all other approaches obsolete, was soon largely rejected as a naïve illusion. Irrationalism has therefore acted as a recurrent challenge to the belief that analytical or deductive reasoning is the beginning and the end of all mental activity. But again, much of what passes for irrationalism in fact does not challenge the validity of reason, but rather opens the possibilities of other realms of investigation that had been previously ignored by the rationalist tradition

Oddly enough, extreme rationalism not only instigated a counter reaction of irrationalism but also prompted developments at the other end of the spectrum: movements such as relativism and skepticism. Once you have concluded that reason alone cannot give certain and ultimate knowledge about reality, the foundation of knowledge based on rationality becomes rather shaky. Let us start with relativism.

Relativists claim there is no absolute truth, because they always think about truth as something relative to some particular frame of reference, such as a particular language or culture or philosophy or religion. Whatever is true for me may be false for you; whatever is right for me may be wrong for someone else. All there is left then are our *opinions* about what is true or false, and about what is right or wrong. There is no room anymore for rational arguments and rational debates about our opinions. All we have left is the right to have our own opinions in matters of truth. But if the world is round, will someone's opinion make it flat?

That's where relativism runs into trouble. If all truth is only a matter of opinion, then relativists can only express what their opinion is, even regarding relativism itself; they cannot coherently claim that relativism is true, for in the world of relativism there is no such thing as absolute truth. Whether their opinion is true or false is no longer a legitimate question, at least not according to their own verdict. Yet, despite its inconsistency, relativism has been on the rise as a truthful opinion about the absence of truth.

Relativism is certainly not a recent invention. The ancient Greek historian Herodotus said in his book *The Histories*, "Everyone without exception believes his own native customs, and the religion he was brought up in, to be the best." Then there is the ancient Greek philosopher Protagoras who is known for the expression "Man is the measure of all things"—which must necessarily include the truths a person may claim. Pontius Pilate would follow soon with his legendary question, "What is truth?" Although the idea of relativism may have a long history, it was never really popular or wide-spread, but nowadays it is receiving more and more traction. It is promoted, for instance, by the late philosopher Richard M. Rorty: "Truth is what your contemporaries let you get away with." In other words, relativism promotes a sort of democratic ideal in matters of knowledge and reasoning.

Relativists basically claim that there are no absolute truths. Taken to its extreme, gravity may be true for you but not for me. As the Boston College philosopher Peter Kreeft put it, "To be a relativist, you must believe that nearly all human beings in history have ordered their lives by an illusion." He also astutely remarks: "There has never been a society of relativists." How can relativists promote relativism by teaching us that relativism is true and absolutism is false? Relativism claims everyone is right, absolutism claims some may be wrong. So either there is a real right and a real wrong, or there is nothing wrong with being an absolutist and nothing right with being a relativist. Kreeft then comes to a powerful conclusion, "Relativism is not rational, it is rationalization. It is not the conclusion of a rational argument. It is the rationalization of a prior action." Once we give up the notion of truth, we have also given up, for instance, on the search for truth in the court room.

But there is more trouble for relativism. Relativists not only deny our capacity to know absolute truth, they also reject the power of human *rationality* to get to the truth. Their reasons for undermining rationality can be manifold, but one of them is that human knowledge and rationality are merely the product of evolution after having gone through the process of natural selection. What we have here is the reductionist agenda of sciences such as sociobiology—which tend to reduce human behavior, including human knowledge, to genes manipulated by natural selection. The end-result is that we end up with mere illusions: social illusions, political illusions, moral illusions, religious illusions—or more in general, *cognitive* illusions. The only thing these relativists acknowledge is that each human being carries a certain amount of knowledge and rationality which does not stem from personal experience, but contains information stored in genes and gathered from the experiences the animal world before us has gone through. But how trustworthy this information is that is for anyone to decide.

More in general, whether in science or elsewhere, it could be said that the statement "all truth is relative" leads to contradiction. If this very statement is relative, then it does not rule out absolutes; on the other hand, if the statement is absolute, then it provides an example of an absolute statement, proving that not all truths are relative. One could even say to a relativist: If there is no truth beyond your belief that something is true, then you cannot hold your own beliefs to be false or mistaken. When you deny that there is something as objective truth, you are in fact insisting in your denial that what you say is objectively true, which makes your original premise false. In short, relativism is an irrational position; it leaves us in a cognitive desert. As Professor David Carlin puts it, "If there is no objective truth, we are free to believe whatever we like, including utter nonsense. And if there is no objective truth, those who have power in society are free to impose, either by persuasion or force or fraud, their beliefs and values on everybody else."

Let's move from relativism to skepticism. Some consider reason so "powerful" that it can put even its own power into question. That's how it can easily turn us into skeptics. Like relativism, skepticism is another doctrine that eats away the foundation of rationality. In the eyes of skeptics, anything we claim to know is suspect and must be doubted. Skeptics deny the validity of nearly all aspects of knowledge, because we are not supposed to know any truth with certainty. Skeptics find a flaw in every argument and every truth claimed—they just glorify doubt. They have this persistent doubt as to how far they can go in trusting the power of reason. No matter where they put their borderline, skepticism ultimately leads to nihilism, claiming that there is no law, no authority, no rationality, no morality, and no purpose to life—and, of course, no God. Nihilism denies the very existence of all these fundamental aspects of life, and declares them non-existent, based on the certainty that nothing is certain. In their search for certainty, they end up with complete uncertainty.

Needless to say that skepticism makes for a very restrained view on the world—actually so restrained that absolute skeptics cannot even know whether they have a mind to doubt with. Like relativists, skeptics too leave us in a cognitive desert. They are so sure that nothing is sure. However, skeptics turn things the wrong way. We often do need to eliminate errors, such as fallacies, in order to get to the truth; yet, our ultimate goal is not to avoid *errors* but to gain *truth*. We want to know, not to know what we do *not* know. The fact that we do make errors in our search for truth should not entitle us to lower our standards of truth. Truth is the ultimate goal of all our searches, and that may include correcting our errors.

Nevertheless, skeptics make it their final goal to avoid errors, in denial of the fact that eliminating errors is only a means to gaining truth—so they end up with an empty shell of complete mistrust. How can one be so sure that nothing can be known to be sure? Skepticism is at best a method to avoid errors, but it never leads to truth. It is an activity, not an achievement. It uses a silly slogan like "It is better to travel hopefully than to arrive"—which, as C. S. Lewis pointed out, is nonsense, because if you believe such a thing, you never travel hopefully because there is no hope of arriving. Once we begin questioning the trustworthiness of our brains and senses and intellect and reason, there is no way of establishing their trustworthiness again independently of trusting them.

Besides, one could argue that talk about making mistakes does not make sense unless there exists also something like finding the truth. The late philosopher Gilbert Ryle used to say that there can be no counterfeit coins without genuine currency. Even those who swear by the "trial and error" method must admit that errors only exist by the grace of truth. Or take the case that two people have a different answer to a specific mathematical calculation. Does this entitle skeptics to state that all answers are worth the same, or that there is no correct answer at all? Even Karl Popper, the champion of falsification and falsifiability, had to admit that the very idea of error is inconceivable without the idea of truth.

The irony is that no one can be certain that nothing is certain. Chesterton diagnosed skepticism very well when he tackled the question whether we can know anything with certainty as follows: "[A] man must either answer that question in the affirmative, or else never answer any question, never ask any question, never even exist intellectually, to answer or to ask." And then he adds, "Most fundamental sceptics appear to survive, because they are not consistently skeptical and not at all fundamental. They will first deny everything and then admit something, if for the sake of argument or often rather of attack without argument." Skeptics are masters of deception; they make us wonder whether we really exist, whether others exist, whether the world exists—and ultimately whether God exists. Skeptics act like criminal lawyers: At trial, they don't have to prove anything in a positive way; all they have to do is raise doubts in the minds of the jurors.

Pope John Paul II summarized all of the above in his Encyclical *Fides et Ratio* (5), in which he says about relativism and skepticism:

> *[They] have led philosophical research to lose its way in the shifting sands of widespread skepticism. Recent times have seen the rise to prominence of various doctrines which tend to devalue even the truths which had been judged certain. A legitimate plurality of positions has yielded to an undifferentiated pluralism, based upon the assumption that all positions are equally valid, which is one of today's most widespread symptoms of the lack of confidence in truth.*

In short, relativism and skepticism lead to an underestimation of reason by undermining all its power. They falsely make us believe there is nothing worthwhile about reason. As a matter of fact, although reason is not all-powerful, neither is it powerless. We just need to find out what its real power is.

2. The Power of Faith

a. Our Religious Nature

Not only are we rational "by nature," we are also religious "by nature." We are "born believers," so to speak. We believe in something above and beyond us. Human beings have a "built-in" tendency to look beyond their own limits. Even when I say about myself, "I am only human," I am comparing myself, not with something "below" me (such as a cat, a dog, or an ape), but with something or someone "above" me and transcending me. Only the "finite" human mind is able to catch a glimpse of the Infinite. This capacity of the human mind is rightly called self-transcendence—referring to the transcendence of something or someone more than our own selves. Belief in the transcendent is at the heart of all religions.

Religious questions about "meaning" are clearly transcendent questions. They presume that life has a meaning beyond itself. Whenever we act, we take a risk on how this act is going to work out; we put ourselves in a larger setting that makes our doings purposeful, although we cannot oversee the total setting by reason alone. Because of our limitations, we act in faith by believing in "tomorrow," hoping for a good outcome and trusting that it makes sense to do what we actually decided to do. In knowing about our limits, we are able to look beyond those limits.

No one can live without some form of basic faith and trust. We were born with some sort of faith. Without any trust in our own doings and in the future ahead of us, we would be completely "paralyzed" in life. Instead we are all "believers"—believers in "tomorrow" and in a wider setting or framework that surrounds and transcends us. Religious believers have faith in something larger than themselves. What individual religions add to this basic faith and trust is that they offer their believers a more specific "outline" or "framework" of this wider setting. Each religion gives an answer to the ultimate questions of life. Other than religion, there is no area of human interest that is concerned with the ultimate meaning and purpose of life.

Religious faith carries us above and beyond our limited capacities by making us aware of the "framework" in which we live. This framework is like the framework surrounding a spider's web—without such a framework, there could be no web. Likewise, religious faith is about the "web" of our lives, and this framework is commonly called God. God is the framework in which "we live and move and have our being," as the Apostle Paul put it (Acts 17:28).

However, it has to be acknowledged that the meaning and purpose of life can be found in a wide variety of items—ranging from money to property, from clothes to cars, from clubs to gangs, from games to gambling, from alcohol to sex, from politics to technology, from magic to witchcraft, from horoscopes to spiritism. Each one of these can become the one and only purpose of someone's life. However, if we consider religion to be related to the ultimate quest for ultimate meaning, most of these kinds of faith and trust would not qualify as religion; at the most, they would qualify as superstition, or second-hand religiosity. They don't give an ultimate meaning to life, a "firm ground" to stand on, a "framework" to live in. They are merely "idols" or "surrogates" that just deceive us with fake or proximate answers to ultimate questions. This is a deception that leads to a religious-like adoration for other gods than God— the gods of the stars (astrology), the god of earthly possessions (Mammon), the god of material goods (materialism), the goddess of nature (Mother Nature), the god of addictions, the idols of sex and food.

However, to be completely oriented on money or sex, to devote one's whole being to the pursuit of beauty or pleasure—in short, to devote oneself unconditionally to anything less than God—is surrendering oneself to an idol. These so-called gods are so human and so little divine, so shallow and so little transcendent, that faith in them doesn't qualify as religious faith—faith in a transcendent and ultimate reality—but at best as a make-believe faith. The real religious faith is about the framework "in which we live and move and have our being." The Judeo-Christian tradition explicitly states that there are many gods, which are called "idols," but there is only one real God. Exodus 20:3 says it clearly, "You shall have no other gods before me." When we don't worship the real God, we must be worshipping idols instead, for we are by nature worshippers. What this leads to is well described by Chesterton: "For when we cease to worship God, we do not worship nothing, we worship anything."

Not surprisingly then, faith and religion set us apart from the animal world. Not only can we be called *Homo sapiens* but also *Homo religiosus*, because we have something like a "religious nature." Only humans have this transcendent dimension. Only humans have this belief in a transcendent framework—a Transcendent Being. This belief is one way of coping with our knowledge that we are limited, that the future is uncertain, and that death is inevitable. Religion diminishes the hurt of death's certainty and the pain of losing a loved one with the prospect of reuniting in another life—not as a form of wishful thinking but as a pillar of religious faith, not as a product of genes but as a given revealed to and embraced by the human mind. Humanity has always known this—intuitively if you will—from its very beginning. In early primeval history, we find already evidence of elaborate burials; such burials with grave goods indicate a belief in an after-life, for the goods are there because they are considered useful to the deceased in their future lives.

How different this is in the animal world. Take, for instance, the observation of female apes—our so-called "close relatives"—who continue carrying their dead newborns around for quite a while, without having any idea of what is going on until at last they give up and drop the dead remains of their newborn. In Guinea, West Africa, chimpanzee mothers were seen in nature carrying and grooming their offspring's lifeless bodies for up to sixty-eight days. By the time the corpses were finally abandoned, the bodies had mummified and developed an intense smell of decay. Ironically, evolutionists gave this observation a peculiar twist: these, they say, must be sixty-eight days of actually mourning the dead! Only human beings could come up with such an explanation. Arguably, this sixty-eight-day period is not a time of "grief," but rather a time of "ignorance." Besides, we should ask such evolutionists where the burial and the grave are once this period of "mourning" was over.

It is because of man's universal drive for self-transcendence that we can find evidence of it even in the earliest archaeological data, such as art and burial rituals. The observation that religion seems universal made some biologists claim it "must" therefore be encoded in our genome. Blaise Pascal—the mathematician, physicist, and philosopher—had a better explanation. He used to speak of a hole in each one of us, an "infinite abyss that can be filled only with an infinite and immutable object; in other words by God himself." It is highly unlikely that this hole is programmed in our genes—and neither is religion. Our universal drive for self-transcendence does not come from genes. Of course, I cannot transcend myself on my own, but because I myself was made in the image of God, I perceive more than myself whenever I perceive myself completely.

It is man's drive for self-transcendence that explains why belief in God as a Transcendent Being is so universal in human history. The rising number of atheists in modern society seems to belie this, but we need to acknowledge that even among the greatest philosophers there is hardly any controversy about the existence of some absolute or infinite being. As the late philosopher Fr. Joseph Bochenski, O.P. put it a few decades ago,

> *The fact that there is such a being is the common conviction of Plato, Aristotle, Plotinus, St. Thomas, Descartes, Spinoza, Leibniz, Kant, Hegel, Whitehead—and even of dialectical materialists, the official present and past party philosophers of communism, if these smaller minds are, in any way, comparable with the greater ones. Although all these philosophers vehemently deny the existence of the Judeo-Christian God, they claim at the same time that the*

world is infinite, eternal, boundless, absolute. And what is more, their attitude is in many ways distinctively religious.

b. Faith Explained

What is faith? The Protestant theologian Paul Tillich was right when he commented that "faith" is the most misunderstood word in our vocabulary. Sometimes, the word faith is used to talk about a person's perspective on ultimate questions. At other times the word faith means a bunch of feelings or convictions that one has about things, i.e. one's deepest "values." At other times the word faith is practically synonymous with one's "philosophy of life." Or faith can be used to talk about any ultimate cause that one really believes in and advocates. Or faith is practically the same as some vague kind of spirituality.

And then there are those who use the word faith for anything that cannot be true. Mark Twain once defined faith as "believing what you know ain't so." The biologist Richard Dawkins expresses the same opinion when he says, "faith is a state of mind that leads people to believe something—it doesn't matter what—in the total absence of supporting evidence. If there were good supporting evidence then faith would be superfluous, for the evidence would compel us to believe it anyway."

Because faith is used in such a vague, general, and often confusing way, it has become difficult to defend or explain "faith in God." So we may have a difficult task here. First we have to explain what we mean by "Faith in God." And next, we need to explain what is meant by a "Catholic Faith" in God. From now on, when I use the word "Faith" (with a capital F), it refers to religious faith or faith in God, rather than to "faith" in the more general sense.

Let's start with the first question. What do religious believers mean when they speak of God? What is the object of their Faith? Religious believers are usually very well able to explain to others what it is they believe in. We referred already to what many believers call the Transcendent. But that might still be a rather nebulous concept. Perhaps a better answer was given by St. Thomas Aquinas. Although he was Catholic to the core, his approach has a much wider implementation.

Thomas understood that God has to be radically different from everything that we see around us, including each one of us. His terminology may seem foreign at first, but it has withstood the test of many centuries. His reasoning starts as follows: we receive our existence; we are *contingent* and could not have been; we don't have to exist, but because we do exist, we can ask for the cause of our existence—God. God alone is the act of existing itself. Or to put it another way, God's essence—what God is—is his existence. God alone is existence by nature. So God is a necessary and eternal being who did not come into existence but always has been. In contrast, all other creatures are not God precisely because their act of existing has been received from God who alone is self-existing. Each creature exists because God who is existence itself holds that creature in existence at every time and place. If God did cease to hold each one of us in existence, we would simply disappear—we would be annihilated.

Thomas very often speaks of God as the *Primary Cause*. What does he mean by that? To explain the concept of a Primary Cause, or First Cause, he uses the example of an infinite series of fathers and sons. Each son's existence is caused by his father, back in time. Theoretically, this sequence can even go back *infinitely* far in time. That would be an example of infinite regress (see 1.b). Although infinite regress is perfectly acceptable in mathematics—negative numbers go on to infinity just as positive numbers do—it is not acceptable when it comes to real beings. Real beings are not like numbers: they need causes. Just like circular causation, infinite causation going infinitely back in time does not really explain anything. Although each son's existence is caused by his father, the cause of that father must go back in time in an infinite way without ever finding a "first father" in the link of fathers—and therefore, without finding a real cause or explanation.

Besides, even if infinite causation would explain something, it certainly does not explain everything about fathers and sons, for a vital question remains: what is it that enables fathers to *generate* sons at all. Moreover, a sequence of events in time may be able to go infinitely forward through the future and back through the past, but the problem would still be that we are dealing here with *time*, which itself must have some other form of cause. Consequently, the explanation for all of this would not take us to another cause in this sequence of *secondary causes*, as Thomas calls them, but to a cause at a higher level, so to speak. That's what Thomas means by the *Primary Cause*. It is a Cause that exists eternally and explains the sequence of secondary causes—a Transcendent Cause, if you will, outside and above the sequence of secondary causes.

And then there is the problem that any part of the chain can only do any causing unless it first *exists*. For something to cause itself to exist, it would have to exist before it came into existence—which is logically and philosophically impossible. Things that exist cannot explain their own existence—they are not self-explanatory nor self-sufficient. In other words, the need for causes must come to an end: There must be a cause that is not itself in need of a cause and does not come into existence—a Primary Cause or First Cause. Peter Kreeft compares infinite regress and infinite causation with an "endless passing of the buck. God is the one who says, 'The buck stops here.'"

One could also say that the Primary Cause provides a "point of suspension" for the chain of secondary causes itself. It is like the framework around a spider's web; without that framework, the web could not exist. Without a Primary Cause there could not be a chain of secondary causes. God as the ground of our being is the "framework" supporting the "web" of our lives, or as we said earlier, God is the framework in which "we live and move and have our being" (Acts 17:28). The Primary Cause brings secondary causes into existence and allows them to be causes of their own.

So God is also the one who brings matter into existence and keeps it in existence. Matter cannot do so on its own. The idea that matter can cause itself and explain itself has rightly been caricaturized by Peter Kreeft as a magical "pop theory" that has things pop into existence without any cause. Nothing can just pop itself into existence; it must have a cause, because it does not and cannot have the power to make itself exist. As they famously say, nothing comes from nothing by nothing. The theologian David Bentley Hart puts it this way: "Physical reality cannot account for its own existence for the simple reason that nature—the physical—is that which by definition already exists."

Secondary causes are contingent—that is to say, they don't have to exist, and so because they do exist, we can ask for the cause of their existence. Any cause in the chain of secondary causes can only do any causing because it first *exists*. Things that exist cannot explain their own existence—they are not self-explanatory nor self-sufficient, but *contingent* instead. In other words, the need for causes must come to an end somewhere: there must be a cause that is not itself in need of a cause and does not come into existence—a Primary Cause or First Cause. St. Thomas discovered that God must be unlike any other being in the world if he is to be its cause. This is how reason can prepare us for "Faith in God" (see 3.d).

Being the Primary Cause, God could never be discovered among the secondary causes of this Universe, for God is not one of them. Science, for instance, is about secondary causes, not the Primary Cause (see 6.b). God is outside the scope of science, just as everything else that is unseen and cannot be counted or measured is beyond the reach of science. God cannot be "seen" through telescopes or microscopes. Because God is "everywhere," it only looks as if God is "nowhere." This calls for a word of caution. God is a Primary Cause, not a super-cause among other causes; he is "above" and "beyond" all secondary causes, brings them into being, and lets them do their own work—acting as a secondary cause, that is. It is only thanks to the Primary Cause that creatures can become secondary causes.

Therefore, when St. Thomas describes God as the First Cause, what he means is not merely "first" in the sense of being before the second cause in time, and not "first" in the sense of coming before the second cause in a sequence of causes, but rather "first" in the sense of being the *source* of all secondary causes, having absolutely primal and underived causal power—a power from which all other causes derive their causal powers. In other words, God is not a deity like Jupiter or Zeus—not a being stronger than other beings or superior to all other beings, not acting like all other beings. Instead, he is the very Source of all being—the Absolute Ground of all that exists. God is the Primary Cause, unlike any other gods who are secondary causes. As Deuteronomy 6:4 puts it, "The Lord is our God, the Lord *alone*"—and no other gods.

Back to our original question, the Primary Cause could be considered the object of religious faith, because that is what religious faith is ultimately about and that is what we mean when talking about God. However, this is still a rather general and abstract description of God. Whether this Primary Cause is identical to God is still to be seen, for these two terms are not necessarily synonyms, but they may turn out to be referring to the same Being. However, it could easily be argued—but not here—that the First Cause cannot be other than God, the Eternal and Infinite, "in whom we live and move and have our being" (Acts 17:28).

From this it should be clear that "faith in God" should not be confused with *superstition*—the belief that semi-divine powers rule the world. It is actually ironic that the Judeo-Christian belief in a Creator—who is outside of nature, and radically distinguished from the world he has created—in fact opposed and discarded any belief in superstition. The first chapter of the Book of Genesis, for instance, is one long polemic against pagan superstition and semi-divine powers. Each "day of creation" in Genesis 1 dismisses an additional cluster of pagan deities. On the first day, the pagan gods of light and darkness are dismissed. On the second day, the gods of sky and sea are smashed. On the third day, earth gods and gods of vegetation take their turn. On the fourth day, it is the sun, moon, and star gods that are on their way out (including astrology). The fifth and sixth days take away any associations with divinity from the animal kingdom (such as sacred falcons, lions, serpents, and golden calves). And finally, even humans (including pharaohs) are emptied of any intrinsic divinity—while at the same time, they are granted a divine likeness. It is obvious that Faith in a Creator, a Primary Cause, changes a Universe with spirits, deities, and goddesses into something "rational." Nature is not divine in itself, only its Maker is—which is quite the opposite of superstition. We are supposed to worship God, not nature or any other deities. That's what "religious faith" is about.

So it is time now to turn to our second question: what do we mean by "Catholic Faith"? It was St. Augustine who gave to the Catholic Church an account of what Christian Faith is that has become standard, even until our own day—his view is presupposed, for instance, by Vatican I and II, the Catechism of the Catholic Church (CCC), and Pope John Paul II's encyclical on faith and reason [*Fides et Ratio*]. Following both the New Testament as well as standard word meanings in ancient Greek and Latin, St. Augustine understood Faith as believing something on the word of a *witness*. The New Testament is full of talk of testimony, of testifying, and of bearing witness to the truth of Christ's life, death, resurrection, ascension, and current presence.

Faith means welcoming this testimony, accepting it, and believing it. The Catechism (166) stresses, "You have not given yourself faith as you have not given yourself life. The believer has received faith from others and should hand it on to others."

Believing something on the word of another's witness is known to all of us. All human beings naturally live by faith in other human beings. It is quite impossible for anyone to go through life without any faith in what others have witnessed. For we all take many things on the word of other people, and we cannot but do so. We must depend to a great extent on others as source of knowledge, for we are practically unable to verify even a small part of our knowledge on our own. As Stephen Barr puts it,

> *For a person to accept as knowledge only what he had discovered and proved for himself from direct personal experience would put his knowledge at the level of the Stone Age. [...] Taking something on authority, then, is not in itself irrational. On the contrary, it would be irrational never to do so.*

Therefore, we must trust in the veracity of those who teach us. Nearly all of our historical beliefs, including our beliefs about where we were born and who our father is, come from hear-say. Even the enterprise of science relies heavily on trusting "eyewitness" reports of others, largely in the case of special experiences and experiments. Most of what we know about science and its findings is from "hear-say," based on these expert reports.

What makes religious faith different, though, is that it is more than just natural, human faith in human witnesses. It is from "hear-say" that is based on the "Word of God." The same God who created human beings comes to meet our questioning by bearing witness to himself and his plan for the world. God explains himself to us, so to speak. In terms of the Catechism (108), "Christianity is the religion of the 'Word' of God, a word which is 'not a written and mute word, but the Word which is incarnate and living.'" Christian Faith is witnessing how God is present and works in human history.

Catholic Faith has at least two different aspects. On the one hand, it is connected with the *intellect*, which makes Faith rationally understandable. This allows one to say, "I *know* Jesus is my Savior." On the other hand, Faith is also connected with the *will*, which turns Faith into a commitment or pledge or surrender. This allows one to say, "I *accept* Jesus as my Savior." When the father of a sick son said to Jesus, "I do believe, but help my unbelief" (Mk. 9:24), he could be understood as saying, "I know what Faith tells me, but I cannot fully surrender yet." Making the step from intellect to will is often called a "leap of faith." It is not a leap from having insufficient reasons for God's existence to a state of greater certitude, but from having an intellectual understanding to a complete surrender in Faith. Faith is more than an intellectual belief—even the demons know and believe that God exists (James 2:19). The difference between what the intellect tells us and what the will tells us explains why we often see in the lives of non-believers a certain disconnect between what they could have known and what they have chosen to know.

Thomas Aquinas was very aware of this disconnect when he said, "Whereas unbelief is in the intellect, the cause of unbelief is in the will." No matter how strong the empirical and rational evidence may be in favor of God's existence, non-believers often decide not to accept God's existence and God's Revelation as a fact because they don't like the way the world looks to them with God in the picture. They act like smokers who know smoking is unhealthy, but nevertheless keep smoking. It is the will, says Pascal, which "dissuades the mind from considering those aspects it doesn't like to see." Psalm 95 puts it this way, "If today you hear his voice, harden not your hearts."

Obviously, Catholic Faith is more than what we can reach by reasoning—there is also surrender involved. That's why atheism is often not a rational conclusion but rather a matter of choice and preference. Even the best arguments won't work for those who are not willing to even listen to them. Atheists often do not will what they know, but they know what they will. They must will to see what they don't like to see. The British philosopher Anthony Flew seemed to be this way. For more than fifty years he scrutinized arguments for and against God before finally abandoning atheism in favor of theism. One could say in general that if someone is not interested in whether God exists, or vehemently rejects God, it is almost impossible for such a person to be won over by any kind of empirical evidence or rational argument. We are dealing here with a choice made before evidence is brought in. Atheists often invest a great deal of time and energy in fleeing the very God they deny or reject. But isn't flight itself the recognition that there is actually something from which to flee? From God we cannot flee—certainly not in the end.

The Catechism (150) describes Catholic Faith as follows: "Faith is first of all a personal adherence of man to God. At the same time, and inseparably, it is a free assent to the whole truth that God has revealed." Religious faith is having confidence in something you may not have experienced with your own senses. As Hebrews 11:1 puts it, "Faith is the assurance of things hoped for, the conviction of things not seen." St. Paul (2 Cor. 5:7) says, "We walk by faith, not by sight." However, even if religious faith is about the unseen, it is not "blind"; it's not an act of "believing without any reason." Just the opposite: religious faith is the act of believing in something unseen for which we do have good reasons. We can reason and argue from what is seen to what is unseen, from what we are familiar with to what we are not familiar with, from secondary causes to a Primary Cause.

There are always two sides to this belief. When we say we love God, we need to know who God is. You cannot love what you do not know, for you want to know the person you love. Knowledge, truth, love, and will are strongly interconnected. Even in religious Faith, faith and knowledge are not contradictory; what we know about God helps us to have Faith in God. Whereas Faith without commitment is actually disbelief (John 8:30- 46; 12:42, 43; James 2:19), commitment without knowledge is actually irrational. Neither one is a genuine option for a Catholic Faith.

To use an analogy, I do not love my wife because I have evidence for her existence. Yet I love her because of what I know about her. It would be foolish to invest a commitment of my love in her without believing and knowing that she really exists and that she is the person I know she is. Just so, I love and obey God because he is God. Therefore, the expression "blind faith" is as deceiving as "blind love"; love is not blind, for it sees the other person's inside, like an X-ray. Something similar could be said about Faith in God; it is not blind but "sees" God, although it is "only a reflection as in a mirror" (1 Cor. 13:12). It would be foolish to invest a commitment of faith and love in God without believing and knowing that he really exists and that he is the God he is. Each time we encounter someone, even God, we want to know whom and what we encounter. Pascal had remarked already, "Human beings must be known to be loved; but Divine beings must be loved to be known."

Bishop Robert Barron of Los Angeles uses a similar analogy: if you are coming to know a person, you will look that person over, assess how she relates to others, Google her, and find out where she went to school and how she is employed, ask mutual friends about her, etc. All of this objective investigation could take place even before you had the opportunity to meet her. When you finally make her acquaintance, you will bring to the encounter all that you have learned about her. But then something extraordinary will happen, something that will, inevitably, reveal to you things that you otherwise would never know: she will speak. In doing so, she will, on her own initiative, disclose her mind, her heart, her feelings to you. Some of what she says will be in concord with what you have already found out, but much of it will be new, beyond anything you might have discovered on your own. But as she speaks and as you listen, you will be faced with a choice: do you believe her or not? You have entered a territory beyond your capacity to control. And you have to decide: do you trust her or not? That's where the will comes in.

It is the same dynamic that applies to our knowledge of

God, the Supreme *Person*, when you listen in faith to God's Revelation. You have to decide whether you trust his Word or not. You have to decide whether this Supreme Person is worth your commitment or not. This step presses beyond reason, though, for it represents the opening of one heart to another. Jesus tells us what the first commandment is: "Love the Lord, your God, with all your heart, with all your soul, with all your mind and with all your strength" (Mk. 12:30). Once you decide to surrender and commit yourself to God, your will has become in harmony with your intellect. And then life changes, for Faith gives you access to a world above you and beyond you, a world that no eye has seen, no ear has heard. It deals with supernatural truths that you could not have discovered through natural means such as science and reason on their own. As the Catechism (157) puts it, "Faith is certain. It is more certain than all human knowledge because it is founded on the very word of God who cannot lie."

It is this very Faith that will show its power when disaster strikes you, when things do not go the way you had planned, when you become a victim of injustice—in short, when self-made people reach their own limits. The existence of suffering and adversity actually shows us that we are *not* in control of our lives but need assistance beyond human power. Isn't it striking that Christianity actually has the Cross at center stage in its religion? It claims there is some mysterious salvation for us in carrying our crosses in life—for the benefit of ourselves and the benefit of others. No wonder the Cross is a touchstone for Christians, but at the same time a stumbling block for non-believers (see 5.d).

It should not surprise us then that the Catholic Faith has profoundly changed the face of the Earth. At *www.catholicscomehome.org*, we find beautifully summarized what we, through the Faith of the Catholic Church, have done for society: we started hospitals to care for the sick; we establish orphanages, and help the poor; we are the largest charitable organization on the planet, bringing relief and comfort to those in need; we educate more children than any other scholarly or religious institution; we founded the college system; we defend the dignity of all human life, and uphold marriage and family; we are ... the Catholic Church ... with over one billion in our family sharing in the sacraments and fullness of Christian Faith.

c. Faith Overvalued

After all the good things we have said about faith, it should not come as a surprise that religious faith has been glorified by some as the one and only source of religion. They speak about Faith mainly in terms of a "leap of faith"—as if Faith is a leap from nothing to everything, a leap into the irrational. It doesn't begin to go "as far as possible" on reason and evidence, and then "the rest of the way" on Faith, but it goes all the way on mere faith. When questioning these believers about their faith, we may get the answer, "You just have to have faith," sometimes accompanied by a shrug.

Indeed some people seem to pride themselves about their belief in the irrational—thinking that this is the most authentic form of "faith." When asked, "Why do you believe in the Bible?" they answer, "Well, I guess I just have faith." Their slogan is, "Don't think, just believe." This protects

Faith from any further investigation by giving it a monopoly position that demands total exclusiveness. But is this really what the Bible means when it uses the word "faith"? It's very doubtful. The Bible does not seem to promote a belief in what is irrational or in any type of unwarranted "blind faith." The Bible has a proverb against blind faith: "A simple man believes anything, but a prudent man gives thoughts to his steps" (Proverbs 14:15). St. Paul says about the Christians in Thessalonica, "they received the word with all eagerness, examining the Scriptures daily to see if these things were so" (Acts 17:11). He also says, "Test everything. Hold on to the good" (1 Thess. 5:21).

Yet, there is still this autocratic view of religious faith that has become popular among many Christians. It is called *fideism*. The Encyclopedia of Philosophy defines fideism as "the view that truth in religion is ultimately based on faith rather than on reasoning or evidence." So fideism is still in search of truth—without advocating total irrationality—but it also asserts that this truth cannot be judged by human standards such as reasoning and logic. What this often leads to, though, is that Faith becomes a mere matter of personal convictions—a matter of personal and private beliefs that cannot be questioned by reason or by anything else. Religious beliefs may be held without any particular reason or evidence, and may even be in conflict with evidence and reason. When Faith is irrational, that may even make it of a better quality. Since fideism has affected many Christians, most modern ideas of Faith are fideistic—they deny, or at least denigrate, the role of reason in Christian Faith.

In short, the "faith-only" perspective of fideism claims that reason plays no, or hardly any, part in matters of Faith. Fideism claims that truths of a certain kind can be grasped only by foregoing rational inquiry and relying solely on Faith. This attitude is sometimes defended with the slogan, "Jerusalem—the city of believers—has nothing to do with Athens—the city of philosophers and non-believers." Tertullian is often quoted as saying, "I believe because it is absurd" (although he actually spoke of being "inapt" [*ineptum*]). This view seems to indicate that the only valid way to know anything about God is solely through Faith, even if or especially when it is irrational. Famous faith-only Christians include not only someone such as Tertullian (160?-230?), but also people like Soren Kierkegaard (1813-1855), Karl Barth (1886-1968), and to a slightly lesser degree, Blaise Pascal (1623-1662). The Protestant theologian Karl Barth took Anselm's motto—"I believe that I may understand"—to mean that we must not wish to understand first so as to believe later, but rather the other way around: believe first!

Fideism fosters the extreme conviction that one must not even look for reasons in making the act of Faith. Fr. Stephen Bevans, SVD testifies, "This was wonderfully expressed by the father of one of my students who, when told that his daughter was learning that theology was 'Faith seeking understanding,' exclaimed: 'But Faith doesn't have to seek understanding—that's why they call it Faith!'" Such people seem to reason (!) that if God's existence were a matter of proof, it would no longer be a matter of faith—therefore, it cannot be a matter of proof either. Some Christians trace this idea back to the German Reformer Martin Luther. Although Luther did not place "Faith" explicitly counter to reason, he did put it in opposition to any human efforts—with reasoning being one of them. He once said, "Reason is the greatest enemy that faith has." Interestingly enough, entirely on his own, Luther added an extra word, "alone" (*allein* in German), to Romans 3:28 in his Bible translation: "For we maintain that a man is justified by faith [alone] apart from observing the law." When challenged about this, Luther responded: "If your Papist annoys you with the word ['alone'], tell him straightway, Dr. Martin Luther will have it so."

The reason for some to embrace fideism is their conviction that God is so "totally other" that we cannot really know anything about him, unless we resort to pure faith. They force us into an either-or dilemma: we either claim that God is like all other entities, albeit infinitely superior in every respect, or we must admit that God in his transcendence is so entirely different that we cannot possibly know anything about him. The former claim is obviously false; God cannot possibly be like all other entities. The latter claim, however, is also untrue; if we don't know anything about God, we cannot even say he exists. So the claim of "faith alone" cannot do the "trick" either.

What is the origin of fideism? The driving force behind fideism is the deep perceived divide between man and God. The assumed "infinite gap" between the finitude of human beings—specifically in regard to reason—and the transcendent, infinite nature of God is supposed to keep us from being able to effectively reason on any spiritual and religious matters. On the one hand, there is the fallen state of man which has left each person's mind, reason, and intellect in opposition to God. On the other hand, there is the infinite greatness of God's power and wisdom, which is totally foreign to human reason and can only present paradoxes to mankind. Because of this infinite abyss between God and man, there must also be an infinite chasm between faith and reason. Therefore, fideism considers religious knowledge far beyond the limits of man's rational faculties and understanding. So reason cannot possibly bring us any closer to God. There is no way to bridge this infinite divide, except by some form of infused Faith.

It is not surprising that fideism can ultimately lead to a form of skepticism—skepticism about the possibility of human knowledge, at least in the area of religious knowledge (see 1.d). So this deep-seated doubt has triggered an appeal to a faith-based knowledge that is no longer supported by any rational evidence. It may sound strange, at first sight, but fideists come very close to agnostics. What agnostics and fideists have in common is that they both underestimate the power of reason. Agnostics believe they have no way to argue either for or against the existence of God, for they see no rational means of finding out either way. When it comes to God, reason is supposed to be entirely powerless. That's where agnosticism and fideism meet: they both deny reason can bring us any closer to God.

What is it that agnosticism stands for? The label of agnosticism may have been a recent invention but the idea behind it is much older. Diogenes Laërtius said already in the 3rd century, "As to the gods, I have no means of knowing either that they exist or do not exist." Agnosticism nowadays applies this idea about pagan "gods" also to the Christian notion of "God"—which is quite a stretch. It asserts that we just do not know whether God does exist or not, and what is worse, we presumably have no way of ever knowing one way or the other. Reason is believed to be completely powerless when it comes to God. So this version is not really atheism in the strict sense, for it also says that we have no way of knowing that God does *not* exist. It just keeps agnostics in limbo; they neither deny God nor affirm God.

Agnostics swear by reason and logic, but in a very truncated way. They claim that logic cannot demonstrate the *falsity* of a belief in God (it is said to be an unbeatable, unverifiable hypothesis), but neither can it demonstrate the *truth* of a belief in God (it is said to be a daring, undecided hypothesis). This makes the biologist Julian Huxley exclaim, "We should be agnostic about those things for which there is no evidence." Agnostics often say that they are not taking any stand pro-or-con God at all and therefore that they are safe, secure, and invulnerable to any attacks from either believers or unbelievers. It has even been said that we are all born agnostics; atheism and theism are considered something "sold" to us.

So how should we assess agnosticism then? It may appear to be pretty harmless at first sight. But there is reason to question this impression. First of all, since agnosticism keeps us in limbo, it refuses to give God the honor and worship he deserves as our Maker. Agnostics just never give God their time to study the evidence that points to him. As they say, if you are not interested in saucers, don't waste your time studying that subject. But when it comes to God, lack of interest is a much more serious case. We owe God our interest—but that assumes already that God exists.

Then there is a second reason why agnosticism may not be as harmless as it looks. Agnostics think that their own logic is so compelling that everyone who disagrees with their agnostic conclusions must be misinformed or just brainless—which is actually a rather arrogant position.

But no matter how we define agnosticism, it should be criticized as a limitation of the mind's capacity to know reality. It actually limits the mind's capacity to know reality to the narrow viewpoint of materialism, scientism, and rationalism. There *is* no God, they say, because we cannot logically or rationally or empirically prove the "God-hypothesis." In short, there is no rational evidence for God and God's existence. However, one of the arguments against agnosticism is that "God" was never intended to be a mere explanation for us to adopt until a better one might happen along, as is done in science. Another problem is that agnosticism usually demands evidence in a materialistic or scientific sense. Pope Benedict XVI accused agnosticism of limiting itself in claiming the power of reason to know *scientific* truth only, at the exclusion of religious or philosophical truths. Therefore, Pope Benedict considers agnosticism "a choice of comfort, pride, dominion, and utility over truth. It is opposed by self-criticism, humble listening to the whole of existence, the patience and self-correction of the scientific method and readiness to be purified by the truth."

The Catechism (2128) summarizes all of this as follows: "Agnosticism can sometimes include a certain search for God, but it can equally express indifferentism, a flight from the ultimate question of existence, and a sluggish moral conscience. Agnosticism is all too often equivalent to practical atheism." In other words, agnosticism tends to stifle the religious sense engraved in the depths of our nature and thus obscures God.

Back to our original question: are fideists similar to agnostics? The answer seems to be a cautious "Yes." They both underestimate the power of reason to bring us closer to God. But then their ways part: agnostics leave it at that, but fideists replace what they consider the weak power of reason with the monopoly of pure faith. Whereas the agnostic says, "I do not, and cannot, know whether God exists," the fideist merely adds to this, "But I accept it by faith." However, the faith-alone position of fideists is very questionable: if we don't know anything about God, we cannot even say God exists. The fideistic slogan "Don't think, just believe" has given agnostics a powerful weapon: "Don't believe, just think." Glorifying Faith at the cost of reason may sound devout but leads ultimately to a dead-end, as we will see next.

d. Faith Undervalued

As to be expected, the Faith of fideism has come under attack from many sides, from the inside as well as the outside of Christianity. It is rather ironic that fideism, popular among many Christians, has also become the prevalent attitude in circles of non-believers—and that's why many of them have become non-believers. There are two parties in this debate: the defenders of "faith alone" and the defenders of "reason alone." They both claim an unassailably superior position.

On the one hand, fideists hold up *faith* as a virtue, which shields them from any rational arguments made against their beliefs. This leads easily to a "surrender or die" attitude. When fideists claim that Faith entirely stems "from above" and cannot be tested by human standards "from below," they actually dispense themselves from the obligation to prove their credentials to others and to at least validate their religious beliefs as reasonable. They claim to be right but refuse to give evidence and arguments for their claim. As the Dutch Reformed theologian Harry Kuitert puts it, fideists like Karl Barth ended up creating "a building without a door; there is no way to get in or out." They claim that Faith ends any further demand for reason. Barth argued that we cannot know God apart from his self-revelation, which requires pure Faith without any input of reason. This basically promotes a "take it or leave it" attitude.

However, faith cannot be the only deciding factor to determine whether a certain faith—in the sense of a set of *beliefs*—is true, or cannot be true. We tend to put all religious faiths under one heading: religion. But this creates a very impoverished view of what religion really is or can be, for there is an enormous variety in this collection: not only what most people regard as religions, but also sects and cults. Each one of them claims to be true. Does that make them true? When defendants in court plead innocent, that does not mean they *are* innocent. Similarly, when religions claim to be true, that does not *make* them true. So should we really treat all of them the same? Do they all deserve our attention, let alone our respect? What they do have in common is a set of *beliefs*, but that does not mean all beliefs are of the same caliber and quality.

As a matter of fact, partly due to the fideistic idea of "faith alone," our contemporary culture has an extremely impoverished understanding of what religious faith really is. On the one hand, religious beliefs are equated with "blind" faith, up to being completely irrational. Religious faith is merely seen as a set of personal feelings and opinions about life, meaning, values, and God. What comes to mind here are sects and cults such as Nuwaubianism, the Scientology Church, the Nation of Yahweh, the Church of All Worlds, the Universe People, and the list is going and growing. As a result, Faith is merely understood as a set of private convictions about these matters at best, but certainly not as a set of convictions supported by evidence and arguments. As a consequence, to many contemporary minds, Faith has little or nothing to do with evidence or truth at all. A person's faith cannot be said to be true or false; at the most, a faith conviction is true for a particular individual—so it is at best one's own personal belief. But, according to rational standards, a religious belief cannot be true all by itself. The fideistic slogan "Don't think, just believe" has had a damaging effect on religion. It made atheists exclaim, "Don't believe, just think."

We find this impoverished view of religious faith in many writings of contemporary atheists. They consider all religious faith irrational, void of empirical evidence and rational arguments. The list of atheists seems to keep growing. Many of them are scientists and use their scientific authority to make their anti-religious case. The neuroscientist Sam Harris: "The faith of religion is belief on insufficient evidence." The astronomer Carl Sagan: "You can't convince a believer of anything; for their belief is not based on evidence, it's based on a deep-seated need to believe." Sam Harris again: "We rely on faith only in the context of claims for which there is no sufficient sensory or logical evidence." The biologist E. O. Wilson: "Blind faith, no matter how passionately expressed, will not suffice. Science for its part will test relentlessly every assumption about the human condition." The physicist Richard Feynman, "Religion is a culture of faith; science is a culture of doubt." Or the biologist Richard Dawkins: "Faith is belief in spite of, even perhaps because of, the lack of evidence."

Their common message is clear: religious faith is just blind faith without any empirical or rational backing. Benjamin Franklin had already stated, "The way to see by faith is to shut the eye of reason." Later on, George Bernard Shaw would say something similar: "It is not disbelief that is dangerous to our society; it is belief." And then he goes on, "There's no point of having faith if you have evidence." Mark Twain put this view in a nutshell: "A man is accepted into a church for what he believes and he is turned out for what he knows."

We cannot blame fideism for all of this, of course, but at least it has contributed to what has happened to our secular society. The final outcome is that there should not only be "freedom *of* religion" but also "freedom *from* religion," because religious beliefs are merely personal and private beliefs on things beyond further inspection, and therefore can easily be dispensed with. Secularism has been given an anti-religious overtone—a vision of the future as devoid of religion, instead of separated from religion. It seeks to eliminate religion, or at the very least to privatize and thus marginalize it. Secularists preach tolerance magnanimously, but only for those who agree with them—

"my way or no way."

Another reason for questioning any faith claims held by religious believers is the fact that there are so many different religions with different truth claims. If fideism were right, each religion could claim truth on merely fideistic grounds. No wonder, many people assume nowadays that religious belief or faith only consists of very diverse opinions and conjectures about what they consider unknown and unknowable. Immanuel Kant claimed to have shown, once and for all, that the existence of God lay forever beyond proof or disproof. So the very fact that there are so many different religions, often with widely differing beliefs and practices, seems to prove to many people that religious beliefs are simply opinions about an unknowable God, and thus are not open to reasonable discussion and investigation. There is no way to decide between them, because each believer seems to claim that one's faith proves one's faith is true.

Some others have come to a different conclusion. They have the strong conviction that the communalities between religions trump their differences by a wide margin anyway. After all, most religions have so much "common ground" that we should no longer focus on their differences. It is based on the notion that if we abstract enough from particular beliefs about God, we will eventually arrive at some "god" on whom we can all agree. All religions must have some part of the truth, and the rest does not really matter. This common "god" refers to some abstraction about which nothing much can be said. Some call this idea "ecumenism," while others, the more broad-minded ones, call it "interfaith dialogue," even across an increasingly wide board, from Catholics to Protestants, from Christians to Jews and Muslims, from revealed religions to Buddhism and Hinduism, from monotheism to polytheism. We are presumably all united in "faith," although our beliefs may differ. The new slogan is "one faith with many beliefs."

In this context, a frequently heard argument is that all monotheistic religions worship the same God—no matter whether they call God by the name of Lord, Allah, Brahman, or you name it. So it must be that each religion only captures part of the truth—and together perhaps the whole truth. From this supposedly follows that all religions are equal in capturing only a small part of the divine truth, if there is any truth to it at all. Popular in this context is the ancient fable of six blind men who visit the palace of the Rajah and encounter an elephant for the first time. As each touches the animal with his hands, each felt a different part of the elephant, announcing an elephant to be all trunk, all tail, etc. An argument ensued, each blind man thinking his own perception of the elephant was the correct one. The Rajah, awakened by the commotion, called out from the balcony. "The elephant is a big animal," he said. "Each man touched only one part. You must put all the parts together to find out what an elephant is like." The message is clear. Each one had only found part of the truth. In an analogous way, the different truth claims of all religions end up being equal, for no one has the entire picture, just pieces of it. Ultimately, all religions are supposedly equivalent in being inadequate.

However, there is a real problem here with this view and position. To come to this conclusion, we must have a full and accurate view of the entire picture—just as the king had of the blind men and the elephant from his balcony. The Rajah was in a position of privileged access to the truth. Because he could see clearly, he was able to correct those who were blind. If everyone truly is blind, then no one can know if he or anyone else is mistaken. Only someone who knows the whole truth can identify another on the fringes of it. In this story, only the king can do that—no one else. The Christian apologist Greg Koukle words it correctly: "If the story-teller is like one of the six who can't see—if he is one of the blind men groping around—how does he know everyone else is blind and has only a portion of the truth? On the other hand, if he fancies himself in the position of the king, how is it that he alone escapes the illusion that blinds the rest of us?"

G. K. Chesterton was eager to debunk the argument that the diversity of religions hampers their different truth claims:

> *It is perpetually said that because there are a hundred religions claiming to be true, it is therefore impossible that one of them should really be true.... It would be as reasonable to say that because some people thought the earth was flat, and others (rather less incorrectly) imagined it was round, and because anybody is free to say that it is triangular or hexagonal, or a rhomboid, therefore it has no shape at all; or its shape can never be discovered.*

Neither does the mere fact that many religions have the same reference, God, entail that all religious conceptions of God are equivalent in being inadequate. Think of the following analogy. You are probably familiar with the Evening Star—a rather bright object in the sky during a clear evening. Perhaps, as an early riser, you are also familiar with the Morning Star, a very prominent object that has attracted many people's attention in the early morning. For centuries, some people have admired the Evening Star, while others enjoyed the Morning Star. It turned out, however, that it is the same object they are talking about—the planet Venus, that is. In calling this object Venus, we have found a better designation for what people see at sunrise and what they see at sunset. Amazingly enough, the same thing can be seen at different moments, by different people, from different perspectives. No matter whether we say "Venus" or "Morning Star" or "Evening Star," we are talking about the same referent in the sky; and yet, the designation "Venus" is much more comprehensive and adequate than "Morning Star" or "Evening Star."

However, there is another side to this story. Monotheism does indeed state that there is only one God. But this can mean at least two very different things—either all religions venerate the same God, or all religions have their own gods, but only one of them is God, the real God. In the latter view, Yahweh and Allah not only carry different descriptions but also different references. To use our example of Venus again, talking about "Venus" may refer for some to a planet, for some to a Greek goddess, for others to a horoscope— which are not only different descriptions but also different references. In this view, the difference between Yahweh and Allah is more like the difference between Yahweh and Baal. Baal is *a* god, but not *the* God. The Old Testament makes very often a distinction between God, on the one hand, and gods, idols, or demons, on the other hand. Only Yahweh is God, but all the other gods are not God but God's creations which rebelled against him and became fallen spirits.

No matter how we look at this, there is still a door to

religion that can let you in or out—it's the door of reason leading to Faith and bringing us closer to God. But obviously this is not the kind of reason as understood by rationalism and agnosticism. Similar to what we said earlier about reason—reason is not all-powerful, but neither is it powerless—we could also say about Faith: Faith is not all-powerful either, but neither is it powerless. We just need to find out what its real power is. Even the master of reason, Thomas Aquinas, was overwhelmed by Faith when he had an experience at Mass in December 1273, which persuaded him to stop finishing his *Summa Theologiae*. In his own words, "All I have written seems to me like straw compared to what I have seen and what has been revealed to me."

3. Faith AND Reason

The twosome of "faith and reason" raises many contentious questions. Are we supposed to rely upon our intellect, drawing rational conclusions, rejecting those things that don't make sense? Or are we to accept instead the teachings of Scripture and Church without regard to logic and reason, even if it does not make any sense? Questions like these have troubled many people, as we discovered in the previous chapters.

The Catholic Church has a very distinctive position on the relationship between faith and reason. She does not see them as competitors or contestants, but as equivalent participants in the search for truth, even so in religion. Reason comes from God as much as Faith does. Peter Kreeft describes it well:

> *Christianity inherited faith ... from the Jews, and reason ... from the Greeks, and the central intellectual project of the whole middle ages was a marriage or a synthesis of these two things. They were different, but they were made for each other, like Romeo and Juliet. It was a storybook marriage, but it was a happy one. And perhaps the best way to characterize the modern world is the word 'divorce.' The two partners have sort of set up houses on their own and produced all sorts of arguments against each other.*

Because of this unfortunate development in recent history, which we partly sketched in the previous chapters, we need to reexamine each one again, to get rid of the many misconceptions about the meaning of both faith and reason. There are truths we know by reason and there are truths we know by faith. Properly understood, faith and reason need and support each other. The two make for a valid *distinction*, which some have turned, unfortunately, into an invalid *contrast*. Let us see how the Catholic Church makes her case.

a. Not Reason-Alone as in Rationalism

Since there are both truths we know by reason and truths we know by faith, it is often said that there are material truths as well as immaterial truths, natural truths as well as supernatural truths. Natural truths come to us by experience and experiment; supernatural truths come to us through Revelation and Scripture. And then there are philosophical truths which we find through reasoning. In his Encyclical "Faith and Reason" [*Fides et Ratio*], Pope John Paul II makes a similar distinction (30):

> *It may help, then, to turn briefly to the different modes of truth. Most of them depend upon immediate evidence or are confirmed by experimentation. This is the mode of truth proper to everyday life and to scientific research. At another level we find philosophical truth, attained by means of the speculative powers of the human intellect. Finally, there are religious truths which are to some degree grounded in philosophy, and which we find in the answers which the different religious traditions offer to the ultimate questions.*

Unfortunately, the fact that there is more to know than what we know through the senses has been obliterated by the "reason alone" view of rationalism. No wonder, the First Vatican Council condemned not only fideism—"faith alone" without reason—but also rationalism—"reason alone" without faith. Let's find out first what the reason-alone view fails to reveal.

As we found out earlier, the truncated version of rationalism is deeply rooted in two faith-unfriendly worldviews: materialism and naturalism. How could this ever happen? *Fides et Ratio* (46) explains: "In the field of scientific research, a positivistic mentality took hold which not only abandoned the Christian vision of the world, but more especially rejected every appeal to a metaphysical or moral vision." While materialism holds that there are only material causes—which excludes any causes of the immaterial kind—naturalism holds that there are only natural causes, and therefore rejects any supernatural causes. Materialism and naturalism are philosophical doctrines. Materialism declares that everything is matter and that matter is all there is. Naturalism declares that everything is nature and that nature is all there is. In other words, these doctrines proclaim there is nothing in the world other than "Matter" and "Nature," and everything else is mere illusion. Is that possible?

If this were true, the doctrine of materialism would condemn itself as an illusion too, because it is not material but immaterial. Besides, if this were really true, what would we do with abstract, immaterial ideas such as justice, with abstract, immaterial concepts such as gravity, and with abstract, immaterial entities such as numbers or geometric shapes? If matter or nature is all there is, then what is the mathematical constant *pi* (π)? If materialism and naturalism were true, then universal, immutable, and abstract concepts certainly could not exist by themselves. And yet they do. Concepts are mental, immaterial entities—they have no mass, no size, no color (see 1.b). To reduce them to a "creation of neurons in the brain" obscures the fact that "neuron" itself is an abstract concept. Such a claim makes for a vicious circle: the very idea that concepts are nothing but neurons firing is itself nothing but neurons firing. As Stephen Barr pithily puts it, "The brain does not infer the existence of the mind, the mind infers the existence of the brain." Those who claim that mental concepts are merely products of neurons should realize that talking about neurons requires the concept of *neuron* to begin with.

How could the infinite universal meaning of an abstract concept ever be inscribed in the finite material system of the brain? Even circles we cannot see, for a "circle" is a highly abstract, idealized concept (with a radius and a diameter). As said earlier (see 1.a), it is through the power of abstract concepts and mental reasoning that we gain access to the "unseen" world of truths and untruths, access to laws of nature and the structure of this Universe. Even the concept of truth itself cannot be a material issue; it too has no mass, size, or color. That's where materialism and naturalism run into trouble. They exclude immaterial entities ahead of time from our discourse, and then "conclude" there are only material entities. They are more often than not based on a choice made prior to reasoning, before evidence and arguments against them are brought in.

Not surprisingly, rationalism based on either materialism or naturalism has a problem in the eyes of the Catholic Church, for with its "reason alone" approach it leaves only room for natural truths and material entities, but rejects all supernatural truths and immaterial entities. The First Vatican Council explicitly condemned rationalism—that is, the "reason alone" approach without faith. When the

Catholic Church defends reason, she is not referring to the "reason alone" version as promoted by rationalism, materialism, and naturalism. Instead she speaks of reason combined with faith. Faith tells us more than we could know by reason alone, so we need to be "faithful" in our reasoning. Reason must be receptive to reality in all of its aspects: both the quantifiable and the non-quantifiable, both the measurable and the immeasurable, both the observable and the non-observable, both the tangible and the intangible, both the natural and the supernatural. We want to know and deserve to know the "whole truth," and not just a truncated part of the truth. If we limit ourselves to truths that we know by reason-alone, we miss out on the truths we could know by faith.

As *Fides et Ratio* (75) puts it, "In refusing the truth offered by divine Revelation, philosophy only does itself damage, since this is to preclude access to a deeper knowledge of truth." Rationalism has curtailed the power of reason to "reason alone." But to get the full power of reason back, we need also the power of Faith. Without the power of Faith, reason on its own becomes the supreme criterion of truth. Indeed, rationalism maintains that human reason alone is the source of truth, and therefore the exclusive judge of what is true and false, good and evil. Pope Leo XIII said about this view: "The fundamental doctrine of Rationalism is the supremacy of the human reason, which, refusing due submission to the divine and eternal reason, proclaims its own independence, and constitutes itself the supreme principle and source and judge of truth." What all forms of extreme rationalism have in common is a belief in the supremacy of reason-alone, and therefore a rejection of Divine Revelation and Scripture.

So it could be said that the trio of rationalism, materialism, and naturalism has united forces with each other to undermine all religious faith by denying any form of Revelation. They leave only room for natural entities at the exclusion of supernatural ones. For this reason, Cardinal Pie, a French Catholic bishop of Poitiers at the end of the 19th century, put it this way: "Naturalism is more than a heresy; it is pure undiluted anti-Christianism. Heresy denies one or more dogmas; Naturalism denies that there are any dogmas or that there can be any. Naturalism denies the very existence of Revelation." It is important to specifically add, though, that the truths we know by religious faith and Divine Revelation are not in violation of reason. As *Fides et Ratio* (76) puts it, "Revelation clearly proposes certain truths which might never have been discovered by reason unaided, although they are not of themselves inaccessible to reason." We will discuss this issue further in the next chapter.

But there is another problem with rationalism. In addition to being associated with materialism and naturalism, there is also the problem that rationalism itself is a belief or faith that can never be proven by rationalism itself. If we believe that reason is indeed reasonable, it should be admitted this is a belief in itself, and thus requires some sort of faith. There is a certain step of faith required in putting all of one's intellectual weight on the pedestal of reason. The most fundamental assumption of the rational mind is that the world perceived through reason is true—that the world itself is reasonable. This presupposes that the mind interpreting the world through reason is somehow apprehending the world as it actually exists.

Because of this, faith is in fact a prerequisite for reason. In order to reason about anything we must have faith that there are laws of logic which correctly prescribe the correct chain of reasoning (see 1.b). Since laws of logic cannot be observed with the senses, our confidence in them is a type of faith—not necessarily a religious kind of faith, but faith it is. Besides, when we come to a logical conclusion by reasoning, we can only do so by starting with premises that we accept on faith, trust, or authority. So faith is clearly at the basis of rationality; it is a necessary component of knowledge and reason since a person must *believe* something in order to *know* it. In other words, all human knowledge and reason is dependent on some kind of faith: faith in our senses, faith in our premises, faith in our reason, faith in our memories, and faith in the accounts of events we receive from others. Accordingly, faith is seen as essential to and inseparable from rationality.

But there is another profound connection between reason and faith. Once we accept the idea that truth comes from conformity with reality, we have to face the following intriguing question: how come there seems to be an almost perfect harmony of thought and being, of rationality and reality? Put differently, what must nature, including man, be like in order for reason to capture truth at all? There seems to be some mysterious conformity between the rationality of our minds and the rationality found in the world around us. Somehow the mind seems to be able to capture reality the way it *is*. Hence, there must be an objective source and foundation for knowledge, reason, and rationality. That source and foundation can be found in Faith—Faith in a personal and rational God who makes the harmony between rationality and reality possible.

The fact that the Universe has an elegant, intelligible, and discoverable underlying mathematical and rational structure calls for an explanation—or otherwise must be left unexplained. Even scientists uphold the conviction—consciously or subconsciously—that there is an intelligible plan behind this Universe, a plan that is accessible to the human intellect through the natural light of reason. Where does this power of reason come from? In other words, what is the reason behind the power of reason? As John Polkinghorne puts it, "Such a reason would be provided by the Rationality of the Creator." Only God's rationality can explain that the world is an objective and orderly entity investigable by the human mind because the mind too is an orderly and objective product of the same rational and consistent Creator. Fr. George Lemaître, who launched the Big Bang theory, once spoke about the God of the Big Bang as the "One Who gave us the mind to understand him and to recognize a glimpse of his glory in our Universe which he has so wonderfully adjusted to the mental power with which he has endowed us."

The conformity and harmony between reality and rationality must be a riddle for non-believers, but for religious believers it would be "a match made in Heaven." The physical order we observe in this world appears to be amazingly "consistent." It is a consistency that must perplex us, for how is it possible that reality can be "grasped" by reason? Not only is our rationality consistent, but so is the world itself. It is hard to believe that this match can only be a product of natural selection or any other natural or material causes—unless one eliminates any other explanation ahead of time. If we presuppose a Universe that simply exists apart from any sort of creation by a rational intelligence, there is no longer any reason to accept reason itself as a valid interpretation of reality.

The case could be made that a basic faith in the power of reason is rather shaky if it is not anchored in religious faith—actually the Judeo-Christian form of Faith as revealed to us through the Bible. That's where Faith must come into the discussion. As a matter of fact, the Judeo-Christian Faith affirms that there is an objective source and foundation for knowledge, reason, and rationality. That source and foundation is found in a personal and rational God who is infinitely wise and all-knowing and created this world in his Wisdom. He created the Universe to reflect a coherent order, and he made man in his image—including his rational faculties—so man is able to discover that intelligible organization. Logic and rationality are then expected features in the Christian theistic worldview. Reason is a divine spark in each of us. By denying this, the reason-alone view would undermine its own foundation. Without faith, reason loses its foundation. We cannot just think and reason, we also need to believe and have Faith. Thanks to Faith we can know what we could not know by reason alone.

b. Not Faith-Alone as in Fideism

The First Vatican Council condemned not only rationalism—that is, "reason alone" without faith—but also fideism—which is "faith alone" without reason. The Catholic Church wants people to use *reason* as vigorously and energetically as possible—and this very much includes scientific reason. But then, at the limits of their striving, it invites them to listen and to trust—in short, to have *Faith*.

But this Faith never involves a sacrifice of the intellect and reason. God wants us to understand all we can about him and about his Revelation by way of reason. St. Augustine famously warned us that it is "dangerous to have an infidel hear a Christian ... talking nonsense." Nonsense is a form of irrationality. Augustine could not have said it more clearly, "Believers are also thinkers: in believing, they think and in thinking, they believe."

As said earlier, there are truths we know by reason and there are truths we know by faith. What about the truths we know by Faith? Are they only based on Faith without any reason? Fideism would say so, but the Catholic Church is of a different opinion. In his 1998 encyclical *Fides et Ratio*, John Paul II warned of "a resurgence of fideism, which fails to recognize the importance of rational knowledge and philosophical discourse for the understanding of faith, indeed for the very possibility of belief in God." And in *Caritas In Veritate*, Pope Benedict XVI writes, "Truth frees charity from the constraints of ... a fideism that deprives it of human and universal breathing-space."

When the Catholic Church speaks of "Faith," she is obviously not referring to the "faith alone" version as promoted by fideism. Instead she speaks of Faith combined with reason. Faith addresses issues beyond the scope of reason-alone—issues that science and reason-alone are inherently incapable of addressing, but that are nevertheless entirely real. Accordingly, Faith is seen as complementing reason, by providing answers to questions that would otherwise be unanswerable. However, although those issues are beyond the scope of reason, they are not unreasonable and cannot be against reason. Accordingly, reason is seen as complementing Faith, by providing reasons why Faith is not unreasonable.

Faith cannot be the only deciding factor to determine whether a certain faith—in the sense of a set of *beliefs*—is true, or cannot be true. As we said earlier, there is an enormous variety under the heading of "religion": not only what most people regard as religions, but also sects and cults. Each one of them claims to be true. So should we really treat all of them the same? Do they all deserve our attention, let alone our respect? What they do have in common is a set of *beliefs*, but that does not mean all beliefs are of the same caliber and quality. We would need another important deciding factor to determine which ones are true, and which ones cannot be true—which is *reason*. Religious beliefs that are against reason cannot be true. Religions that are irrational and incoherent cannot be true. And that might eliminate quite a few of them.

So what is the role of reason when it comes to Faith? St. Thomas summarizes what reason does for Faith as follows: (1) reason prepares the mind for Faith; (2) reason explains the truths of Faith; (3) reason defends the truths of Faith. This perspective on reason has a long history in the Catholic Church. It can be traced back to St. Anselm's two famous phrases, "Faith seeking understanding" and "I believe in order that I might understand." But it goes even further back to St. Augustine's two famous formulas (Sermons, 43, 9) which express the coherent synthesis between faith and reason: "believe in order to understand" [*Crede ut intelligas*], but also, and inseparably, "understand in order to believe" [*intellige ut credas*]. In other words, in order to find God and believe, you must scrutinize truth. *Fides et Ratio* (53) says, "Against the temptations of fideism, however, it was necessary to stress the unity of truth and thus the positive contribution which rational knowledge can and must make to faith's knowledge."

The first role of reason is preparing the mind for Faith. In fact, it is by reason that we come to know and understand what faith and belief are. Reason opens the gate to Faith and leads us to God. Reason is the vehicle, which, if driven correctly, takes us to the door of Faith. While reason in and of itself, apart from God's special grace, cannot cause Faith, the use of reason is normally a part of a person's coming to Faith, and serves to support Faith in innumerable ways. Reason can establish the rational grounds for belief by proving God's existence, his authority or credibility as all-wise and trustworthy, and by proving that God has actually made a revelation since he confirmed the fact by working miracles that testify what God has spoken to human beings, especially in the person of Jesus Christ. Augustine made this very clear when he stated:

> *For who cannot see that thinking is prior to believing? For no one believes anything unless he has first thought that it is to be believed. [... It is] necessary that everything which is believed should be believed after thought has preceded; although even belief is nothing else than to think with assent.... Believers are also thinkers: in believing, they think and in thinking, they believe.... If faith does not think, it is nothing.*

The second role of reason is explaining the truths of Faith. St. Augustine called such a crucial intellectual and spiritual activity "Faith seeking understanding." Believers should strongly endeavor to use God-given reason to explore the depths of their Faith and to discover its doctrinal truth. The

Bible itself encourages the attainment of knowledge, wisdom, and understanding (Job 28:28; Prov. 1:7) and promotes such rational virtues as discernment and testing (Acts 17:11; Col. 2:8; 1 Thess. 5:21). Stretching mental and spiritual muscles to apprehend such doctrines as the Triune nature of God and the Incarnation of Jesus Christ moves one from an initial stage of Faith to a deeper stage of reflection and a greater sense of God's majesty, and an even deeper and clearer understanding of the divine mysteries (see 5.a). In the words of *Fides et Ratio* (79), "Faith grows deeper and more authentic when it is wedded to thought and does not reject it." We can certainly use our reason to better understand our Faith. In fact, that's a classic definition of theology: Faith seeking understanding.

The third role of reason is defending the truths of Faith. Augustine said that the authority of the Christian Faith is Scripture. However we should not be satisfied with simply resting on any authority, but we should seek to understand the authority in which we have placed our faith. In other words, we should not just believe, but we should seek to understand why and what we believe. Reason can show us that the mysteries of Faith are in harmony with naturally known truths; besides, it can defend their validity against the charge of being contrary to reason. What Christians believe is not irrational but can be explained to and defended against non-believers by using something we all have in common—reason.

Nevertheless, religious faith also comes with mysteries. Mysteries are beyond full comprehension. Yet, this poses serious questions. How could we ever believe something we don't fully understand? If there is no room for "blind faith" in the Catholic Church, how could we ever deal with mysteries? Well, we said earlier the expression "blind faith" is as deceiving as "blind love." Something similar could be said about Faith in God; it is not blind but sees God as in a mirror. This does not mean, of course, that we can understand everything in religion completely. Can God be understood to the fullest, for instance? The answer is a clear No. "If you understood him," Augustine declares, "it would not be God."

So religious faith necessarily deals with mysteries that cannot be understood completely. But although the mysteries of our Faith may be beyond reason, they are not against reason—they are not unreasonable. They can be defended, though not proven, by arguments based on reason. A mystery is not something about which we can't know anything, but something about which we can't know everything. God gave us brains and expects us to use them to understand the mysteries of Faith, to the extent such understanding is possible. The reason that there must be mysteries is that God is infinite and our intellects are finite. The fact that total comprehension isn't possible doesn't mean you have to "check your brains at the door" any more than your failure to entirely grasp quantum physics does.

One might also wonder whether we could ever believe something that goes *against* reason. The truth is that Faith tells us more than we could know by reason alone, yet it can never contradict reason. Christian truth-claims never violate the basic laws or principles of reason. Christian Faith and doctrines (for example, the Trinity and the Incarnation), though they often transcend our finite human comprehension, are not irrational or absurd. St. Thomas is very definite in defending that Faith cannot be against reason. When something is against reason, God cannot create it, he says. St. Thomas is so adamant on this issue because God is reason himself, so he cannot act against his own nature by doing what is contradictory. God is absolutely free, but his freedom is not arbitrary, so he cannot go against what he has declared true and right. We know this, because our own power of reason is rooted in creation and thus participates in God's power of reason. Our reason is a reflection of God's Reason. Reason has its origin in God as much so as Faith does.

As a consequence, God being all-powerful does not mean that God is able to do what is logically contradictory. St. Thomas gives many examples: God cannot create square circles; God cannot make someone blind and not-blind at the same time; God cannot declare true what is false; God cannot undo something that happened in the past; and the list goes on and on. To use a silly example: God does not even have the power to make a stone so heavy that he himself cannot lift it—that would be contradictory, and therefore against reason. Doesn't this put God at the mercy of our own reason, though? Not at all. God cannot act against his own nature, which includes Reason. In Islam, Allah can change his mind any time, but not so in Christianity.

When St. Thomas talks about Faith—and he does so constantly in his *Summa theologiae*—he cannot do so without using reason. So even his style reflects this permanent dialogue between Faith and reason. He uses a question/answer (Q&A) format, but his answer is always embedded in a web of dialogue with alternative views. He starts with a specific question [*quaestio*], usually divided in separate articles. After stating his question, St. Thomas always first considers the reasons for the view he will ultimately reject. He then says "On the contrary," and states the opposite view, which is usually closer to his own view. So each article contains arguments pro and con a certain position. Counterarguments are then given and counteracted again. In the response [*responsio*], St. Thomas explains his own position. After explaining his view more fully, he then gives replies which show why the reasons given for the view he rejects are inadequate. All in all, it is a perpetual dialogue between Faith and reason.

Thanks to our intellect, with its power of reason—that means, without any special assistance from God—we can know many things about ourselves, about the material world, and about God; or, as St. Thomas says, "about things that are beneath us, things that are in us, and things that are above us." Blind faith and cold reason are both dangerous guides. The balanced Catholic seeks to have the body of reason animated by the fire of Faith. Without reason, Faith loses its credibility. We cannot just believe and have Faith, we also need to think and reason. Thanks to reason we can know what we could not know by Faith alone.

c. No Double Truth

Why should we believe something? The reason is not because others believe it or because it feels good, but the only valid reason must be because it is *true*. So if there are truths of faith and if there are also truths of reason, does this mean there can be a "double truth"—making something true according to faith but false according to reason, or vice-versa?

The Catholic answer is a definite no. When we speak of faith and reason—or theology and philosophy, or religion and science—we are making a distinction, not a separation. We can distinguish them without putting them in contrast to each other. There are two key types of truth—there is divine truth and there is human truth—and these are always to be kept distinct when we think about faith and reason. Human truth comes from so-called "natural" revelation based on reason, while divine truth comes from so-called "special" revelation based on Faith. Something similar can be said about science and religion: science masquerading as religion is as unseemly as religion masquerading as science. Instead, they convey two very different kinds of truth. Science has *theories* to help us understand, but they are subject to change—so we should not make science more than what it is. Religion, on the other hand, has *truths* we try to understand, but they never change—so don't make religion less than what it is.

St. Thomas was emphatic that when both natural revelation and Special Revelation are rightly understood, the truth learned from one of these two will never contradict the truth learned from the other. Thomas claimed that Special Revelation and natural revelation—or faith and reason, or theology and philosophy—play, in his own words, "complementary roles in the quest for truth. Grace does not destroy nature but fulfills it." He clearly stated that all aspects of God's revelation are complimentary. We have St. Thomas to thank for constantly reminding us that all truth is God's truth and is therefore both universal and permanent. God has revealed Himself both in the Scriptures and in the natural world. Therefore, if we find a seeming contradiction between the two, we have not understood correctly either the Scriptures, the natural world, or both.

Perhaps a few examples may demonstrate how important the rejection of "double truth" is. Since there are truths of reason as well as truths of Faith—which can never contradict each other—it cannot be that the earth is flat according to faith and religion, but at the same time round according to reason and science, for that would create a contradiction. In a similar way, if science tells us that the earth circles the sun, it cannot be that faith has the sun circle the earth. But also, Faith or Scripture cannot tell us that the plants were created on the third day before the sun on the fourth day, whereas science tells us that plants cannot exist without light from the sun. In all such cases we are dealing with contradictions which cannot be both true if there is no "double truth." When we detect a "double truth," either one or both must have been claimed in error and must be reevaluated.

One word of caution, though. Sometimes we might think we have a double-truth issue, when in fact we do not. For instance, creation as understood by faith versus evolution as understood by science do not contradict each other. Creation is about how secondary causes are related to God, the Primary Cause, whereas evolution deals with how secondary causes are related to each other through reproduction and natural selection. The same can be said about randomness in science and Providence in faith. Randomness is about how events are related to each other, whereas Providence is about how events are related to God. So we do not need to make a choice between two truths in these cases because there is no problem of "double truth" here.

How important the rejection of "double truth" is can be shown when we weigh it against contrary views. Some believers—like the Protestant Reformer Martin Luther in his more excitable moments—have held that Faith at all times trumps reason. Others have held—especially so nowadays—that science must always trump Faith if religion is to apply in the modern world. Contrary to these views, St. Thomas claims that the truths of Faith must agree with the truths of science, because God is author of both, and so any apparent conflict shows that we have failed to understand one or the other or both. This denial of the theory of "double truth" brings an end to the claim of some that something can be true in philosophy and science but false in religion and faith, or vice-versa.

According to St. Thomas, if something is true in philosophy or science, it must also be true in the Christian Faith. You cannot have one thing being true in one area and it being false in another area. Truth is truth—all truth is God's truth. So there's no real opposition between truths of reason and truths of Faith, only an apparent one. When scientists propose as fact what is only an unproven hypothesis, or when theologians mistake their personal opinions for issues of divine revelation, the impression is left there's a conflict between the two realms, but this isn't the case. It only appears to be so because someone has erred.

In fact, St. Thomas' view is a bit more intricate than

sketched so far. On the one hand, he did say that there are certain truths that can be known through Special Revelation and cannot be determined by investigating the natural world, while at the same time there are certain truths learned from the study of nature that are not found, for example, in the Bible. Some truths can be found in nature but not in Scripture—for instance, the working of DNA. Other truths can be found in Scripture but not in nature—for instance, the Triune nature of God. On the other hand, Thomas did add a third set of truths, a set of "mixed articles." These are truths that can be known from the Bible as well as by a study of nature—for instance, the knowledge of the existence of a Creator (see 3.d).

St. Thomas says about these "mixed articles" that one could attain truths about religious claims without Faith, but then we are dealing with truths that are incomplete. St. Thomas called this "a twofold truth" about religious claims, "one to which the inquiry of reason can reach, the other which surpasses the whole ability of the human reason." Yet, even in those cases, no contradiction can stand between these two truths. On the other hand, something can be true for Faith but inconclusive in philosophy (though not the other way around). This entails that a non-believer can attain to truth, although not to the "higher" truths of Faith.

What does this mean for religious faith more in specific? Faith builds on reason and reason builds on faith. Since faith and reason are both ways of arriving at truth—and since all truths are harmonious with each other—faith and reason are consistent with each other. Reason covers what we can know by experience and logic. From reason, we can know that there is a God and that there is only one God;

these truths about God are accessible to anyone by experience and logic alone, apart from any Special Revelation from God. So there is a twofold mode of truth in what we profess about God. Some truths about God exceed all the ability of the human reason—such as the truth that God is Triune—but there are some truths which the natural reason also is able to reach—such are that God exists, that God is one, and the like. In fact, such truths about God have been proved demonstratively by many philosophers, guided by the light of natural reason (see 3.d).

All of this raises the famous question Pontius Pilate once posed: What is truth? The matter of *truth* is at the core of this discussion. Long ago, Aristotle famously worded the issue as follows: "To say of what is that it is or of what is not that it is not, is true." This dictum has been the starting point for all philosophical discussions about truth. It talks about something that is said or stated, on the one hand, and something that is or is not, on the other hand. So this raises the question what the relationship is between what is said or stated, usually called a *statement*, and what is or is not, commonly referred to as a *fact* in reality. So the question is: what is this relationship like?

Aristotle was of the opinion that the two have a relationship of *correspondence*—sometimes called the correspondence theory. St. Thomas, walking in Aristotle's footsteps, speaks more specifically of a correspondence between reality and intellect [*adequatio intellectus et rei*]. The correspondence theory may sound trivial, but basically it only asserts that there must be a correspondence between the way reality is and what we say about reality. However, the term "correspondence" is still ambiguous. It can be taken in the sense of "corresponding *to*" the facts, meaning that a statement is linked to a fact, like a ledger entry corresponds to a sale. Or it can be taken in the sense of "corresponding *with*" the facts, meaning that a statement conforms or squares with a fact, just like a key corresponds with a key hole. The latter interpretation is harder to defend than the former, for the intellect always processes sense-data in order for perception to become cognition, but let's leave it at that. More recently, at least two rival theories were developed as alternatives to the correspondence theory: the consensus theory and the pragmatist theory. What do they claim differently?

The *pragmatist* theory considers statements true, not so because they correspond to what is the case in reality, but because most of us accept them as true, mainly because they have been so successful. A common reason for accepting them as true is that they "work" in a satisfactory manner, which is more specifically the standpoint of pragmatism. However, the problem with this view of equating "true" with "successful" or "useful" is that true explanations may indeed be successful and useful, but successful or useful explanations are not necessarily true. The geocentrism of Ptolemy was as successful in its predictions as the heliocentrism of Copernicus, but Ptolemy had it wrong, in spite of the fact that with the help of his system, ships had been able to navigate the seas for centuries, and astronomers had been able to predict eclipses quite precisely. In other words, Ptolemy's geocentrism was successful and useful but not true. Truth is often not particularly useful, and many an illusion proves useful. However, the most important point against pragmatism is that even success depends ultimately on truth in terms of correspondence, since success implies that a prediction "comes true" and corresponds to what is actually the case in reality. Which takes us back to the correspondence theory.

The other theory, the *coherence* theory, declares a statement true if it is part of a coherent axiomatic system. However, this would entail that a statement being true in one system may be untrue in another system. Consequently, this kind of truth is self-made, depending on the chosen axioms—which is like saying, what is "true" in chess is not "true" in checkers. Admittedly, this idea may be helpful in mathematics and logic, but it is pretty useless when dealing with reality as done in the empirical sciences. Einstein said it right, "As far as the laws of mathematics refer to reality, they are not certain; and as far as they are certain, they do not refer to reality." When we add 1 to 1 in math, the result is 2; but when we add 1 drop of water to another drop of water, the result is not 2 drops but 1 drop. Also, whether we choose either a Euclidean or a Riemannian geometry is completely up to us, but when it comes to cosmology, we need the kind of geometry that has the best correspondence between our theories and the facts. The problem is that the choice between coherent systems cannot be made on the basis of coherence but must be made on the basis of correspondence again. Maurice Merleau-Ponty said it right, "the real is coherent and probable because it is real, and not real because it is coherent." So we are back again with Aristotle and St. Thomas.

Their conclusion—that truth is ultimately based on correspondence—is probably something practically all people nowadays, including scientists, would agree with, although perhaps reluctantly. They do in fact maintain, as a working assumption, that they are dealing with objective reality, even though they do not always say so. Any understanding of reality has to *correspond* to that reality. Although some sociobiologists seem to claim we believe what we believe because what we call "truth" emerges from brains shaped by natural selection, they must admit that natural selection itself does operate depending on the way the world "is." Besides, if their claim entails that our beliefs are mere artifacts, such a claim would act like a boomerang that destroys its own truth claims. Beliefs like these contradict the fact that scientific proofs of something being true come from conformity with reality, not from systems of ideas. Regardless of the fact that neither human reason nor the Universe can be explained by themselves, the most surprising thing in all of this remains the perfect harmony of thought and being, truth and reality. Perhaps the only possible explanation for this harmony would be that we have here "a match made in Heaven" (see 3.a).

As to the issue of truth, it is safe to say that St. Thomas uses a solid theory to define truth (how to determine truth is another issue). It is clear again that Thomas Aquinas strives for real and objective knowledge—a perfect harmony of thought and being, truth and reality, that is. His understanding is firmly based on senses, intellect, and reason—on something we all have in common. We have no direct access to what the world is "really" like, other than through our senses. Yet our knowledge goes beyond that, while remaining real, truthful, reliable, and "veridical"—after being tested versus reality, of course. *Fides et Ratio* (83) rightly stresses that "reality and truth do transcend the factual and the empirical."

We should probably underscore that Thomas' viewpoint cannot be confused with "naïve realism," which assumes that perceptions based on the senses create carbon copies of reality. If that were the case, all we would need in order to perceive and observe something is taking a "picture" of it. However, the mind with its intellect and reasoning does not simply create an exact replica of things in the world but abstracts from this its own "picture." Such "pictures" correspond to reality, but not in all respects and aspects; they are not an exact replica of what they "picture"; even photographs are not two-dimensional replicas of reality. Perception is not a passive process of monitoring sense-data but rather the result of some mental reconstruction process. Even though our perceptions are mental and intellectual constructions—rather than direct recordings of reality—they clearly are neither arbitrary nor illusory. Although we know the world through sensations or sense impressions, they are just the media that give us access to reality. Knowledge does rest on sensation, but that doesn't mean it is confined to it.

Obviously, St. Thomas' conception of truth is the best antidote against current ideologies of relativism and skepticism. We discussed already (see 1.d) that the statement "all truth is relative" leads to contradiction. When you deny that there is something as objective truth, you are in fact insisting in your denial that what you say is objectively true, which it cannot be by its own verdict. Nevertheless, relativism is on the rise, in spite of the fact that science is currently one of the (perhaps last?) strongholds where truth is still respected in our culture.

Why does science still hold on to its truth claims? Well, if truth were at the mercy of some individuals, science had to abandon all its universal claims. It is reality that sometimes forces scientists to revise their theories in order to come closer to the truth. They constantly need to adjust the "speculations" in their minds to the "data" of reality. The so much heralded idea of falsifiability and falsification in science says that a theory is in trouble when its predictions turn out to be false—that is, not matching the way the world is. Who would ever want to drive across a bridge designed by engineers who believed their calculations are merely based on opinions instead of truths?

Ironically, it is the very same science—heralded as a stronghold in search of the truth—that has also been used to promote relativism. Sociobiologists, for instance, claim we believe what we believe because what we call "truth" emerges from brains shaped by natural selection. They consider human knowledge and rationality to be merely the product of evolution after having gone through a process of natural selection. They basically reduce reason to genes manipulated by natural selection. What they seem to forget is that, even if we invoke natural selection as a determining force, it must operate depending on the way the world "is"—reality, that is. Truth, on the other hand, is often not particularly relevant to survival. Besides, if their claim entails that our beliefs are mere artifacts or illusions, such a claim would act like a boomerang that destroys its own truth claims as well. The end-result is that we end up with mere illusions: social illusions, political illusions, moral illusions, religious illusions—or more in general, illusions about reality and truth. That would not be good news for sociobiology itself. Claims like these contradict themselves—if they are considered true, they become false.

Even though most scientists still have faith that reality can be known through reason (see 8) and that their scientific questions have rational answers, they still easily give in to relativism when it comes to issues outside of the scientific realm. Some of them limit the mind's capacity to know reality and truth to the narrow viewpoint of materialism, scientism, and rationalism. They give reason the power to grasp "scientific" truths, but deny there are any other truths to be apprehended—which is basically the viewpoint of rationalism as discussed earlier (see 3.a).

Contrary to this claim, it could be argued that there are many more truths than scientific truths—truths about beauty, love, morality, and religion. There are arguably many more perspectives than what science tries to capture with its barometers, thermometers, and spectrometers. Science may have its own window on the world, its own scientific point of view, but there are many other windows, views, vistas, perspectives, or whatever you wish to call them. Reality is like a jewel with many facets that can be looked at from various angles, with different "eyes." Just like the "physical eye" sees colors in nature, so the "artistic eye" sees beauty in nature, the "rational eye" sees truths and untruths, the "moral eye" sees rights and wrongs, and the "religious eye" sees everything in relationship to its Creator. All these "eyes" claim to be in search of reality and truth.

So what remains standing is this: truth is truth, even if you do not accept it; and untruth is untruth, even if you claim it. Truth is truth—for everyone, anywhere, at any time. Knowledge is about reality, not about knowledge. To know is to know things in the real world, not to know mental abstractions in the mind. Either we conform our minds to reality, or we shape reality to conform to our thinking. St. Thomas tells us that we must choose the former, not the latter. Contrary to what relativists and skeptics believe, we are dealing here with truth and reason, not sentiment and habit. G. K. Chesterton once firmly asserted "that truth exists whether we like it or not, and that it is for us to accommodate ourselves to it."

In April 2005, in his homily during Mass prior to the conclave which would elect him as Pope, then Cardinal Joseph Ratzinger said, "relativism, which is letting oneself be tossed and 'swept along by every wind of teaching,' looks like the only attitude acceptable to today's standards. We are moving towards a dictatorship of relativism which does not recognize anything as certain and which has as its highest goal one's own ego and one's own desires." The truth remains that truth cannot be established by a majority vote. The idea of "many truths" is as detrimental to our cognitive health as the notion of "double truth."

Let us come to a conclusion. Why should we believe something? Because others believe it? Not so! Because it feels good? Not so! The only reason is: because it is *true*. How do we know what is true? Faith tells us so "from Above"—but Faith can never tell us what is against reason—and reason tells us so "from below"—but reason can never tell us what is against Faith. Yet, reason tells us more than we could know by Faith alone, and Faith tells us more than we could know by reason alone. Reason needs to purify Faith, and Faith needs to purify reason. Discovering the truth through reason can never destroy Faith. Discovering the truth through Faith can never destroy reason. Therefore, we should always be "faithful" in our reasoning, and "reasonable" in our Faith.

The Catechism (159) summarizes all of this well: "Though faith is above reason, there can never be any real discrepancy between faith and reason. Since the same God who reveals mysteries and infuses faith has bestowed the light of reason on the human mind, God cannot deny himself, nor can truth ever contradict truth." In the words of Pope John Paul II, "Faith and reason are like two wings on which the human spirit rises to the contemplation of truth; and God has placed in the human heart a desire to know the truth—in a word, to know himself—so that, by knowing and loving God, men and women may also come to the fullness of truth about themselves." In other words, we need to carefully navigate between the extremes of fideism, with its faith-alone approach, and of rationalism, with its reason-alone approach.

In his address to a group of U.S. bishops visiting Rome, Pope John Paul II expressed very clearly that he wished to defend the capacity of human reason to know the truth:

> *This confidence in reason is an integral part of the Catholic intellectual tradition, but it needs reaffirming today in the face of widespread and doctrinaire doubt about our ability to answer the fundamental questions: Who am I? Where have I come from and where am I going? Why is there evil? What is there after this life?... The result has been a pervasive skepticism and relativism, which have not led to a more 'mature' humanity but to much despair and irrationality.*

d. Proofs for God's Existence

As we discussed in the previous section, St. Thomas taught us that some things about God can be known by Faith, based on Special Revelation, but other things about God can be known by reason, based on natural revelation—that is, by studying God's revelation in nature. And then there is a "mixed" version: some things about God we can know not only from Special Revelation but also from natural revelation. An example of this "mixed" approach is our knowledge that God exists. This can be shown by natural revelation through the power of reason as well as by Special Revelation through the power of Faith.

In this chapter, we will see how we can know that God exists, based on natural revelation alone. The advantage of reasoning over Faith is that one can communicate reasoning much easier than Faith to other people. There are at least two ways of how we can know and show others that there is a God, without relying on any Special Revelation: one is based on *empirical* evidence, another one proceeds through *logical* reasoning.

There is indeed *empirical* evidence for God's existence. The Catholic Church declared during Vatican I that "God, the beginning and end of all, can, by the natural light of human reason, be known with certainty from the works of creation." This conviction has strong biblical roots. The Bible testifies that "The heavens are telling the glory of God" (Ps. 19:1) and that God "did not leave himself without witness" as St. Paul worded it (Acts 14:17), and that "since the creation of the world his invisible nature, namely, his eternal power and deity, has been clearly perceived in the things that have been made" (Rom. 1:20).

As we found out in the first chapters of this book, our Universe shows many clues of God's existence, including the fact that there is order, intelligibility, rationality, and morality. For those who are able to "connect the dots," a new world opens up—the world of religion, an unseen world that can be "seen" through the visible world. Let us make clear first that the existence of God is a factual issue of yes or no: God either exists or he doesn't—that's not a matter of opinion. You can have your own opinions, but you can't have your own facts. God's existence is either true or false. Well, there is much evidence to indicate it is true. We have empirical evidence "beyond reasonable doubt."

Why does not everyone see this evidence? There are arguably many reasons. First, science has given us natural explanations of this evidence, suggesting there is no room and no further need for any supernatural explanations. This has made some scientists claim that science can ultimately explain everything in the world, making any other explanations redundant, or even obsolete. Second, we have become increasingly critical as to what counts as evidence. Often evidence is only considered evidence if it is of an experimental nature, backed by experiments. Obviously, there is no way God's presence can be tested in the laboratory. Third, some require evidence not only beyond reasonable doubt but beyond any doubt. Even in court that is hard to do, let alone in religion. Fourth, we have lost interest in why the existence of God is important. God somehow has vanished from our radar screen, for we have learned to understand the world apart from God. And there are probably many more reasons why we don't see or want to see any evidence for God's existence.

Because of all such reasons, some have chosen the road of *logical* reasoning instead, hoping to attain the same certainty as we can gain in geometry and mathematics. Most well-known are the "proofs of God's existence" that come very close to mathematical proofs and seem to share a similar kind of certainty. They became very popular from the Middle Ages on.

God's existence was to some extent obvious for medieval theologians—they simply knew he existed. Nevertheless, they attempted to prove his existence anyway to show that his existence is "reasonable." The basic strategies they employed are the ones used ever since. Some philosophers—such as St. Anselm of Canterbury, Descartes, Spinoza, Hegel, and a number of others—suppose that God's existence can be inferred in an *a priori* way, regardless of any experience of finite entities—by means of mere thinking, so to speak. Just as the properties of a triangle can be derived from its definition, God's existence can presumably also be inferred in a similar way.

Let us take the "proof" by St. Anselm of Canterbury as an example. It is perhaps the most puzzling one. While it has not been all that popular with the average believer, it has fascinated philosophers, and even today there are respectable philosophers who accept it. Anselm defined God as "that than which nothing greater can be conceived," and then he argued that this being must exist in the mind—even in the mind of the person who denies the existence of God. He suggested that, if the greatest possible being exists in the mind, it must also exist in reality. If it exists only in the mind, then an even greater being must be possible—

that is, one which exists both in the mind and in reality. Therefore, this greatest possible being must exist in reality.

One good way to understand Anselm's argument is to see it as a *reductio ad absurdum* (see 1.b), where the claim to be reduced to absurdity is the claim that God exists in the mind, but *not* in reality. Here is a more formal analysis:

(1) God is that than which nothing greater can be conceived. (Definition);
(2) God exists in the mind, but not in reality. (Premise to be reduced to absurdity);
(3) Existence in reality is greater than existence in the understanding alone. (Premise);
(4) It is conceivable that God exists in reality. (Premise);
(5) It is conceivable that there is a being greater than God. (Follows from 2, 3, and 4);
(C) It is conceivable that there is a being greater than that than which nothing greater can be conceived. (Follows from 1 and 5).

What the argument tries to "prove" is that the conclusion (C) is clearly false. So there must be a problem in the argument which led to it, since sound arguments cannot have false conclusions. Anselm's idea is that the problem with the argument which leads to (C) is that (2) is false: God exists in reality, as well as in the mind. That sounds rather compelling, doesn't it?

However, St. Thomas, and later Immanuel Kant, refuted St. Anselm's proof. Thomas argues, "Now from the fact that it is conceived by the mind what is indicated by the name 'God,' it does not follow that God exists, except in the intellect." Kant dubbed it the *"ontological* argument" and declared that what exists in thought does not necessarily exist in reality. His famous remark was that a hundred real coins do not contain the least coin more than a hundred possible coins—or more technically, he argued that "existence" is not a predicate. Kant's point is that stipulating existence as a predicate to its subject does not give the subject actual existence. Since then, there is some general consensus that Anselm's argument is indeed not valid.

Yet, nearly all of the great minds of Western philosophy have found the argument worthy of their attention and criticism. If God is defined as "that than which nothing greater can be conceived," it follows, for instance, that if one god is greater than another, then the lesser god isn't God. Many have tried to reformulate the ontological argument, including giants such as Norman Malcolm, Alvin Plantinga, and Kurt Gödel. Plantinga, for example, writes: "Our verdict on these reformulated versions of St. Anselm's argument must be as follows. They cannot, perhaps, be said to *prove* or *establish* their conclusion. But since it is rational to accept their central premise, they do show that it is rational to accept that conclusion."

The question that remains, of course, is how metaphysics could ever use reason to "reach into Heaven, where God resides." How could reason ever bring us closer to God? Basically and rather simplified, St. Thomas' answer is twofold. Reason alone can never reach God in his very own Being—only Faith can. The other part of his answer is that Faith is consistent with reason, so it can never be unreasonable or irrational, since all truths are harmonious with each other. It is especially from this latter viewpoint that St. Thomas formulated his five arguments for the existence of God. He called them actually "Five Ways" (the

Quinque Viae in his *Summa Theologiae*).

Here are his five arguments in a nutshell. In the Argument from *Motion*, St. Thomas argues that since everything that moves is moved by another, there must thereby exist an Unmoved Mover. In the Argument from *Efficient Cause*, he argues that the sequence of causes which make up this Universe must have a First Cause. In the Argument from *Contingency*, he argues that since all existent things depend upon other things for their existence, there must exist at least one thing that is not dependent, and therefore is a Necessary Being. In the Argument from *Gradation*, he argues that since all existent things can be compared to such qualities as degrees of goodness, there must exist something that is an Absolutely Good Being. In the Argument from *Design*, also known as the "Teleological Argument," he argues that the intricate design and order of existent things and natural processes imply that a Great Designer exists.

Let us focus for a moment on the first argument, the "argument from motion." It starts with the principle that "nothing can move unless it is moved by something else." St. Thomas argues from this that there has to be a "First Mover," which he identified as God. Seen through modern eyes, this argument can easily be misunderstood. We tend to think of billiard balls that impart motions to each other in a series of collisions, which requires a cue ball that sets all the other balls in motion. However, such a sequence of moving objects is not at all what St. Thomas had in mind. When he says that A "moves" B, he is saying that A "causes" B and thus "explains" B. There is no movement through space here; St. Thomas is rather thinking in terms of cause and effect.

Although it looks like everything in this sequence has been explained by a previous cause, really nothing is ultimately explained, for the question remains what enables A to be a cause, which calls for another cause and explanation—not at an earlier time but at a different level. This would not take us to another cause in a sequence of causes, but to a cause at a higher level, of an altogether different order, outside and above the sequence of causes—a cause that explains this very sequence and makes it possible. That's where the "First Mover" comes in, if understood correctly.

As St. Thomas expressed it, "God is to all things the cause of being." Everything that exists can only exist because the "First Mover" causes it to exist. The "First Mover" is not the cue ball in a long sequence of causes that sets all the other balls in motion, but it is the Primary Cause that makes this very sequence of secondary causes possible. Secondary causes may act one after another in time and space, but the Primary Cause is not a spatio-temporal entity that is the starting point of a series of motions. As Stephen Barr words it: the "First Mover" is not first in a temporary sense but in an explanatory sense. It is about causal priority, not temporal priority.

Let us discuss one more argument, the "argument from contingency," because the four other Ways that St. Thomas mentions could be taken as variations of this one particular Way. The point of departure is that our Universe need not be the way it is, and it need not even exist. We are *contingent* beings who could easily not have existed, as the reason for our existence cannot be found within ourselves—we cannot make ourselves exist. Therefore, we depend for our existence on an overarching, transcending "ground"—a Necessary Being. As contingent beings, we depend on God, no matter how much we want to be independent. Existence is something received. However, if there is no inherent necessity for the Universe to exist, then the Universe, including everything in it, is not self-explanatory and therefore must find an explanation outside itself. Obviously, it cannot be grounded in something else that is also finite, contingent, and not self-explanatory—for that would lead to infinite regress—so it can only derive from an unconditioned, infinite, and necessary ground, which is a "Necessary Being," not self-caused but un-caused.

Some may wonder what then caused the First Cause, or worded differently, who created the Creator. The idea behind this question is probably that "everything needs a cause," so why not the Creator? However, thinking that way would lead to an infinite regression. Instead we should rephrase the question as follows: "Everything that has come into existence needs a cause." Something that does not exist cannot bring itself into existence. But God, on the other hand, never came into existence—that is, God is the uncaused cause, the eternal cause who has always been in existence, so God is not even self-caused. Therefore, the question "Who created God?" is illogical, just like the question "To whom is a bachelor married?" is illogical. It makes no sense to ask "What is God's cause?" because God never began to exist, and only that which begins to exist needs to have a cause. We could perhaps say again, "The buck stops here."

So the entire argument from contingency runs like this:
   (1.) Every contingent entity must have a cause;

(2.) Such causes cannot run in an infinite regress;
(3.) Consequently, there must be a Primary Cause;
(4.) Obviously, this Primary Cause must itself be uncaused;
(5.) Because of (1), this Primary Cause must be a necessary rather than a contingent being. It is this Necessary Being that we call *God*.

The late philosopher Ralph McInerny points out that St. Thomas is very aware of the difference between 'God' used as a proper noun, and 'god' used as a common noun. The ambiguity is pronounced in Latin which lacks the indefinite article 'a', where in English we can disambiguate between 'God' and 'a god.' The situation is worsened by translations that simply translate the Latin word *deus* in the Five Ways as 'God' in English. In the Five Ways, St. Thomas does not use 'god' as a proper name, but as a common noun having five different nominal definitions. So each of the Ways merely concludes that there is "*a* god." Somewhere else, Aquinas asks the question whether there is "a God" [*utrum deus sit?*]. Thus, it is also true that the Five Ways do not as such prove that there is only one god. It is for this reason that St. Thomas himself thinks one must actually argue additionally that a god must be utterly unique, and thus that there can be only one, which he does in several questions after the Five Ways. Of course, once the utter uniqueness of "a god" has been shown, one can begin to use "God" as a proper name to refer to that one and utterly unique Being, revealed to us in Scripture, as Thomas subsequently does in his *Summa Theologiae*.

It is not very likely that St. Thomas really thought one can demonstrate or prove the existence of God with the Five Ways. It is rather telling that he does not call them "Five

Proofs" but "Five Ways." He does not end each "Way" with QED [*quod erat demonstrandum*], like we often do in math and logic, but by the less overreaching statement "And this we think of as (a) God [*et hoc dicimus deum*]." Apparently, St. Thomas himself did not have the presumption of logically *proving* God's existence. He is somehow clarifying what we mean when we speak of God, and what this entails. Nonetheless, these "ways" certainly are compelling in a *rational* sense, working like powerful "pointers" to a Creator God. They show us that speaking of God and referring to God is reasonable—and certainly not against reason. They also show us what Christians mean when they speak of God—certainly not the gods or idols of pagans which are *not* primary, necessary, and absolute beings.

This takes us back to St. Thomas' saying: "We must believe that God [a god] exists, which is clear by reason." What St. Thomas means by this statement is that *reason* leads us to assume a Primary Cause, whereas *Faith* in God discovers that this very concept refers to the God of our Faith—that's the point where general revelation and Special Revelation meet. This does not mean that reason can fully fathom God, for elsewhere he says, "We cannot understand what God is, but what he not is." In other words, our philosophical knowledge is limited to knowing *that* God is, more so than what or who he is. Yet, reason tells us that this Universe cannot explain itself, but needs an ultimate non-contingent explanation. So these "Ways" are more like "insights" than "proofs." We should not forget that St. Thomas also remarked: "To one who has faith, no explanation is necessary. To one without faith, no explanation is possible."

Does all of the above mean that we have confirmed the

claim of atheists that there is *no* full-proof logical argument for God's existence? The answer is yes and no. The Catechism (35) acknowledges that the reasoned proofs of God's existence "can predispose one to faith and help one to see that faith is not opposed to reason." However, it is not an undisputable proof with logical certainty, but it surely is a very powerful rational argument in favor of God's existence. While we may attain knowledge of the existence of God via our reason, God is still not directly visible to our senses.

On the other hand, no matter whether we deem these "proofs" valid or not, the atheist philosopher Kai Nielsen correctly states, "To show that an argument is invalid or unsound is not to show that the conclusion of the argument is false. It's only to show that the argument does not warrant our asserting the conclusion to be true." In short, to show that the proofs do not work is not enough by itself to deny God's existence. It may still very well be the case that their conclusion is true.

How is it possible for non-believers to deny these so-called "proofs"? One reason is, of course, that atheists may be missing the will to accept a world with God in the picture, for often atheism is not a reasoned thing—not a rational conclusion, that is—but more of a preferential choice. Another explanation is that these "proofs" are not real compelling proofs in the technical, mathematical, or scientific sense. Yet, they could still be accepted in a *rational* sense: they offer strong reasons or arguments for God's existence, which makes them work as powerful pointers to a Creator God as the best possible—and arguably only—rational explanation for the fact that this

Universe does exist and is the way it is. The physicist and Anglican priest John Polkinghorne calls them "pointers to the divine as the only totally adequate ground of intelligibility."

The fact that there is any world at all, or any causality at all, or any order at all, or any law at all, is the proper starting point of an argument for God as the Primary Cause. Clouds, trees, plants, animals, human beings, societies, buildings, planets, and stars certainly exist, but they don't have to exist. St. Thomas saw very clearly that their being is not self-explanatory, but depends, ultimately, on some primordial reality which does exist through the power of its own essence. This "necessary" being is what St. Thomas called "a god," and identified eventually as "God."

St. Thomas makes an important distinction between demonstrative reasoning and persuasive reasoning. As we saw earlier, demonstrative reasoning yields a conclusion that is undeniable for anyone who grasps the truth of the argument's premises. In such cases, believing the argument's conclusion is not a voluntary affair, but a logical consequence. If I know that the sum of all rectangles' interior angles equals $360°$ and that a square is a rectangle, then I cannot help but believe that the sum of a square's interior angles equals $360°$. In such cases, knowledge of a demonstration's premises is sufficient to guarantee assent to the demonstration's conclusions. However, the situation is different when it comes to Faith. Were a person to grasp the truth of sacred doctrine by means of this sort of reasoning, belief would be forced and the merit of Faith destroyed, says St. Thomas—which would not be acceptable.

Persuasive reasoning, on the other hand, does no such thing. We might think of persuasive reasoning as playing a game of apologetics for theological purposes. In "persuasive reasoning," we rather deal with "credibility arguments" that corroborate the truth of what Faith teaches us, but they are ultimately unable to move one to assent to the articles of Faith. In other words, the arguments used in persuasive reasoning may provide reasons for accepting certain doctrines, but they cannot compel acceptance of those doctrines. Faith is certainly a matter of knowledge, but understood as knowledge *of* God, more than knowledge *about* God. To know there must be a God is one thing; to believe in this God and then live and act as if he is real is another. One still needs the grace of Faith in order to embrace them. It is the interior movement of grace and the Holy Spirit which is primary in making a person see that these truths have been divinely revealed and are to be believed and lived by. This is why St. Thomas insists that human investigation into matters of Faith does not "deprive faith of its merit," or render Faith superfluous.

Needless to say that the God of the "Five Ways" is the "God of philosophers and scholars"—and not, as Blaise Pascal put it in his *Memorial*, the "God of Abraham, the God of Isaac, and the God of Jacob"—and the "God of Jesus Christ," we should add. For Pascal this awareness was a conversion experience. Romano Guardini describes that experience as follows: "He had thought about God with concepts, but without arriving at any reality. He had exerted himself, but had not gotten off the ground—now he stands before the reality of God." To make that final step we need also the input of Faith and grace based on Special Revelation. But again, it is not a matter of either faith-alone or reason-alone. Reason takes us to the door of Faith, but only Faith can take us through that door. It is in the harmony of these two that we come to a deeper understanding of God. Faithful reasoning and reasonable Faith go hand in hand.

Guardini describes Pascal's conversion to the God of his Fathers in more depth when he says,

> *Religious thought endeavors to learn the mode of thinking which corresponds to the living nature of God; it is that of Scripture and the saints.... When Pascal lived through that experience, of which the Memorial informs us, he did not cease to be a mathematician, a physicist, an engineer, a psychologist, and a philosopher.... For Pascal, the world remains the world, philosophy remains philosophy. But everything is called into a new coherence, and thought is challenged to a new effort through the discovery that God, grasped by the 'philosopher' merely as 'the absolute,' is in truth the Living God, who enters into history in Jesus Christ; and that the relation of man to him, conceived by the philosophical theory of being as 'relation to the absolute,' is in truth the very life, oriented towards God, of him who is called by God.*

Gerard M. Verschuuren

4. Natural Theology

We discovered earlier there are two spheres of knowledge: Special Revelation guiding reason—preserving it from mistakes and indicating the final solution it must come to—and reason serving to clarify, explain, and defend the mysteries of Faith. The result of this collaboration is theology.

Some beliefs could never be demonstrated by mere reason (for example, the mystery of Trinity or the Incarnation), but reason can serve to explain and clarify them. Other beliefs, such as the basic beliefs of Faith—the existence of God and the immortality of the soul—can be arrived at by reason, but they come to their fullest and deepest meaning when guided by Faith and by Special Revelation. So there are two roads leading to God: the road of religion (Faith) and the road of philosophy (reason).

Thus it is necessary to distinguish two types of theologies: on the one hand, a rational, philosophical, or *Natural* Theology, which reaches God from a purely rational perspective, and on the other hand, a revealed, supernatural, or *Dogmatic* Theology, which is based on Faith and on revealed doctrines, while using reason as a clarifying tool. Whereas Natural Theology starts with reason in search of Faith, supernatural Theology begins with Faith in search of reason. Coming from two opposite ends, they may meet in the "middle"—guided by the supernatural light of Faith and the natural light of reason.

St. Augustine sought believing in order to better understand, but he also sought understanding so as to better believe.

To use another analogy, we can start at either end of a continuum. We can start on our end and "dig a tunnel" towards God hoping to find answers—which is sometimes called natural or general revelation. Or we can start on God's end, hoping that God will "dig a tunnel" towards us who are waiting for answers—which is sometimes called Special or Divine Revelation.

As said before, there is evidence for God in nature. The first Christians knew this very well: God "has not left himself without testimony," as the Apostle Paul worded it (Acts 14:17); and "God did this so that men would seek him and perhaps reach out for him and find him, though he is not far from each one of us" (Acts 17:27). The early Christian theologian St. Augustine gave a name to this kind of revelation of God through creation: Natural Theology.

Natural Theology is a branch of philosophy that investigates what human reason can tell us concerning God, without any input from Revelation. Thus it aims to demonstrate the existence of God, to establish the principal divine attributes, to vindicate God's relation to the world as that of Creator to creature, and, finally, to throw some light on the problem of evil and on the action of divine providence. There are some other endeavors that are closely associated with Natural Theology. One of them is *apologetics*, which tries to present a rational basis for the Christian Faith and to defend it against objections. Another one is *theodicy*, which is a rational attempt to justify God's existence in light of the apparent imperfections of the world, especially with regards to evil. In general it could be said that the conclusions Natural Theology reaches are somehow limited. They relate to God purely and solely in so far as he is the First Cause of Being. A study of God as known in his own essential nature is entirely beyond the scope of reason alone.

Given its very limited range, why would we need philosophy and reason with regard to Faith? The explanation is that there are certain truths which Faith presupposes—St. Thomas calls them "preambles to faith"—for example, truths of the existence of God, that God is one, that God is good, and the like. So, reason and philosophy can *prepare* the way to Faith. Before we can believe what God has revealed to us, we must first know that there is a god, that we have a soul capable of grasping philosophical truth, that there is a God who knows all things, and that we have good reasons for believing that God has spoken to us, revealing truths which otherwise would not have been known.

In *Fides et Ratio*, Pope John Paul II mentions the most important moments in the encounter of faith and reason during the early history of the Church. He refers to St. Justin Martyr and later apologists who used philosophy as a "preamble" to the Faith. He also mentions St. Clement of Alexandria who called philosophy a "stepping stone to the Faith." *Fides et Ratio* (36) also points out that "The Acts of the Apostles provides evidence that Christian proclamation was engaged from the very first with the philosophical currents of the time."

From early Christianity on, reason and philosophy have been used to show us that there is a God and to demonstrate his primary attributes such as his power, knowledge, and presence. This can be done by reasoning from what we know rather than by starting from what Faith tells us. This way, reason lays the foundation for Faith and makes revelation "reasonable," but most of all "credible." Reason is thus the common ground between believers and non-believers, so it is an important apologetic tool. Unlike Islam, Christianity believes in the power of reason, not the power of the sword (the word "islam" is best translated by "submission"; the word "salam" means "peace").

It should not surprise us then that Pope John Paul II in his Encyclical *Faith and Reason* stresses the role of philosophy for the study of theology:

> *I wish to repeat clearly that the study of philosophy is fundamental and indispensable to the structure of theological studies and to the formation of candidates for the priesthood. For the reasons suggested here, it has seemed to me urgent to re-emphasize with this Encyclical Letter the Church's intense interest in philosophy—indeed the intimate bond which ties theological work to the philosophical search for truth. From this comes the Magisterium's duty to discern and promote philosophical thinking which is not at odds with faith.*

Not surprisingly, there has been controversy as to what philosophy and Natural Theology can do for religious faith. There are two extreme positions, as we found out earlier. We either claim that God is like all other entities—which is obviously false, for God cannot possibly be like all other entities—or we must admit that we cannot possibly know anything about him—which is also untrue, for if we don't know anything about him, we cannot even say he exists. St. Thomas took a middle position in this debate by introducing the idea of *analogy*, implying both similarities and dissimilarities between the Creator and his creatures.

When we say that God "sees," this is to be understood neither as a claim that God has eyes as humans do nor that God is incapable of seeing because he does not have such eyes. What we mean instead is that he perceives in a manner analogous to the way humans perceive with their eyes. The Psalmist could not say it more clearly, "Does the one who shaped the ear not hear? The one who formed the eye not see?" (Ps. 94:9).

So whatever perfections reside in us must be deficient likenesses of what exists perfectly in God. When we say, "God is good," the meaning is not that God is the cause of goodness, or that God is not evil, but the meaning is, in the words of St. Thomas, "Whatever good we attribute to creatures, pre-exists in God, albeit in a more excellent and higher way." So, natural knowledge of God is mediated by our knowledge of the created order. Hence we must admit, in conclusion, that our knowledge of the Infinite is inadequate, and necessarily so since our minds are only finite. Yet, we can say something positive about God based on what he created. We argue from the existence of causes that are familiar to us in sense experience to the existence of a Primary Cause who is unfamiliar to us. So we reason from finite causes to an Infinite Cause. In a similar way, we argue from our finite imperfections to God's Infinite Perfections. Being the ultimate cause of our own existence, God must have all the perfections we find imperfectly in ourselves. From the experience of our own imperfections, we glean certain principles about the Perfections of God.

According to St. Thomas, God—from whom everything else is created—"contains within Himself the whole perfection of being." Obviously there can be only one infinite being, only one God. When we say that God is infinite, we mean that he is unlimited in every kind of perfection, or that every conceivable perfection belongs to Him in the highest conceivable way. If several infinite beings were to exist, none of them would really be infinite, for if there were several, each should have some perfection not possessed by the others. Well, if God is Infinite Perfection, then he must have infinite powers, more in specific the powers of being all-powerful (*omnipotent*), all-present (*omnipresent*), and all-knowing (*omniscient*). These attributes are essential to God—without them, God would not be God. A god who is not all-powerful or not all-present or not all-knowing cannot be God. Of course, it should be added that those terms are predicated of God imperfectly and analogously as God's creatures are imperfect images of him.

Again, do not take these perfections or attributes as super-traits. God's power is not like our power raised to the power of a zillion. Instead, God's power is the Source and Origin that all human power depends on and derives from; other powers are not "next" to God but "under" God. We would not have any power if God did not give us some power. The same holds for God's omniscience; it is not the sum total of all human knowledge, but surpasses it in an infinite way. And this also holds for God's omnipresence; it is not the presence of all individual creatures combined, for it is of an entirely different magnitude and scale. Only in that particular sense can it be said that God is all-powerful, all-knowing, and all-present. He is infinitely greater than all his works. Put differently, the step from man to God is infinitely greater than the step from beast to man. Let us see what this entails.

a. God Is All-Present

There is a double dimension to God being *omnipresent*: God is all-present in both space and time. Seen in terms of *space*, he is everywhere. He is not located in any specific spot; therefore, any attempt to identify him with particular locations, or the sum of all locations, necessarily fails. He transcends all spatiality. That's why it may seem that God is nowhere, because he is "everywhere." Being the Primary Cause, he is not tied to any secondary causes. As someone has metaphorically and paradoxically expressed it, "God's center is everywhere, His circumference nowhere." That God is truly present in every place or thing or situation—in other words, that he is omnipresent or ubiquitous—follows from the fact that he is the ultimate cause and ground of all reality.

Not only is God all-present in terms of space, but also in terms of *time*. This is often expressed as God being eternal, which means he has neither beginning nor end. He is at the beginning of everything but has no beginning, and he is at the end of everything without having an end. There is no past or future for God—only an eternal present. Time being a measure of finite existence, the Infinite One must transcend it. God's self-existence is timeless. In that sense, he is the Alpha and the Omega by enclosing everything in between. God is not somewhere "in" time but he is the Creator of time; without God, there would be no time.

Albert Einstein had already showed us that both time and space are part of the physical world, just as much as matter and energy. In point of fact, time can be manipulated in the laboratory. The presence of mass (and more generally energy) causes space-time to curve. Since both space and time are measures of the finite, God's infinity transcends all temporal and spatial limitations. This may sound highly abstract, but it can be boiled down to this: God is an infinite power outside and beyond the spatio-temporal dimensions of our Universe. God did not create the world in time, but with time—or having time in it. God did not create the world in space, but he created space in the world—or a world full of space. From out of his very Being, God gives being to the whole world and all things in it, including time and space.

C.S. Lewis tried to explain this when he noted that "If there was a controlling power outside the Universe, it could not show itself to us as one of the facts inside the Universe—no more than the architect of a house could actually be a wall or staircase or fireplace in that house." Every analogy is limited, but just as architects and builders are not part of their buildings, yet are somehow "part" of every part of them, so is God *transcendent*—that is, not a physical part of what he created—and yet he is *immanent*—that is, actively involved with each and every part of it at each and every moment. God transcends creation and yet is fully present to it—all-present, that is. We are just God's creatures—not "next" to God but "under" God, not "outside" God but "in" God. "Outside" God, there is nothing—no space and no time. As St. Hilary of Poitiers put it, "He is outside of all things and within all things." So when people venerate Jupiter, the Pharaoh, the Roman Emperor, a Golden Calf, or a spirit in some particular tree, they are venerating idols, but certainly not God, who is all-present Infinity.

This might raise the question for some why the Primary

Cause should be identified as God. Why not as Matter with a capital M, as is done in materialism? Matter seems to be all-present too—matter is everywhere. For materialists, matter is indeed almost literally "all-present"—something that simply *is*, of which nothing else is the cause and which is itself the cause of everything we see around us. In this view, matter deserves the position of "primary cause." However, matter may be everywhere, but it is not all there is. There are also immaterial things, if only for the simple reason that the very idea of materialism is something immaterial. Yet, for some enigmatic reason, materialism has quite a spiritual appeal to it. Materialists may not explicitly express it that way, but for them matter is a "primary cause" that needs no further explanation, and is responsible not only for things coming into existence, but also for their continuing in existence, because nothing can exist without the materials out of which it is made, so they say. But can materialists really maintain this position as an alternative to God being the Primary Cause?

It is very doubtful they can. Matter is anything that has mass and takes up space and time, so it is subject to motion and change. The Primary Cause, on the other hand, cannot be subject to motion and change, or space and time. The philosopher Michael Augros brings this argument to a close, "Matter itself is a *product*, receiving its very existence from the action of something before it." So God as the only Primary Cause, uncaused and motionless, remains standing; it is God who brings matter into existence and keeps it in existence. Matter cannot do so on its own. The idea that matter can cause itself and explain itself we referred to earlier as a magical "pop theory" that has things pop into existence without any cause. Nothing can just pop itself into existence; it must have a cause, because it does not and cannot have the power to make itself exist. For something to cause itself to exist, it would have to exist before it came into existence—which is logically and philosophically impossible. God, on the other hand, did not come into existence, for he is eternally present—all-present, that is.

Materialists are not the only ones to deny God is the Primary Cause. Others claim that Fate also qualifies as "all-present," for it rules the world and therefore deserves to be considered the "primary cause." They often speak of the "goddess of Fate" or the "blind deity of Doom." In this view, everything in this world is ruled by chance, randomness, destiny, or karma. However, if randomness is the basis for change in the Universe, it must be a secondary cause and cannot be itself a primary cause. Chance events actually occur *within* nature, so chance itself cannot be a primary cause. That's why it makes no sense to capitalize "Chance" and declare it a self-explanatory principle of nature. Randomness plays a very legitimate role in the sciences, but it is just a feature of *created* things, another secondary cause—and therefore cannot be the ultimate explanation of everything else in this Universe. So reason forces us to choose God over randomness as an ultimate explanation of the Universe we live in. Besides, if everything were simply a matter of chance, how could the Universe be so orderly and coherent?

In both of these cases—whether it is materialism or fatalism—reason could make the case that the Primary Cause cannot be some abstract entity, but must be a Person. God being a Person follows from his Infinite

Perfection. A person is the highest entity in this Universe that we know of. Not only can we talk about persons in terms of causes, but also in terms of intentions, thoughts, reasoning, and so on. If God, the Primary Cause behind all secondary causes, is infinitely more than each one of us—that is, more than any person on earth—then God must at least not be less than personal. A person is the highest being of creation, and therefore the closest in resemblance to God. How can he who formed the eye not be able to "see"? But again, this is language of analogy.

As said earlier, whatever imperfections reside in us must be deficient likenesses of what exists perfectly in God. Our intellect and will are part of being a person, and as such they are finite reflections of God's perfect and infinite Will and Intellect. Analogous to the way we are intelligent and free and distinct from the things we create and produce, God is a personal being who is intelligent and free and distinct from the Universe he created.

b. God Is All-Knowing

What also follows from his infinite perfection is that God is *omniscient*—that is, he possesses the most perfect knowledge of all things. In the first place, he knows and comprehends himself fully and adequately, and in the next place he knows all created objects and comprehends their finite and contingent mode of being. Everything which to our finite minds signifies perfection and completeness of knowledge may be predicated of God's omniscience: it is on himself alone that God depends for his knowledge. To make him in any way dependent on creatures for knowledge of created objects would destroy his Infinite Perfection. Being all-knowing is essential to being God.

As creatures, we know of "past" and "future," but past and future do not apply to an eternal God. If there were something God did not know yet, his knowledge would be imperfect and not perfect. His knowledge does not change, analogous to the way mathematical truths do not change. Humans can change their minds, but God cannot change his Mind, for that would involve a contradiction, namely that his Perfect Knowledge would also have an imperfect part of "reconsidering things he may have missed the first time around." If God were not all-knowing, he would not be God.

First we need to find out how reason leads us to think that God is all-knowing, or omniscient. Following the early Christian writer Boethius, Aquinas held that God's position with respect to time is such that, unlike us, he does not have to wait for the future to unfold in order to know its contents. God is in no way a temporal being, but he is rather the creator of time, with complete and equal access to all of its contents. If he were in time, even God could not know what has not yet happened—for to think differently would create a contradiction. But if God exists entirely outside of time—in a kind of eternal present to which all that occurs in time is equally accessible—he would indeed be able to comprehend all of history, the past and the present as well as the future, just as though they were now occurring. For this reason, an all-knowing God would have "fore-knowledge" of future events, decisions, and actions because his fore-knowledge is situated outside time, external to time. It comprises all that ever was and ever will be.

Obviously, new questions arise. If God is really all-knowing, then his knowledge must include the very future that we are trying to shape ourselves. If that is the case, then one of the two has to go it seems: either an all-knowing God or a free human being! Put differently, how can an all-knowing God know which decisions and actions his creatures will engage in, without losing the idea that those decisions and actions are done *freely*? How can God know "ahead of time" what we will end up doing if we are supposedly free to make our own choices in life?

The answer is actually rather straightforward. Perhaps a simple analogy may help us understand that there is no contradiction between God's fore-knowledge and human freedom. If you were watching a video of certain events of your past life, you may get the impression that these actions were in fact predetermined and preordained, and yet you know that they were freely decided upon when they were taking place. Well, God in his eternity is like someone watching the "video" of what is taking place on earth without taking any freedom away from the "actors on the stage." Again, this is just an analogy, and therefore inadequate, of course.

Aquinas would explain the apparent conflict between God's activity as Creator and ours as free creatures by again using his powerful distinction between Primary Cause and secondary causes. We are prone to think of God's activities as some kind of secondary cause, situated at the same level as our own free decisions. We think, for instance, that God creatively wills that I decide to do something, and his willing then causes me to make a decision—as if his will were a secondary cause. In this scenario, God's creative fiat would be an event independent of my decision, which would indeed rob me of my autonomy. I would no longer be a free agent but a puppet manipulated by God.

In contrast, God as a Primary Cause works in such a way that we are not acted upon as if God were a secondary cause, but instead exercise our own free will as a secondary cause of our own decisions and actions. God is not the direct cause of my decisions—I am—but he is the indirect cause that lets me be the cause of my own decisions. Seen in this light, our human freedom need not be in conflict with an all-knowing God at all. God is the complete and Primary Cause of a free act, whereas the human agent is its complete secondary cause. God's willing that I decide as I do does not make my decision God's. God's willing does not take away from me the operations of my will, or the actions founded upon them; they remain my own. God as the Primary Cause is in fact the one who gives us decision-making power; he allows us to become secondary causes of our own. In short, God is not the direct cause of my decisions—I am.

That God knows infallibly and from eternity what a certain person, in the exercise of free will, will do or actually does in any given circumstances, and what he might or would actually have done in different circumstances is mandated by natural reason, since it is a consequence of the eternal actuality of God's omniscience, including his foreknowledge. So to speak, God has not to wait on the contingent and temporal event of a person's free choice to know what that person's action will be—he knows it from eternity. However, God's infallible knowledge of our future does not mean he has some kind of secret knowledge that makes our free choices not really free but already chosen for us. Again, St. Thomas argues that God's infallible knowledge of our future is not some secret predictive power because there is no such thing as the future for God. Rather, in his transcendent eternity, which is outside the flow of time, all events from any time are present to him in one eternal now. But seen from our "temporary now" perspective, we are still free actors who freely decide to cause things to happen.

c. God Is All-Powerful

Not only is God all-present and all-knowing, he is also *omnipotent* (all-powerful)—but again, as long as we do not misconstrue this term. God's power does not exceed other powers in degree but it completely transcends other finite powers. His is an Infinite Power completely unlike our finite powers. It is not a worldly power raised to the zillionth power, but it is an "other-worldly" power—all-powerful, al-mighty, omni-potent. But we always need to keep in mind that the Infinite Primary Cause is analogous to, but not identical to, finite secondary causes.

There are several analogies to describe the relationship between God and his creation. Let us just look at two of them. One analogy, used by Stephen Barr, has God as the author of a novel. Characters in a novel have effects within the novel's plot by means of acting within the plot in accordance with the internal rules of the novel. The author of the novel, on the other hand, causes things to happen as they do in the novel not by being an actor in the plot, but by simply conceiving of the plot. This analogy stresses that there could not be a novel without an author (although one can read a novel without giving any thought to its author). So the strong point of this analogy is that there can only be a novel because there is an author. But one of its drawbacks is that the actors in the novel are not really free human beings; they must follow the plot. That is a serious weakness.

Therefore another analogy might be needed as well: the analogy of God as the author or producer of a playwright. When we ask about the "origin of the play," we are not asking about its first words, we are asking who wrote it and why. In this analogy, the actors on the world stage can still be free actors, who may not act the way the author or producer of the play would like them to act. The actors of the play may even speak and act on their own as if there were no playwright or script, or they may do so by deciding to deviate from the script. This analogy leaves space for human freedom, but it has another important drawback: there could be a play without a playwright or script. A play does not necessarily require a playwright, so God would not be necessary for a cosmic play. That is serious weakness too.

No matter how we conceive of the relationship between God and his creation, we do have to make sure we don't lose either an all-powerful God or the freedom of human beings. So it is of utmost importance to reconcile God's sovereignty and omnipotence with human freedom. Not everyone thinks his is possible. Jean-Paul Sartre, for instance, would say that an almighty God doesn't leave room for free human beings, so free human beings would leave no room for an almighty God. If our world were fully preordained by God, our brains would automatically refuse to enforce what our free minds would like to do. That would be a travesty of human freedom: "a toy world which only moves when He pulls the strings," in the words of C.S. Lewis. On the other hand, according to Sartre, our freedom to make our own decisions would entail that this freedom takes away from God's sovereignty.

After what we have seen, this seems to be a false dilemma. The Infinite Power of God resides on a level completely different from where the finite powers of humans reside. If God does absolutely everything, then no real secondary causality would exist; we couldn't do anything, for every apparent act would really and fully be God's act. Yes, if God and humans were on the same level, they could perhaps be in a power battle, but not in a world of Primary and secondary causes. Therefore, Sartre created a false dilemma: we do not have to question God's omnipotence, or even his existence, if there is human freedom. Why assume, like Sartre did, that God and Man are in a power battle? That amounts to thinking that if God does something, then nothing or no one else is doing it, and if something else is doing it, then God is not the cause of it. Finite human beings can never compete with the Infinite God, for it is God's power that is the source and origin of human power. Michael Augros uses this analogy, "There is no competition between the carpenter and his tools in order to take credit for the house being built." It is thanks to the Primary Cause that secondary causes can act as causes according to their own nature as received from God. It is also thanks to the Primary Cause that human beings can become free causes of their own.

By becoming free causes of their own, humans do not take

anything away from God's sovereignty, but they exercise the free will that was given to them by God himself. God makes his creatures movable by nature so that they can move themselves. Therefore, submitting ourselves to God, the Maker of Heaven and Earth, is not like submitting ourselves to a dictator, who is just another person in our midst. Yet, that's how some people think of God—a sort of benevolent dictatorship. On the contrary, the more we become like God, the more we become like ourselves, since we were made in his image. We tend to think that our freedom is compromised by God's will, so we take it as a threat to our freedom against which we should rebel. We think of freedom in terms of complete autonomy, meaning that we are entirely self-determining, that we can become whatever we please, and that we are answerable to no one. We think we are only free when we are free of God. Instead, following God's will—which is our free choice—would be an opportunity for us to become more like our deepest self.

The fact that we do have freedom actually points to a Creator after whose image we were made. For how could we be free if there were no God who has freely created us after his image? Again, human freedom is an imperfect reflection of the perfect Freedom God has in his Divine Sovereignty. St. Hippolytus once stressed "the significance of the proverb, 'Know Yourself,' that is, discover God within yourself, for he has formed you after his own image." God does not rob us of any decisions we make ourselves. He is in fact the one who gives us decision-making power; he allows us to become causes of our own. Without a Primary Cause, we could not even be a secondary cause.

Let us use one more analogy to rationally explain how an

almighty God can give us freedom. A sovereign king can pass a law that makes him no longer sovereign—which is somehow what God did for the world. God sets limits to his own omnipotence by setting no bounds to human freedom. When it comes to our salvation, we are certainly at *God*'s mercy, but he has also chosen to be at *our* mercy. Otherwise, we would be nothing more than puppets on the world scene. Instead, God lets the actors on the world stage be free actors, who may not act the way the Author of the play would like them to act. God *wills* perfection in us but *allows* imperfection. Dictators may take human freedom away, but God made us in his image and thus he created us, not as marionettes, but as beings endowed with freedom as well. Since God made us after his own image, we cannot just be marionettes or automata. Because we are rational beings, made in God's image, we have been created with free will and are master over our acts—the right to choose is ours.

In addition to the issue of human freedom, there is a much more serious problem for God's sovereignty—it is the existence of evil. The existence of evil certainly poses a huge problem for a belief in an all-powerful God. Long ago, the Greek philosopher Epicurus worded the problem as follows: "Is God willing to prevent evil, but not able? Then he is not omnipotent. Is he able, but not willing? Then he is malevolent. Is he both able and willing? Then whence cometh evil? Is he neither able nor willing? Then why call him God?" Objections like these have been made many times since and by many different people. The British philosopher David Hume, for instance, is one of them: "Is God willing to prevent evil, but not able? Then he is impotent. Is he able, but not willing? Then he is malevolent.

Is he both able and willing? Whence then evil?"

When we talk about evil, we should at least distinguish between physical evil and moral evil. As far as *moral* evil is concerned—that is, evil that humans cause themselves—the answer can be found in what we said earlier about human freedom: moral evil is a consequence of human freedom. God could perhaps have chosen to eliminate the possibility of evil and evil-doing, but then God would have also taken away the possibility of good and doing-good—as well as the possibility of free choices. It is clear that the possibility of moral evil is a consequence of this human freedom. How could God ever give us freedom without accepting its consequences up to the point of us freely choosing the wrong outcome?

But there is more than moral evil. What about *physical* evil—evil not caused by human beings, evil that seems to come with nature, such as natural death, famine, diseases, earthquakes, tsunamis, and other catastrophes? They are usually not our doing—or are they? Several answers have been given to this haunting question as to why an all-powerful God allows physical evil to exist.

It is certainly not easy to answer such questions. Many rational answers have been sought. One of them runs as follows. Nature is bound to "obey" its God-given laws of nature. If intelligent and free agents are to exist, then the laws of nature must operate as they do. One simple example of this is that God made a Universe in which small objects would be attracted to larger ones, which we call the force of gravity. Gravity is a secondary cause. By allowing such "inferior" causes to operate, God made a Universe in which he does not have to be the direct cause of every stone falling to the ground. Thus we are able to know what the outcome is of certain contingent events like stones falling. We do not have to wonder about God's will every time a stone falls to the ground, even if it strikes us on the head. God has given us a secondary cause—the force of gravity—which is the direct cause of each stone's earthly plummet. This way, we live in a world that we can trust and count on because it follows some God-given laws of nature. Knowing this helps us make decisions that are not only free but also based on sound predictions.

Obviously, human beings, as part of nature, are also subject to these contingent events. They feel pain, they get sick, they fall victim to disasters, they are rich or they are poor. Human beings get in the way of all these secondary causes that God has established in his Omnipotence. The evolutionary biologist Francisco Ayala rightly places this in a wider context: "As floods and drought were a necessary consequence of the fabric of the physical world, predators and parasites, dysfunctions and diseases were a consequence of the evolution of life." Such explanations cause events like these to happen without making God directly responsible.

Yet, you may wonder why God allows a stone, following God's laws of nature, to hit you of all people on the head. Is God powerless to stop otherwise lawful events from happening? If so, then he seems not to be all-powerful. It looks now as if the all-powerful God has become the victim of his own all-present laws. Thomas Aquinas, for one, denies this. God could indeed have created a perfect world in which he was in control of everything, but he decided not to. Instead he made a world that is on its way to perfection.

Aquinas says that it was in God's wisdom to ordain not to be responsible for all contingent events. And it was also in God's wisdom to allow that there be "defects" in certain secondary causes—such as a falling stone hitting your head or an earthquake destroying your home. As Michael Augros puts it, "If secondary causes, unlike the Primary Cause, are not infallible, if they are defectible, then we might well blame them, rather than the first cause, for any flaws we find (or think we find)."

Yet, the question remains how God could allow such defects to happen then? Here is Aquinas' famous answer: if all evil were prevented, much good would be absent from the Universe; a lion, for instance, would cease to live, if it could not kill its prey. Whatever may be evil for the individual, the prey, is good for the larger picture, the Universe. Environmentalists are very aware of this fact; even "dangerous" animals such as poisonous spiders and snakes play an essential role in their ecosystem; taking them out would disrupt the system. Or think of something like pain: we could be in real danger if there were no pain to alert us of harm. So God allows "defects" in secondary causes to exist because this contributes to the greater good of the whole, so that the defect in one thing yields to the good of another, or even to the universal good.

Seen in this light, God's creation is in a state of journeying toward an ultimate perfection yet to be attained. The first chapter of the Book of Genesis calls God's creation "good," but it does not use the word "perfect." God's creation is not perfect yet, but it is on its way to perfection—and we, human beings, have been made participants in God's creation; we are his "co-workers" in bringing his creation to perfection. God *wills* perfection but *allows* imperfection on the journey to perfection. So physical evil is part of the imperfection we are still surrounded by. Moreover, when speaking about perfection, we should always realize that we can only have a sense or idea of perfection if we look "down" from a heavenly perspective where Infinite Perfection is residing in God's Mind.

This makes the distinction between what God wills and what he allows even more important. Aquinas says that God "neither wills evils to be nor wills evils not to be; he wills to allow them to happen." God does not will earthquakes, but he allows them when they are a consequence of the laws of nature—in the same way as God does not will wars but allows them when humans use their freedom to start them. In other words, there is God's positive or *providential* will and then there is God's *permissive* will; therefore, not everything that happens in this Universe is directly willed by God. To say that God "allows" or "permits" evil does not mean that he sanctions it in the sense that he approves of it, or even "wills" it, let alone causes it. (But there is much more to it, of course; in 5.d, we will delve deeper into the mystery of suffering, but that requires Special Revelation.)

To wrap up our discussion, all the above questions and answers are based on the power of mere reason, and are part of Natural Theology. Reason opens the gate to religious faith, but only Revelation can let us in through that gate. But before we can enter Dogmatic Theology, Natural Theology must have done some groundwork: we must have some sufficient rational grounds for believing that there is in fact a God, that he can be known by man, and that he has Divine Imperfections such as being all-present, all-knowing, and all-powerful. Only then can we enter the territory of Dogmatic Theology. Natural Theology may get us halfway but Dogmatic Theology takes us the rest of the way.

5. Dogmatic Theology

It would be a grave error to confuse Natural Theology with Dogmatic Theology. These two view God under different aspects: even when they teach the same truth, e.g., the unity of God, they reach it by totally different paths. It belongs to Dogmatic Theology to deal with many subjects which are beyond the scope of Natural Theology, such as the mysteries of the Trinity and the Incarnation. These are mysteries because God is infinite and our intellects are finite. Dogmatic Theology does not pretend to fully explain these doctrines—for the mysteries of the Godhead are of necessity beyond the reach of man's intelligence—but it analyses their precise meaning, establishes their mutual relations, and demonstrates that they are not contrary to reason. Mysteries go beyond reason, but that does not make them unreasonable.

One of the truths that reason can discover is that God is a person. Now the central claim of the Bible is that this person has not remained utterly hidden to us but has, indeed, "spoken" to us in the history of mankind. The decision to accept in trust what God has spoken about himself is what the Church means by "Faith." It is the Faith we received through witnesses. As we found out earlier, St. Thomas clearly distinguishes between "preambles of Faith," which can be established by philosophical principles, and "articles of Faith" that rest on divine testimony alone. Everything we could say about God from a philosophical perspective would also be accepted by religious people; the only difference is, religious people know much more about God than the greatest minds in philosophy.

Faith is about what learned about God by God's Special Revelation to us (which comes through the Bible and Christian Tradition). When the Apostle Paul was in Athens and saw an altar inscribed "To an Unknown God," he invited the Athenians to take the step from a "God of reason" to a "God of Faith": "What therefore you worship as unknown, this I proclaim to you" (Acts 17:23). By Faith and Special Revelation, we know that God came into the world through Jesus Christ and that God is Triune (Father, Son, and Holy Spirit). These truths about God cannot be known by reason alone.

Yet, reason does play an important role in Dogmatic Theology. In his encyclical *Fides et Ratio* (93), Pope John Paul II could not say it more clearly, "The chief purpose of theology is to provide an understanding of Revelation and the content of faith." Reason cannot discover on its own that God is Triune, but reason can help explain what it means that God is Triune and it can demonstrate that a Triune God is not against reason. In *Fides et Ratio*, Pope John Paul II makes this very clear:

> *[65] Theology is structured as an understanding of faith in the light of a twofold methodological principle: the auditus fidei [hearing the Faith] and the intellectus fidei [understanding the Faith]. [66] With regard to the intellectus fidei, a prime consideration must be that divine Truth "proposed to us in the Sacred Scriptures and rightly interpreted by the Church's teaching" enjoys an innate intelligibility, so logically consistent that it stands as an authentic body of knowledge. [77] Theology in fact has always needed and still needs philosophy's contribution.*

> *As a work of critical reason in the light of faith, theology presupposes and requires in all its research a reason formed and educated to concept and argument. Moreover, theology needs philosophy as a partner in dialogue in order to confirm the intelligibility and universal truth of its claims. It was not by accident that the Fathers of the Church and the Medieval theologians adopted non-Christian philosophies.*

What we see here again is the strong interaction between Faith and reason. Even religious faith is something we can reason about. As it was said about St. Paul, "He entered the synagogue, and for three months debated boldly with persuasive arguments about the Kingdom of God" (Acts 19:8). Let us see how this alliance works out for some important theological issues such as Trinity, Incarnation, Providence, Salvation, Predestination, Suffering, and Dogma.

a. Holy Trinity

The Catechism calls the Holy Trinity "a mystery that is inaccessible to reason alone" (237), and declared it "the source of all the other mysteries of faith" (234). It is for sure one of the most challenging mysteries of the Christian Faith. It took the Church several centuries to battle the heresy of Arianism which denies the Trinity. Although mysteries of Faith may be beyond reason, they are not unreasonable; they can be explained and defended, although not proven, by arguments based on reason. As said earlier, a mystery is not something about which we can't know anything, but something about which we can't know everything.

The mystery of the Holy Trinity is described by the Catechism (258) as follows: "one God and Father from whom all things are, and one Lord Jesus Christ, through whom all things are, and one Holy Spirit in whom all things are." Then it explicitly states, "Christians are baptized in the *name* of the Father and of the Son and of the Holy Spirit: not in their *names*, for there is only one God, the almighty Father, his only Son and the Holy Spirit: the Most Holy Trinity" (233). Very early in Christian history, St. Hippolytus (around 200 AD) would describe this mystery as follows, "God is One. It is the Father who commands, and the Son who obeys, and the Holy Spirit who gives understanding: the Father who is above all, and the Son who is through all, and the Holy Spirit who is in all." In other words, in the Trinity, the Father is not the Son; the Son is not the Father, and the Spirit is neither Father nor Son. They are all "one" precisely by not being each other—one in being, diverse in person.

In order to articulate the dogma of the Trinity, the Church had to use reason to develop her own terminology with the help of certain notions of philosophical origin—notions such as "substance," "person" or "hypostasis", "relation" and so on. With the help of these concepts, the Church could make clear she does not confess three Gods, but one God in three persons, the "consubstantial Trinity." Each of the three persons in the Godhead possesses the same eternal and infinite divine nature; thus, they are not "three Gods," but the *one*, true God in essence or nature.

This mystery has been declared by some as illogical and against reason, but it is not. A mathematical analogy may help explain this: not $1+1+1=3$, which would amount to polytheism, but $1 \times 1 \times 1 = 1^3 = 1$, which defends monotheism. Or with the help of a geometric analogy: the fact that we distinguish three dimensions in space does not mean that we can separate those three dimensions. St. Patrick famously explained the doctrine of the Holy Trinity to his flock in Ireland by using the three leaves of the shamrock: each leaf represents one of the three persons, but yet it is still only one shamrock. St. Augustine used another analogy to help us understand how you can have relational distinctions within one being, when he said, "I cannot love love unless I love a lover; for there is no love where nothing is loved. So there are three things: the lover [Father], the loved [Son], and the love [Holy Spirit]." Somewhere else, he uses another analogy:

> *I speak of these three: to be, to know, and to will. For I am, and I know, and I will: I am a knowing and a willing being, and I know that I am and that I will, and I will to be and to know. Therefore, in these three, let him who can do so perceive how inseparable a life there is, one life and one mind and one essence, and finally how inseparable a distinction there is, and yet there is a distinction.*

Not surprisingly, the Trinity may appear to be in violation of monotheism when not properly understood. That is one of the reasons why it had to be rationally secured from attacks and heresies. The Eleventh Synod of Toledo in Spain (AD 675), for instance, had to clarify—against Muslim allegations that a Triune God is contrary to monotheism—what a Trinitarian belief entails: "We acknowledge Trinity in the distinction of persons; we profess Unity because of the nature or substance. The three are one, as a nature, that is, not as person. Nevertheless, these three persons are not to be considered separable, since we believe that no one of them existed or at any time effected anything before the other, after the other, or without the other." Later on, the Fourth Lateran Council (1215) would add:

> *The Father is from no one; the Son is from the Father only; and the Holy Spirit is from both the Father and the Son equally. God has no beginning; He always is, and always will be. The Father is the progenitor, the Son is the begotten, the Holy Spirit is proceeding. They are all one substance, equally great, equally all-powerful, equally eternal.*

What we see here is that reason has been used to explain what a Trinitarian belief stands for and how we can and should talk about God. From now, it can no longer be said that all monotheistic religions worship the same God, for the God of Christians is very different from the God of Muslims. The title of a recent book raises the crucial question, "Is the Father of Jesus the God of Mohammed?" It could easily be argued that both religions may refer to the same God in Heaven, but the way they talk about this common reference is very different. The "common ground" approach of the interfaith dialogue obscures some essential differences between the two. Both religions may refer to the same God, but the way they talk about this "common reference" is very different. Any kind of dialogue between religions must be honest about the differences that separate them—sparing us a false impression of common ground.

At the same time, it is clear that reason can never fully explain the mystery of the Holy Trinity. It remains ultimately a matter of Revelation. It is not a natural truth revealed by natural revelation, but a supernatural truth revealed by Special Revelation. Some have expressed it this way: God himself is the revealer ("Father"), the revelation ("Son"), and the being-revealed ("Spirit") in both indestructible unity and indestructible difference. St. Thomas gave equal praise "to the One who begets, and to the Begotten One, and to the One who proceeds from them both." So, though equal, there is an order in procession, with the Father "greater" as source, but equal in dignity to Son and Holy Spirit. This may not make for easy understanding, but at least it determines what can, and what cannot, be said about the Triune God. Christians cannot talk about God without mentioning that Jesus is the Son of God.

b. Incarnation

Incarnation is the mystery and the dogma of the Word made Flesh. The Church calls "Incarnation" the fact that the Son of God assumed a human nature in order to accomplish our salvation. The Catechism (464) says, "The unique and altogether singular event of the Incarnation of the Son of God does not mean that Jesus Christ is part God and part man, nor does it imply that he is the result of a confused mixture of the divine and the human. He became truly man." As Pope St. Leo the Great put it in 451, "Invisible in his own nature, he became visible in ours. And he whom nothing could contain was content to be contained."

Not surprisingly there have been heresies that denied either Christ's divinity or his true humanity. In response, the Church had to explain clearly and proclaim explicitly that Jesus Christ is Son of God by nature and not by adoption, that the Son of God is "begotten, not made, of the same substance (*homoousios*) as the Father." The Nicene Creed stated very explicitly that Jesus is "of a *same* substance" [*homoousios*], not "of a *similar* substance" [*homoiousios*]. This requires very specific terminology: "The Incarnation is therefore the mystery of the wonderful union of the divine and human natures in the one person of the Word" (CCC

483). When the Second Person of the Trinity became incarnate, he took on a human nature, while still retaining his divine, transcendent nature. So he renounced his dignity, as it were, not his divinity.

Once we accept in Faith the mystery of Incarnation, we might feel the need of reason to ask *why* the Word was made Flesh. One of the earlier attempts to pose and answer this question comes from St. Anselm of Canterbury (1033-1109). In one of his major works, "Why God Became Man" [*Cur Deus Homo*], Anselm offers a theological explanation for Christ's incarnation and crucifixion in terms of "atonement"—that is, how human beings can be reconciled to God through Christ's sacrificial death. Christ's saving death involves a satisfaction for sin to God as a form of debt—the repayment of what man owes God but is not able to pay God. Anselm argued that the insult given to God through sin is so great that only a perfect sacrifice could satisfy, and that only Jesus, being both God and man, could be this perfect sacrifice. Therefore, the reasoning would be that Jesus gave himself as a "ransom for many," to God the Father himself, because only the God-Man can offer the satisfaction required to avert the punishment.

In essence, Anselm argued that God had to act that way because it was the only logical course he could follow, given the divine attributes of Omnipotence and Justice. On the one hand, God had to redeem humankind, or else the eternal purposes for this would have been thwarted, and then God's *omnipotence* would have been compromised. On the other hand, humankind also had to be punished for the Fall, or else God's *justice* would have been compromised. It was the purpose of Anselm's argument—

which explained the course of sacred history not only in broad outline but in excruciating detail—to make the whole mystery more accessible to human reason, perhaps even too accessible according to some.

Later theologians suspected that rationality was achieved in tis case by trapping God within the rational structures of the created world. In the final analysis, God's actions were explained by assuming God had to follow the same rules we do. In this view, a program of salvation became a program of punishment, the mediator became a substitute, and the Cross became a means of payment. Peter Abelard (1079-1142), writing somewhat later, suggested that the world was, after all, God's creation and he could do as he pleased with it. If he wanted to forgive humankind, why couldn't he simply forgive what had gone wrong? Dogmatic Theology cannot ignore this question.

In a recent interview, Pope Emeritus Benedict XVI asked the same question, "Why the cross and the atonement?" After mentioning all the evils we have witnessed now and in the past, he continues, "This mass of evil cannot simply be declared nonexistent, not even by God. It must be cleansed, reworked and overcome.... God simply cannot leave 'as is' the mass of evil that comes from the freedom that He Himself has granted. Only He, coming to share in the world's suffering, can redeem the world." Therefore, "When the Son struggles in the Garden of Olives with the will of the Father, it is not a matter of accepting for himself a cruel disposition of God, but rather of attracting humanity into the very will of God."

The main point of this discussion is that suffering can be used for redemption, atonement, and reparation of all sins.

Redemption is actually a culmination point in the Bible. We find it already in the Jewish Scriptures when some take upon themselves the sins and burdens of others so that all will be free of the consequences of sin. This is sometimes called "vicarious atonement." We find this belief, for instance, in the well-known story about Abraham's plea for Sodom. He asks God, "Will you indeed destroy the righteous with the wicked?" Then Abraham starts negotiating: suppose there are fifty righteous within the city, would you then destroy the place and not spare it for the fifty righteous who are in it? Next Abraham whittles this farther down: What about forty-five? What about forty? What about thirty? Suppose twenty are found there? And at last he gets God down to ten: "For the sake of ten I will not destroy it."

The previous story even has a sequel, counting down from ten to one, when God says to the prophet Jeremiah: "Run back and forth through the streets of Jerusalem.... Search her squares to see if you can find a man, one who does justice and seeks the truth; that I may pardon her." Ultimately, that one man will be found in Jesus of Nazareth, the Son of Man, the Son of God. It was the High Priest Caiaphas who spoke to the Sanhedrin these prophetic words: "One man should die for the people" (John 11:50). There is something very peculiar going on here: God is asked not to treat the just the way the unjust deserve to be treated, but instead God decides to treat the unjust in the same way as he treats the just, as if they too were just. Somehow, God decided to pardon the unjust majority because of the just minority. That was also the "mission" Jesus Christ had—through him humanity can be pardoned. Jesus gave us our dignity back, but at the cost of his own.

Christians see the story of Abraham and Isaac as a profound allegory for the sacrifice of Jesus on the Cross. Like Isaac, Jesus was a father's only beloved son. Like Isaac, Jesus carried uphill the wood for his own sacrifice. Even Abraham's words proved prophetic. Since there was no punctuation in the Hebrew original, verse 8 could be read as follows: "God will provide Himself, the Lamb, for a burnt offering"—the Lamb being Jesus Christ, God himself. That would be a theological explanation of the mystery of Incarnation—as to "Why God became man."

c. Providence

The "God of reason" has sometimes been caricaturized as the God of deism. In the 17th and 18th centuries, during the Enlightenment—the "Age of reason"—deism became popular among intellectuals who, raised as Christians, believed in the one God of Natural Theology but rejected all forms of revealed religion (theism). The God of deism— "nature's God"—has often been described as a God who once made the world, but more like a watch-maker who makes a watch, lets it run its own course, and then abandons it to itself—the "hands-off" approach of an absent landlord, so to speak. This means that the God of *deism* does not intervene in the affairs of the world, and contrary to what is maintained in *theism*, no supernatural events or miracles can be ascribed to God. However, this is not necessarily the way Natural Theology sees it. If God were to take away for one instant his sustaining power, the entire creation would at once fall back into nothingness. So everything fully depends on God, even in Natural Theology.

God preserves and governs the world, so nothing happens without the will or permission of God.

Nevertheless, the "God of Faith" takes us much further than the "God of reason." What Faith "adds" to reason is that the "God of reason" has not remained utterly hidden for us but actually "spoke" to us and still keeps "speaking." He is actively involved with his creation and with each one of his creatures. The "God of Faith" is the God of history who is intimately and perpetually involved with the affairs of humanity. He is not a God merely of the past but also of the present and the future. He is the eternal "I AM" (Ex. 3:14), the One "who is and who was and who is to come" (Rev. 1:4).

This is how Divine Providence is understood: as care exercised by God over the Universe, his foresight and care for its future. Though the term itself hardly occurs in the Scriptures—or at least it is translated in various ways—the closest comparison can be found in Genesis 22, when Abraham takes his son Isaac to a mountain so as to sacrifice him to the Lord, and then is asked by his son, "where is the lamb for the burnt offering?" Abraham answers him "God will *provide* for himself the lamb for the burnt offering, my son." And then, when the angel of the Lord stops him from sacrificing his son, Abraham finds a ram in the thicket. So he calls this place "The Lord will provide"—which means, God will take care of it.

That passage reflects basically how we understand Divine Providence: God, by his providence, is in charge of all that happens to his creation and to all its creatures—he takes care of everything. His providence is not just some general oversight of the world, leaving the details worked out by someone or something else. Rather, he is behind every detail of the Universe—from the falling of a sparrow to the number of hairs on your head. Through his Providence, God orders all things.

A distinction is sometimes made between "general providence," which refers to God's continuous upholding the existence and natural order of the Universe, and "special providence," which refers to God's extraordinary intervention in the life of people. Providence by which the entire Universe is ruled clearly follows from the fact that God is the "author" of all things and that order and purpose must characterize the action of an intelligent creator. If God is not in control of all things, then he is not sovereign, and if he is not sovereign, then he is not God. But in addition, God also takes care of us individually: "For God is at work in you" (Phil 2:13). We can do nothing without God. When the Apostle Paul says (Phil 4:19), "My God will fully supply whatever you need," he is basically saying the following: do all you can and let Divine Providence take care of all the rest. The Catechism (303) summarizes this as follows:

> *The witness of Scripture is unanimous that the solicitude of divine providence is concrete and immediate; God cares for all, from the least things to the great events of the world and its history. The sacred books powerfully affirm God's absolute sovereignty over the course of events: "Our God is in the heavens; he does whatever he pleases."*

Of course, the question for Dogmatic Theology is how we can rationally understand and explain God's Providence. It is through Divine Providence that God accomplishes his Will. To ensure that his purposes are fulfilled, God governs the affairs of humanity and works through the natural order of things. The laws of nature are nothing more than

God's work in the Universe. The laws of nature have no inherent power; rather, they are the principles that God set in place to govern how things normally work. They are "laws" only because God decreed them; they are somehow the "commands" he gave to the Universe. The primary means by which God accomplishes his Will is through secondary causes (e.g., laws of nature and human choices). In other words, God usually works indirectly to accomplish his Will. It is in and through secondary causes that Providence ordinarily works.

This raises the rational question why there seem to be so many imperfections in the creation of a Perfect God. The answer of the Catechism (302) is that God's creation is perfect, but not complete yet:

> *Creation has its own goodness and proper perfection, but it did not spring forth complete from the hands of the Creator. The Universe was created "in a state of journeying" [in statu viae] toward an ultimate perfection yet to be attained, to which God has destined it. We call "divine providence" the dispositions by which God guides his creation toward this perfection.*

In this process towards perfection, we ourselves as God's creatures become co-workers who must participate in God's Providence. The Catechism (323) confirms this, "Divine providence works also through the actions of creatures. To human beings God grants the ability to co-operate freely with his plans." And it also says, "To human beings God even gives the power of freely sharing in his providence by entrusting them with the responsibility of 'subduing' the earth and having dominion over it.... They then fully become 'God's fellow workers' and co-workers for his kingdom" (CCC 307).

In spite of all of this, most of us do have the opinion that a perfect world from the very beginning would be better than an imperfect world on its journey to perfection. We tend to assume in our reasoning that God's providence should have created an ideal world, a hedonistic paradise, a place in which comfort and convenience are maximized, a world in which everyone has an electrode implanted to cause intense euphoria and ecstasy with a simple push of the button.

But if that is considered a perfect world, then we should also ask ourselves whether we really admire those who appear to have a life of ease. What we do admire instead are lives of courage and sacrifice; we have a high regard for people who overcome hardship, deprivation, or weakness so as to achieve some notable success; people who stand against some great evil, or who relinquish their own happiness to alleviate the suffering of others—in short, people who take up their crosses. A life without challenge is a life without interest. Seen this way, the maximization of creaturely pleasure does not seem to be a top priority in most lives—let alone in God's Omnipotence and Providence for us. It is only in a world where daily life is divorced from its supernatural end that suffering loses it redemptive value.

Apparently, there are always two sides to the Good News story of God's Providence: we have to do our part in order for God to do his part. There is obviously a strong interaction between the two. Since we were given freedom, we have to use the gift that was given to us. Free creatures are of greater value than puppet creatures, because their greater likeness to God would be an improvement to creation. But after doing our part, we must leave the rest up to God's Providence and Grace. We may not know what the future holds, but we do know that God holds the future. The future of the Universe is in the hands of its Maker. Everything in this Universe unfolds in accordance with God's plan. God orders all things, and nothing eludes God's care for the world.

This still leaves the question as to how Divine Providence can be reconciled with all the randomness and all the coincidences we see around us. Some even say, "I wish you good luck," as if we are ruled by luck. Well, in religion, there is no place for good or bad "luck." As a matter of fact, Thomas Aquinas once said, "Whoever believes that everything is a matter of chance, does not believe that God exists." And St. Padre Pio was apt to say in various ways that it is God who arranges the coincidences. Once he asked a man who claimed such-and-such event had happened by chance: "And who, do you suppose, arranged the chances?" Apparently, anything that seems to be random from a "natural" or "scientific" point of view may still very well be included in God's eternal plan of Providence. Randomness is about how things in this Universe are related to each other. But when we speak of Providence in religion, we are talking about how things in this Universe are related to God—not to each other. When it comes to God, randomness has lost its regular meaning.

Just as we on our own can steer the laws of nature to achieve our own purposes, so does God work through natural causes and human intentions in order to achieve his purposes and salvation plans, because he is "part" of all that happens in this Universe, without being a physical part of it. It is God's Providence that allows us to see events in their inter-connectedness. Believers of the Judeo-Christian tradition know very well that God does work this way—constantly, faithfully, and lovingly.

How can this be? As discussed earlier (see 4.b), Thomas Aquinas would argue that God's position with respect to time is such that, unlike us, he does not have to wait for the future to unfold in order to know its contents. God is in no way a temporal being, but rather the Creator of time, with complete and equal access to all of its contents. But if God exists entirely outside of time—in a kind of eternal present to which all that occurs in time is equally accessible—God would indeed be able to comprehend all of history, the past and the present as well as the future, just as though they were now occurring. As the Book of Proverbs (16:33) says, "The lot is cast into the lap, but its every decision is from the Lord." Anything that seems to be random from a human or natural point of view may still very well be included in God's eternal, providential plan.

For this reason, religion does not have to be "intimidated" by randomness. The Bible has several examples of chance being used for divine purposes by casting lots. The eleven apostles used chance to have God elect a new, twelfth apostle: "Then they gave lots to them, and the lot fell upon Matthias" (Acts 1:26). In Palestine, temple priests were chosen by lot: "According to the custom of the priesthood, he was chosen by lot to enter the temple of the Lord and burn incense" (Luke 1:9). The Old Testament mentions another case: "Then Saul said, 'Cast the lot between me and my son Jonathan.' And Jonathan was taken." (1 Sam. 14:42). Apparently, there is no fundamental conflict between randomness and Divine Providence. God even rules through what we consider randomness and coincidence.

One more challenging question might be as to how God's Providence can work in the seemingly "closed" system of our Universe. We will discuss this question further later on (see 9). For now, let this suffice: the proposition that the physical Universe is a closed system that does not allow for Divine Providence "from outside" is not itself a law of physics, but an assumption that can be traced back to ideologies such as materialism, naturalism, and scientism. These ideologies preclude Divine Providence ahead of time—*a priori*, if you will—from even being possible. They rule out beforehand what they don't want to accept.

d. Suffering

Why is there suffering? Why the evil of suffering? Theology certainly needs to face these questions. We already did so briefly through Natural Theology (4.c), but here lies also a task for Dogmatic Theology, for the Bible reveals to us that there is a much deeper root for evil and suffering than Natural Theology could ever discover on its own: it is the existence of Original Sin. This doctrine is rather central in Catholic Faith, for if there is no Original Sin, then the Cross is a hoax; if the Cross is a hoax, then the whole economy of salvation is up for grabs.

So where does Original Sin come from? The answer is very straightforward: from the Fall in Paradise. That's when the first humans decided with their free will that they wanted to follow their own commandments, not God's—and thereby they started a cascade of evils that keeps going on and on.

The Catechism (403) explains this further by telling us that Adam "has transmitted to us a sin with which we are all born afflicted." Not only is sinfulness hereditary but it is also contagious, and is passed on like we pass on the flu. Because of the unity of the human race, the Catechism (404) can state,

> [A]ll men are implicated in Adam's sin, as all are implicated in Christ's justice.... By yielding to the tempter, Adam and Eve committed a personal sin, but this sin affected the human nature that they would then transmit in a fallen state.... And that is why original sin is called 'sin' only in an analogical sense: it is a sin 'contracted' and not 'committed'—a state and not an act.

What we have here could easily be expressed in terms of heredity. If you come from a dysfunctional family, chances are you will start another dysfunctional family. We "inherited" a state of being "dysfunctional," so to speak. This idea follows the biblical principle that the sins of the fathers are visited onto the children to the third and fourth generations (Ex. 20:5; 34:6-7; Num. 14:18; Deut. 5:9). There is probably no better term to capture this than "Original Sin"—it is not genetic, but it is hereditary. C. S. Lewis even argued that the existence of Original Sin is perhaps one of the most obvious facts of human life, even so to non-believers. G. K. Chesterton called it "the only part of Christian theology which can really be proved." You don't have to be a rock scientist or a brain surgeon to know there is something wrong with humanity, something that is "rotten" to the core. But the Bible tells us it's not God's doing, it's ours—and it goes back to the very beginning of humanity.

Do we really have to call this evil? For some people, evil belongs to a superseded and superstitious world of black and white. They think we don't *do* anything wrong, but things just *go* wrong—due to genes, hormones, or mere "fate." They consider evil some kind of disease located somewhere in a gene or temporal lobe or whatever. They even tell us that we can evade moral responsibility by saying that our glands made us act the wrong way. However, morality is about choices each one of us constantly makes based on moral values and laws (see 6). As a consequence, evil is often the outcome of a corrupted morality. At the very moment that we let self-interest become the driving force behind all our actions, evil will take over and control us. Without the compass of morality, we would head down a dangerous blind alley. It would be a world without good and bad, right and wrong, good and evil.

The Book of Genesis tells us that evil and suffering are real—a consequence of the Fall, when God said to Eve "I will greatly multiply your pain in childbearing; in pain you shall bring forth children" (Gen. 3:14-16). This makes one wonder if there was a physical change in the world as a result of the Fall. Were there "thistles and thorns" *before* the Fall? St. Thomas Aquinas makes a very astute remark here: "Some say that the animals, which are wild now and kill other animals, were not that way [in paradise].... But this is entirely unreasonable. The nature of animals was not changed by the sin of man." And yet, since the Fall, there is not only mental suffering (grief, hatred, frustration, heartbreak, guilt, humiliation, anxiety, loneliness, misery, self-pity) but also physical suffering (pain, illness, disability, hunger, poverty, and ultimately death).

Especially the last part of the previous sentence may cause

some to wonder whether there was *death* before the Fall. The Book of Genesis seems to assume there was. As a matter of fact, carnivores were created with organs expressly intended for causing the death of other animals. When God threatened Adam and Eve with death for disobedience, the Bible seems to imply they had some knowledge of what death is, as they had seen it among animals. Yet, before the Fall, Adam and Eve were preserved from death and suffering by special graces given them by God.

How can this be? The material world is subject to decay and death, but humans are not because they have been endowed with an immortal soul. For an immortal soul, the death of the body would be a punishment undeserved, prior to sin. Adam and Eve were created for immortality, but then lost the eternal life of the soul in the moment they sinned, and physically died many years later. After the General Resurrection, God will restore to us the grace needed to prevent our bodies from breaking down over time. Although spouses won't be reunited after the Resurrection—"When they rise from the dead, men and women do not marry, but are like the angels in heaven" (Mk. 12:25)—body and soul will.

So the "thorns and thistles" may have always been there, but since the Fall in Paradise, they were felt not only as painful but also as distressing, as something "evil." St. Thomas is right; after the Fall the *world* did not change, but *we* did. Seen this way, not only the cause of moral evil but even the cause of physical evil has to be traced down ultimately to sin. Without sin, physical evils would not rankle or embitter us, but because of Original Sin they do.

We know of "evil" because we have an idea of "good" and of what things should be like, if everything were "good"—the way God intended them to be before the Fall. Evil—and hence suffering—has everything to do with sin. When a paralytic was brought to him, Jesus said, "your sins are forgiven" (Mk 2:5). The paralytic wanted to be able to walk, not to be delivered from his sins, but Jesus saw the man's real need. Forgiveness of sins is the foundation of all true healing.

Whenever we ask why bad things happen to good people, we could as well ask the reversed question: why do good things happen to bad people. Who is to say we are good people anyway? Because of Original Sin, there is not only much good in the worst of us, but also much bad in the best of us. Looking at things this way gives us a completely different perspective on evil and suffering: we are no longer "good" people who suffer "bad" things; we are "bad" people who enjoy so many "good" things. So we should never turn misery into self-pity. As Jesus once said, "No one is good but God alone." And besides, who is to say suffering is all bad, or bad forever? God is certainly able to use suffering for a better purpose, for something good. There is actually something therapeutic about suffering—it has the potential to redeem us, transform us, and transfigure us.

Interestingly enough, only humans take diseases and catastrophes as something that "should" not be. This is something no animal would be able to do. A prey does not consider the predator "evil"—perhaps painful, literally, but not evil. When giving birth, animals may experience physical pain but not suffering in the sense of something "bad" or "evil." Humans, on the other hand, do. Only humans can get depressed. Animals may "dislike" these things, but they do not question them in terms of "Why *me*?" They do not have a "me," and since animals do not know about good and bad, they cannot ask why bad things happen to good animals. Only humans can have knowledge of God, so they ask the question "Is something wrong between God and me?" or "Why do bad things happen to good people?"

Because we are able to ask *whether* there is something wrong between God and us, we are also able to see *what* is wrong between God and us—Original Sin is the answer coming from Special Revelation. The consequence of Original Sin has been unending misery, a pit from which no one can escape by their own efforts. Only God can provide a way for human beings to return to their original status from before the Fall, as we discussed earlier (5.b). Until this salvation appears on earth, suffering remains the endemic state of humanity. The hopeful side of this doctrine is that with the coming of God's Son, who alone can remove Original Sin, it will eventually be possible for a redeemed humanity to live in an ideal world free from suffering—which is the Kingdom of Heaven, a broken world restored. The restauration began with the Incarnation of God's Son and will eventually lead to the General Resurrection, when God will restore the immortality with which Adam and Eve were created.

This is a dramatic turn; it shifts the theological focus from Original Sin and human suffering to Christ's Incarnation and his Crucifixion. Jesus the Messiah went to the full depth of sin and suffering on Golgotha by identifying himself with our suffering in order to eradicate the effects of sin. The Good News of Jesus Christ is actually the "reverse side" of the doctrine of Original Sin (cf. CCC 389). So the real answer to the question of "Why suffering?" does not come from abstract theological explanations but from a person called Jesus of Nazareth. It is an answer that comes directly from the Man of Golgotha: God is love—and love wants to share to the very end, with all its consequences. God's love wants to share everything with us, even our sufferings.

So Jesus came, not to abolish, but to sanctify suffering with his presence. Jesus did not save us *from* the cross, but instead he saved us *by* the Cross. Anyone who offers love without sacrifice, anyone who offers Christ without the Cross, is just selling snake oil. Even in suffering—or particularly in suffering—we can find the Glory of God, for Jesus is the human face of God—and a human face comes with tears. Seen from this angle, even suffering can at times become a blessing. As the late Fr. Benedict Groeschel put it, "This is the mystery of the Incarnation. Christ comes and weeps with us. He suffers with us."

In other words, Golgotha has become a "meeting place" for all those who suffer. From now on, in the words of the Catechism (1521), "Suffering, a consequence of Original Sin, acquires a new meaning; it becomes a participation in the saving work of Jesus." In him, we are able to "offer up" our sufferings, for we are participants and co-workers in his creation. Needless to say that this is so much counter to our modern mindset. We live in a world that runs away from suffering; our bathroom cabinets are filled with painkillers. Since the time of our youth, we have been conditioned to view suffering as an impediment to happiness. This worldview, which is so deeply embedded in our culture, tells us that the less we suffer, the happier we will be. Yet, we could be missing out on another dimension of suffering, for suffering has this mysterious potential of redeeming us, transforming us, transfiguring us. You might think the less we suffer, the closer to God we will be—but it might actually be the opposite. Suffering provides those who suffer the ability to participate in their own and others' redemption from sin. That's how suffering can become very therapeutic.

As a matter of fact, whenever we suffer we can find the best therapy in Jesus. Where else would we go if not to Jesus? It is in Jesus, the Son of God, that we can find comfort in our sufferings. Jesus is the human face of God, and a human face comes with tears. Our tears are his tears, for God is not a God of evil but a God of love. Through the Incarnation, he entered space and time, which includes our suffering. Pope Benedict XVI summarized this well during his *Urbi et Orbi* blessing on Christmas Day 2011 with one single sentence: "Jesus Christ is the proof that God has heard our cry." Indeed, he is a compassionate God.

However, this raises other theological questions: Can God really suffer with us? Is God really a "suffering" God? Natural Theology seems to tell us that God cannot suffer, for any change in God would take away from his Perfection. That the Divine nature is essentially incapable of any internal change is an obvious consequence from Divine Infinity. Being able to change, on the other hand, implies the capacity for increase or diminution of perfection, which entails imperfection. But since God is infinitely perfect and is necessarily what he is, from this follows that God is immutable and impassible, that he cannot change and cannot suffer. God cannot be altered by anything a creature does. We depend on him, but he does not depend on us. He affects us, but we do not affect him, so our suffering cannot make him suffer either. Since God does not undergo emotional changes of state either, he cannot suffer.

But Natural Theology is not the end of the story. The rest of the answer must come from God himself. What is it then that Biblical Revelation tells us about God? Put in a nutshell, it would be that God is not only all-knowing, all-present, and all-powerful, but also all-loving. He is the God who created the world and humanity out of *love*. He is the one in search of us! He has a plan for his creation, a plan for all he created, including each one of us—which is called Divine Providence. God revealed himself to be a personal, loving, and compassionate God who has freely engaged himself in human history. He mercifully heard the cry of his enslaved people in Egypt and determined to rescue them. He revealed himself, especially in the Prophets, to be a God who grieved over the sins of his people. He was distressed by their unfaithfulness, and suffered over their sinful plight. So disheartened was God by their hard-heartedness that he actually expressed his anger at times. In short, it is a long love story of God's concern for and involvement with us.

In order to accentuate God's positive biblical attributes of perfection, love, goodness, and faithfulness, the early Church Fathers spoke of God with a whole cluster of negative attributes such as not-able-to-change (immutability) and not-able-to-suffer (impassibility). Do the positive and negative attributes clash with each other? Not really. When the Church Fathers call God immutable and impassible, some people take this to mean that God is therefore "callous," "heartless," or "indifferent"—the opposite of love, goodness, and faithfulness—but such a conclusion does not follow at all. Stating that something is not-white does not mean that it is black, as these two make an incomplete disjunction; there is much in between not-white and black—all the colors of the rainbow. To say that God is immutable is not the same as to say that God is static; to say that God is impassible is not to say that God is uncaring. Stating that God is immutable and impassible is only meant to protect his transcendence by asserting that his Goodness and Faithfulness can never change.

However, there is another important reason why God cannot suffer. If the suffering of creatures would really cause the Creator to suffer, this idea would place both on the same level. As a consequence, there would be no hope for us of ever being freed from suffering. What human beings cry out for in their suffering is not a God who suffers, but a God who loves wholly and completely. A god-in-pain, on the other hand, is no longer God, let alone a God-in-charge. If God were as vulnerable as we are, we would be in real trouble. But God does not suffer, he is not a suffering God. If he were, that would rob him of his transcendence and make him like one of us. We need a God-in-charge, not a God-in-pain. Because God the Father is in charge, God will not be devastated by suffering. It will not affect his faithfulness and sovereignty. God is impassible, not because he is uncaring, but because he is unwavering in his loving salvation. The impassibility of his nature is, therefore, a guarantee that he will always be there for us.

This led St. Bernard of Clairvaux to his statement that God

cannot "suffer," but surely God can "suffer with"—in his own words, although God is *impassibilis*, he is not *incompassibilis*. God is perfectly compassionate—in fact infinitely more compassionate than any human being ever could be—not because he suffers like those who suffer, but he "suffers with" those who suffer and he does so in his Love that fully and freely embraces those who suffer. It is love and not suffering that ultimately is at the heart of compassion. In the end, God's immutable Love will be superior to all the cruelties and absurdities of this world. So as to the question "Are we suffering alone?" the answer is No: God is suffering-with-us. This does not mean, though, that God is a suffering God. A god who suffers is not God. If suffering would affect God as much as it affects us, there would be little hope left for all of us who are suffering.

But did not God himself suffer through the suffering of his Son, you might ask. To think that God himself suffered in the suffering of Jesus is called *Patripassianism*: it is the Father [*pater*] himself who suffers on the Cross [*passio*]. It states that God the Father was incarnate and that whatever happened to the Son happened to the Father, and so the Father co-suffered with the human Jesus suffering on the Cross. It asserts that God the Father—rather than God the Son—became incarnate and suffered on the Cross for our redemption. When the Son suffered, it was actually God who experienced the sufferings. When Jesus was in pain, God himself was in pain. When Jesus died on the Cross, God died on the Cross.

The early Fathers and the early Church councils strongly rejected this as a heresy, because it is based on the erroneous idea that there is only one Person in the

Godhead, so that the Father, the Son, and the Holy Spirit are all one person—rather than three Persons (see 5.a). So it is in essence an anti-Trinitarian heresy. As a consequence, it claims that both the Father and the Son suffered on the Cross in one Person. In reaction to this threat posed to Orthodox Trinitarian theology, the Church spoke of "the Son of God in two natures, but in the singleness of one person, incapable of suffering and immortal in divinity; but in humanity for us and for our salvation suffered in the true passion of the body" (Denzinger 344). Jesus is God, but God is not Jesus. With Jesus' suffering, the Son of God was in pain, but God the Father was in charge.

To hold that the Son suffered as God would mean that he experienced our human suffering in a mitigated divine manner, and thus that he did not experience suffering as human beings do experience suffering. In other words, to place the significance of the Son's suffering within his *divine* nature is to relegate his human suffering to insignificance, and thus to demote all human suffering to insignificance. Ironically, those who advocate a suffering God have actually locked suffering within God's divine nature, and thus have locked God out of all human suffering.

Instead, it needs to be stated that God the Father "suffered with" his Son at the Crucifixion—not by becoming a God-in-pain on the Cross of his Son, but by remaining a God-in-charge who watched the suffering of his Son with divine compassion. The Infinite Power of God the Father is witnessed in raising God the Son gloriously from the dead. The bodily resurrection testifies that Jesus' offering of his human life was for our salvation, and thus that the *human* suffering and death he bore were of the utmost importance for the suffering of all of us. Jesus showed us in his suffering that we do not suffer alone. He made our tears his tears. Through Special Revelation, we know that the compassion of the impassible God the Father has become flesh in the passible God-Man (see 5.b). As Pope St. Leo the Great said about Jesus's suffering, "Being God who cannot suffer, he did not disdain to be man that can suffer."

e. Salvation

Because there is sin in the world—as a consequence of the Fall in Paradise—we have to face the question how sinful people can ever be saved. How could that even be a valid question? In the Bible, God reveals himself not only as a God of Love but also as a God of Justice. Love and Justice are divine attributes that are essential to God—without them, God would not be God. God is both Love and Justice; he is both loving and just. So when God is just, he is also loving, and when he is loving, he is also just.

Yet, there is a certain tension between these two when it comes to God's relationship with sinful people. That's where the concept of *mercy* comes in. On the one hand, *Justice* might require that sinful people should not be saved, so there would at best be salvation only for some, perhaps not even one person. On the other hand, *Love* might require that sinful people are forgiven their sins so all can be saved; it would entail salvation for many, if not all. Hence, it should not come as a surprise that this "tension" has stirred quite a rational and theological debate in Christianity.

Not too long ago, Pope Francis added to this controversy—at least for some of us, especially in the media—when he said, "The Lord has redeemed all of us ... not just Catholics.... Even the atheists." Many in the press heralded this as breaking news: no longer does it seem important which road we take to Heaven, for everyone can be saved. Like there are many mansions in Heaven (Jn. 14:2), it was at last acknowledged by a major Church leader that there are also many roads to Heaven—all equally valid. Really?

Indeed, at first sight, this stands in sharp contrast to the centuries-old Church teaching that there is no salvation outside the Church. But then it could be added that not everyone had a chance to become acquainted with the Gospel, the Church and her teachings. Although the document *Lumen Gentium* (LG 16) from Vatican II still confirms that those who have been given knowledge of Christ, but fail to act, "could not be saved," the Council also expressed,

> *Those who, through no fault of their own, do not know the Gospel of Christ or his Church, but who nevertheless seek God with a sincere heart, and, moved by grace, try in their actions to do his will as they know it through the dictates of their conscience—those too may achieve eternal salvation.*

Earlier, the late theologian Karl Rahner had introduced the term "anonymous Christian"—similar to the much older notion of a "virtuous pagan" or a "righteous gentile." Although some took the phrase "anonymous Christian" as derogatory for non-Christians and even paternalistic toward those who have not expressed any desire for it, it does convey an important message by declaring that people who have never heard the Christian Gospel, including the ones who lived before Jesus was born, might still be saved through Christ. It accepts that, without Christ, it is impossible to achieve salvation, but it does not accept that people who have never heard of Jesus Christ would *not* be saved. This is like repeating Jesus' words, "Forgive them for they do not know what they are doing."

Is this a cautious way of saying there is eternal salvation for everyone regardless of their religion? Not so if one reads these texts carefully and focuses on their exact wording. Vatican II and all the Popes since (and before) speak of "*redemption* for all" but not of "*salvation* for all." Let us not confuse these two notions: redemption is universal, but salvation is not. Redemption is indeed for all, because Christ "died for all," in the words of St. Paul (2 Cor. 5:15). The Catechism (605) puts it very emphatically, "There is not, never has been, and never will be a single human being for whom Christ did not suffer." But again, redemption is not the same as salvation. Salvation results from accepting Jesus' redemption and living one's life accordingly. But those who do not accept this gift of universal redemption—unless it is "through no fault of their own"—may still miss out on salvation. The Catechism (55) makes it very clear that God gave us "the hope of salvation, by promising redemption."

Let us pose the question one more time: did Pope Francis stray away from Church teaching and from what his predecessors had stated? In light of the above, we can now say he only confirmed that redemption in Christ is for all, not just Catholics—even for atheists. However, it does not follow from this that people from other religions, not to mention those without a religion, have actually accepted this gift of redemption and therefore will "automatically" receive salvation. Again, redemption is universal but salvation is not. Redemption has opened Heaven for all, but that does not mean that all will end up in Heaven. So it could be said that Pope Francis used Saint Peter's Square as a present-day "Areopagus": he was evangelizing—trying to bring salvation within the reach of as many people as possible. His message was not a declaration of universal salvation but a universal invitation to salvation—in an effort to make salvation as universal as possible.

The issue of salvation is certainly not a new topic in Dogmatic Theology. It has a long history in which the Catholic Church had to defend her theology against various opposing claims and interpretations. It is an age-old contentious controversy that had its roots in a perceived antagonism between God and man. It led to questions such as: Does salvation come from what *we* do or from what *God* does? Is salvation something we can *earn* or something we must *receive*? Does salvation come from our *works* or from God's *grace*? Can we buy our way into Heaven or must God invite us into Heaven? The keyword in all these questions is the word "or"—suggesting that a choice has to be made and that only one choice is correct.

Like with many other theological debates, extreme either-or positions put God and man in a power battle against each other. The underlying assumption is that whatever we give to God, we must take away from man; that whatever we give to man, we can only take away from God. However, God and man can never be in competition with each other for they are on entirely disparate levels. To think differently creates false opposites, contrasts, or dichotomies and would be a complete misunderstanding of God's Omnipotence (see 4.c). Yet, the reasoning behind it seems rather attractive or even compelling: if God is *all-powerful*, he can choose freely who will be saved and who will be damned, so it doesn't matter what we do on our own.

By putting human freedom against God's sovereignty, certain groups of Christians have made this issue into an either-or dilemma: either God wins and we lose all, or we lose and God wins all. Whereas the heretic Pelagius (354-420) held that we alone are responsible for our salvation (through our works), the Protestant Reformers in particular argued the opposite—that God alone is responsible for our salvation (through grace). Martin Luther went as far as denying free will in his Heidelberg Thesis: "'Free will' after the fall is nothing but a word, and as long as it is doing what is within it, it is committing deadly sin." And John Calvin declared that the human merit of works would "make void the Cross of Christ." The Catholic Church rejects both extreme positions as the outcome of a false dilemma. She stresses that there are always two sides to it, for both God's grace and our works are intricately connected. Leaving either one out does injustice to the theological discussion of salvation and God's Omnipotence.

First, there is God's grace. God's part comes first, of course. Without grace we cannot do anything—if only because all secondary causes are fully dependent on the Primary Cause; without creation there would not even be any creatures, for we are contingent beings. Everything is grace, and without it, we would fail. Without God we could not do anything—we could not even exist! We could not love if we were not loved first by God. We could not have reason without God's Reason. Grace, which literally means "gift," is God's favor to us. In other words, it is not something received in return for anything given from our side—it is free and unmerited. So when people say that our salvation depends on what *we* do ourselves, they should realize that salvation ultimately comes from God's grace, not from our doings. Even when we do "good works," on our side, they are always a fruit of grace, coming from God's side first. Jesus emphasizes this with the imagery of the vine. "I am the vine, you are the branches ... apart from me you can do nothing." While good fruits do require constant care on our part, the power to grow comes from God.

But there is also another side to all of this—the human part. Branches need to be cultivated to bear good fruits, so they require constant care and hard work on *our* side. We need to do our part, our works, to let God's grace work. God's grace does not take away any responsibilities on our side. Although we do not earn salvation—for it is a gift based on grace—we do have the choice to accept or reject that gift through our works. What we do on our side does not take anything away from what God does in his Sovereignty. We are free to either cooperate with or go against God's grace. But grace is not a once and for all event; it must be preserved, nourished, and cherished—which is a task of a life-time. In other words, God's grace is captivating but not irresistible. God's plan does include the possibility that we could throw away the gift we have been given. We do have that "power."

Obviously, the Catholic Faith rejects false dilemmas. It rejects putting our "work" in opposition to God's "grace." These two are not in competition with each other but they grow in union. St. Ignatius of Loyola used to put this in the following terms: work as if everything depends on you, but trust as if everything depends on God. Applied to the theological notion of salvation, this would entail that God provides "sufficient" grace for everyone to be saved, but whether it is "efficient" and put into effect (efficacious) depends on us. Thomas Aquinas would say "grace changes the will without forcing it." God offers salvation to all, but this may not produce salvation for all. In other words, not only does salvation depend on God's grace, it is also dependent on our works.

This "balanced" Catholic view about "grace and works" has often been rejected by other Christian denominations. They wonder whether human beings are really free to reject God's grace. In their view, God's grace is irresistible, otherwise God's Sovereignty would be in danger. But again, that puts God and us in a power battle. God gave us the freedom to decide as to whether we accept grace and do good, or whether we reject it and do evil. If Adam and Eve could fall from grace, certainly all of us can fall from grace as well. If grace were irresistible, Adam and Eve could never have rejected God's grace.

God would never force people against their will to come to him. That is not God-like, and not Biblical besides. Yet, it may sound strange or even offensive to some that the sovereign, all-powerful God of Christianity made himself dependent on us—for instance, on Mary's fiat so God's Son could be born in her womb. Nevertheless, that is the way God works. The only way God could redeem humanity was by means of a free "yes" of a human being, Mary, "full of grace." God's power is tied to the unenforceable "yes" of a human being, of someone like Mary, and of human beings like you and me.

Because we are free human beings, we will be held accountable for our choices in life—and that is where Hell and eternal damnation come in. God's Love calls us to Heaven, but God's Justice may also have to send some into Hell. Without God, injustice in this world would be permanent and unfixable. However, God does not cast anyone into Hell against their will. No one wants Hell to exist; no one wants evil to exist. But Hell is just evil eternalized. If there is evil and if there is eternity, then there can be Hell—it is a consequence of our own free choice. C. S. Lewis called Hell "the greatest monument to human freedom." He also says, "There are only two kinds of people—those who say to God, 'Thy will be done,' or those to whom God says in the end, 'Thy will be done.'" Although redemption is for everyone, salvation is not. For some there is salvation, for some there is damnation. Heaven is for those "on his right," while Hell is for those "on his left" (Mt. 25:34, 41).

f. Predestination

The previous theological dispute about "grace and/or works" also has had another related outcome. Not only did some theologians argue that if God is *all-powerful*, then he can choose freely who will be saved and who will be damned, but also did some of them conclude that if God is *all-knowing*, then he must know also who will be saved and who will be damned ahead of time, so he must have foreseen who will go to Heaven and who will end up in Hell. This issue is usually referred to as *predestination*.

Needless to say that this may easily lead to unnerving questions: Could it be that some people are his favorite ones from the very beginning? Were some people perhaps chosen and others rejected from the very start, before they were even born? Some Christians, particularly of the Calvinist tradition, have come to the conclusion that some of us are indeed predestined—in the sense of pre-determined, pre-arranged, pre-planned, pre-elected, or pre-ordained—to go to Heaven, while others are predestined to Hell, no matter what they did on their own.

Although Christian churches differ in their interpretation, all believe in some form of *predestination*, because the Bible uses the term. The Apostle Paul says, "these whom he predestined [*praedestinavit*], he also called" (Rom. 8:30) and "he predestined us for adoption to himself through Jesus the Messiah, according to the pleasure of his will" (Eph. 1:5). Predestination is definitely part of God's Providence in Christianity. But does this mean some of us are predetermined to be winners and others to be losers? Thomas Aquinas does not think so; he identifies predestination with salvation through God's mercy. He put it this way:

> *The reason for the predestination of some, and reprobation of others, must be sought for in the goodness of God.... God wills to manifest his goodness in men; in respect to those whom he predestines, by means of his mercy, as sparing them; and in respect of others, whom he reprobates, by means of his justice, in punishing them. This is the reason why God elects some and rejects others.*

St. Thomas uses two keywords here: mercy and justice. *Mercy* may lead to election, predestination, and salvation, whereas *justice* may lead to rejection, condemnation, and damnation. God first intends the purpose of the Universe, so it might manifest his Infinite Goodness, which includes his Love as well as his Justice—for he is a God of Love as well as a God of Justice. The *Magnificat* proclaims this very clearly, "His mercy is from age to age," but it emphatically adds, "to those who fear him" (Lk. 1:50). It is certainly important to mention God's mercy. But this information could also obscure that we must first acknowledge that we can do what is wrong. As Fr. James Schall, S.J. puts it, "Mercy without judgment bypasses free will."

St. Paul, for instance, makes no bones about it. Paul was a realist. In long-ago Galatia—but it could be anywhere else—he found "immorality, impurity, licentiousness, idolatry, sorcery, hatred, rivalry, jealousy, outbursts of fury, acts of selfishness, dissension, factions, occasions of envy, drinking bouts, orgies, and the like" (Gal 5:19-21). And then he speaks of the consequences: "Those who do such things will not inherit the Kingdom of God." He knew very well that people do such things, often even frequently. Christianity is initially presented to us because we are sinners who "do such things."

There is indeed God's Infinite Love, but not unconditionally, for he is also a God of Justice. God's Infinite Justice is not merciless, for he is also a God of Love. His just actions are loving, and his loving actions are just—similar to the way a father may punish his child out of love. Therefore, God intends that there should be salvation as well as damnation, so that both his Love and his Justice might be more perfectly manifested—neither one without the other. Since God's grace is not irresistible, God does not choose who will be saved and who will not, but he does save those who choose to accept his grace and his call for salvation. Salvation is God's choice, of course, but God's choices are based on our choices.

Could God not have done this differently? It is hard to see how. It would really be meaningless to suppose that God would have shown greater love toward the ones who have chosen to be lost by omitting them from creation—for what is not there cannot be loved. Equally, it is meaningless to think the lost would be better off had they not existed, for what does not exist is neither well nor bad off. And it is as good for the lost as it is for the saved to have the opportunity for salvation, and to have a choice as to whether to accept God's salvation. But what is certainly not good for the lost is the fact that they decided to reject God. Yet that is fully their decision, and its consequences are fully earned. We should never accuse God of arbitrarily rejecting those people. St. Augustine would say, "God created us without us: but he did not will to save us without us." The Catechism (600) adds to this, "To God, all moments of time are present in their immediacy. When therefore he establishes his eternal plan of 'predestination,' he includes in it each person's free response to his grace."

So who will make it to Heaven? Is it only an elect group of the happy few? No, God wants everyone to go to Heaven, but everyone also has the free will to decline or accept his offer. As we said earlier, redemption is for everyone, but salvation may not. Theologians such as the Protestant Reformer John Calvin, however, keep maintaining that our capability of choosing would be a direct violation of God's Sovereignty. They claim that if human beings are able to frustrate God's desire to bring us to salvation, then God's will would not be all-powerful. Human beings would supposedly be more powerful than God, as they have the power to frustrate God's power. From this they conclude that, if certain people are not saved, then it is apparently not because they chose not to answer the call for salvation, but because God, in his Sovereignty, had decided ahead of time that they would not be saved anyway. If the saved ones happen to do good work, according to this view, their "good works" are certainly not a means toward salvation, but they are merely signs of their predetermined election.

What this amounts to is turning pre-*destination* into some kind of pre-*determination*. While studying for a defense of Calvinism, around 1600, the Dutch Calvinist Jacob Arminius became convinced that he was defending an illogical position and sought to modify Calvinism so that God might not be viewed the author of sin, nor man an automaton in the hands of God. Arminius and his followers, the so-called Remonstrants and Arminians, concluded that if we let God alone be responsible for everything, then not only do we make God completely responsible for the salvation of the saved ones, the "elect," but also for the damnation of the lost ones, the "reprobate," even to the point of directly willing their sins. If so, the elect would be saved with no merit of their own, and the reprobate would be damned for no fault of their own. This may perhaps "save" God's Sovereignty, understood in a very warped sense, but surely not our freedom and not God's Goodness, Love, and Justice.

So where does this leave us? On the one hand, we need to keep God's Sovereignty and human freedom together as two sides of the same coin. It needs to be stated again that the ones who make it to Heaven are not the ones God had already chosen and elected ahead of time based on some kind of sovereign and arbitrary selective will, but they are the ones who answered his call and accepted his grace. When it comes to salvation or damnation, God has a choice, of course, but so do we. And God's choice is based on our choices. By his own Will, God has chosen to limit the realm of his own power, creating beings that have a free will that can frustrate his own Will. As a matter of fact, it is hard to see how a loving God could do anything but honor our choice in matters of right and wrong.

So if we do end up in Hell, we are not "rejects" arbitrarily rejected by God from the start, but we have rejected ourselves. The Catechism (1037) teaches that "God predestines no one to go to hell; for this, a willful turning away from God (a mortal sin) is necessary, and persistence in it until the end." If salvation were really dependent solely upon God's sovereign preordaining Will, then what is the point of Christ's Sacrifice on the Cross?

On the other hand, we need to keep a clear distinction between predestination and predetermination—they are very different concepts. In the words of St. Augustine, "Predestination is nothing else than the fore-knowledge and fore-ordaining of those gracious gifts which make certain the salvation of all who are saved." God's fore-knowledge cannot force our free will, for the simple reason that it is basically nothing else than the eternal vision of the future of human decisions, as we discussed earlier (4.b)—which does not deny or exclude free will at all. God knows with certainty his elect, but we do not. God fore-sees, as in an eternal pre-view, the free activity of everyone precisely as that individual is willing to shape it. So pre-destination should not be confused with pre-determination of the human will. No one is predetermined to get saved or lost; everyone is called to salvation, but everyone also has a choice to accept it or reject it. Rejecting it is not God's choice but ours. God's *knowing* of the outcome is not his *causing* of the outcome. As we said earlier, God is not the direct cause of my decisions—I am—but he is the indirect cause that lets me be the cause of my own decisions (see 4.b).

If pre-destination were actually a matter of pre-determination, then we would have no reason to better our lives, for nothing we would do could change the outcome anyway. Compare this with watching the replay of a game on TV. Does it matter whether the players were trying to win? Of course it does, but when you watch a replay, it has already been determined who the winners are. God knows the outcome of the "game" we are in, so to speak, but we are still in the game and have no way of knowing what the outcome will be, for it partly depends on what we decide we are going to do. "Strive to enter…," says the Bible (Lk. 13:24). We are all invited to win. It is clear that we know ahead of time there are winners, but we do not know yet who they will be. We all have to "run" to see who will make it to the finish line. Although election and salvation are known already in God's infallible and timeless fore-knowledge, his fore-knowledge did not pre-determine and cause the outcome.

If pre-destination were just a matter of pre-determination, another erroneous consequence would be that grace could only be given to the "pre-elected" ones, forcing them into a state of permanent grace that presumably can never leave them until they die. Grace would indeed be irresistible—a gift that you cannot refuse. It is exactly because of this line of thinking that some Christians have come to believe they can no longer "fall away," since they are predetermined from eternity to be saved anyway. They sometimes call themselves "born-again," and believe that a profession of Faith is all that is necessary to procure salvation. But there is something missing here, just as there is something missing when you profess your marriage vows and then think you no longer need express your love through a lifetime of loving actions. Salvation cannot be secured ahead of time.

Again, pre-destination is not pre-determination: if Adam and Eve, who possessed grace and a perfectly intact nature, could freely sin, how much more so is it possible to sin for all their descendants—including those who call themselves born-again Christians, for they too possess not only grace but also a wounded nature and a darkened intellect. If Adam and Eve could fall from grace, surely all of us can fall from grace as well. Hence, do not confuse "the elect" with the "born-again." The elect are those who persevere to the end, but not necessarily those who were once "born again" and started out the right way, but stopped half-way. Reality is that born-again Christians can and, sadly enough, do fall away sometimes. As St. Paul says, "Do you not know that in a race all the runners run, but only one gets the prize? Run in such a way as to get the prize" (1 Cor. 9:24).

g. Dogma

The Church's position on many theological issues is laid

down in so-called dogmas. Dogmas are truths that are proclaimed by the Church as divinely revealed, and must be held by all the faithful as matters of divine and Catholic Faith. They determine the correct interpretation of the Scriptures. They are about truths, but the supernatural ones.

As we found out earlier, supernatural truths are very different from natural truths. Supernatural truths come from Revelation, which makes them infallible, whereas natural truths come from reason and are fallible, because reason is fallible. That's why they should be treated very differently. Scientific truths, for instance, are natural truths that are open to revision and may have to be adjusted to new developments in research; so what is true today may have to be revised tomorrow because it turned out to be false. But supernatural truths are very different from scientific truths: what is true of Catholic doctrine today will also be true tomorrow. Whereas scientists must submit their minds to the data of experiment, religious believers must submit theirs to the data of Revelation and the Church's teaching. No matter what happens in society and science, the Church can never deny in one age what she had affirmed in a previous age as essential dogma. Dogmas don't evolve. Scientific theories can and will be revised, but dogma cannot.

Yet, Divine Revelation is progressive in nature—that is, over time, we are granted a fuller and fuller knowledge of God in general, including a fuller understanding of the meaning of prior Revelation. The New Testament, for instance, does not abolish the truth of the Old Testament but extends and deepens it. Although Revelation came to its fullest manifestation in Jesus, the Son of God, its understanding would still need further completion. Many of the central doctrines of Christianity—including the communion of Saints, the Resurrection of the body, the Trinitarian nature of God, the Divinity of Jesus, the Perpetual Virginity of Mary, and the Eucharistic Transubstantiation—only gradually became more transparent following Jesus' death. According to the Gospel of John (16:12-13), Jesus told his disciples,

> *I have many more things to say to you, but you cannot bear them now. But when He, the Spirit of truth, comes, He will guide you into all the truth; for He will not speak on His own initiative, but whatever He hears, He will speak; and He will disclose to you what is to come.*

Roy Schoeman, a convert from Judaism to Catholicism, gave a good description of this process in his book *Salvation Is from the Jews*:

> *Abraham was given a fuller knowledge of God, and a greater intimacy with him, than any of his predecessors had since the Fall. Then, when God revealed himself to Moses in the burning bush, he gave Moses a yet fuller revelation of the divine Name, which had been withheld from mankind until then.... Similarly, the Messianic prophecies in the Old Testament contain veiled information about the Messiah that became clear only later, through the life of Jesus himself and through the inspiration of the Gospel writers. And so it is throughout the rest of salvation history.*

In other words, Christianity came into the world as a single idea, but time was needed for believers to perceive its multiple aspects and to spell out its full meaning. It is for this reason that the doctrine of the Faith undergoes a process of development through time. The formulation of Revealed Truth develops through the discernment of new truths that are formally implicit in what the apostles handed over to us. This process of growth resembles the way a river growths—it gets wider and deeper, while remaining the same river. Such truths, once they are proclaimed by the Church as divinely revealed, are called dogmas. Hence, the Church cannot deny in one age what she has affirmed in a previous age as essential dogma. G. K. Chesterton once said, "Truths turn into dogmas the instant that they are disputed." And the late, great Dorothy Sayers would add to this that the drama is in the dogma, for which our ancestors were willing to die:

> *Official Christianity, of late years, has been having what is known as bad press. We are constantly assured that the churches are empty because preachers insist too much upon doctrine—dull dogma as people call it. The fact is the precise opposite. It is the neglect of dogma that makes for dullness. The Christian faith is the most exciting drama that ever staggered the imagination of man—and the dogma is the drama.*

Only truths proclaimed by the Church as divinely revealed are called dogmas, to distinguish them from more optional interpretations. Dogmas must be held by all as essential for Catholic Faith. True, the Church did change her interpretation of certain passages in the Bible every once in a while, but such interpretations are not unchanging dogma; they were never proclaimed as divinely revealed. Obviously, geocentrism has never been declared a dogma, and creationism can never be declared a dogma. Our salvation does not depend on whether we believe in heliocentrism, evolution, global warming, or any other scientific theory. The Church can change her position on such issues without affecting any dogma—they are dogma-neutral. But dogmas she cannot change.

The question remains, though: Why would we need more

than Scripture? Why would we need Dogmatic Theology in addition to Biblical Theology? Isn't the Bible all we need for Christian Faith? Especially since the Reformation, we often hear that the Bible is our main and sole guide—*Sola Scriptura*, in the words of Martin Luther—which seems to entail that our Faith is only and completely defined by Scripture, not by Church tradition and Church interpretation as well. However, Luther's notion of *Sola Scriptura* is an egg without a shell, so to speak. When St. Paul was preaching the Gospel, he was not carrying a book of four gospels around; such a book did just not exist at the time. To him and other early Christians, the term "Scripture" meant the Old Testament. In the meantime, the New Testament was in the making, right in the middle of the living Church.

So how then did the New Testament come along and what determined which books and letters were to be included in it? In other words, when the Holy Spirit fell upon the apostles at Pentecost, the purpose was to give birth to the Church, not to deliver a manuscript. It was the Church's task to first develop the New Testament by writing down what Jesus had taught his followers and what they had experienced in living with him. And then the next step was to determine which written down accounts were reliable and which were not. This means that the Early Church had to establish what is called the *canon*—an official list of inspired New Testament books. She had to separate the inspired wheat from the uninspired chaff. In other words, every Bible has a very important page that did not come with all the books we find in the Bible—and that is its table of contents.

Many questions abounded during early Christianity. One of them was: should the Jewish Scriptures be part of the Christian canon? The answer of the early Christian Church was a definite yes. All of them? In their later rabbinic canon of AD 70, the Jewish community decided not to accept the two Books of the Maccabees, for example, but Christians did because those had played an important role in their own communities. And the same holds for the Book of Ecclesiasticus (also called the Wisdom of Sirach, not to be confused with Ecclesiastes). It was not the Bible, of course, that decided what should be included in the Bible, but rather a group of Pharisees in AD 70. They suppressed books that did not comply with their tradition—rabbinic orthodoxy, that is.

The next question for Christians was what should be included in the canon of the New Testament. The tradition of the Church decided to omit a few Gospels of gnostic origin because they went against her tradition and were not used in her liturgies. In 367, St. Athanasius, the Archbishop of Alexandria, published a listing of orthodox, canonical books, identical to the one we find in our current Catholic New Testament. Later, Martin Luther would reject some of these books in his own Bible, particularly the Letter of St. James, because it went against his stand of "grace only" [*Sola Gratia*] in rejection of "works."

We should be careful, though, not to use a certain scriptural interpretation to form a set of doctrines, and then use this set of doctrines to authorize our selection of canonical books. That comes close to a vicious circle. Again, it is not the New Testament that decided what should be in it, but people did—for instance, Protestant Reformers like Luther.

So when it comes to the canon of the Bible, we cannot simply say that whatever is in the Bible is "biblical." The fact that something is, or is not, in the Bible is not the decisive point. The fact that the word "Trinity," for instance, is not in the Bible does not mean it is unbiblical. The question is rather reversed: what is "biblical" enough to be in the Bible?

Before the idea of a "canon" of the New Testament had been formulated, the Church had already developed her own concept of what was canonical. As a matter of fact, the Scriptures of the Old Testament needed a canon of New Testament interpretation—a living interpretation by means of the Faith handed down from the apostles, which was the tradition of the *apostolic succession.* Scripture did not come along all by itself. It is a product of tradition—the tradition of the early Church, more in particular the apostolic succession. First of all, the Church's tradition determines what belongs to Scripture. Second, the Church's tradition had determined, and still determines, how to read and interpret Scripture. Any text, even a text in Scripture, can have multiple interpretations. So Scripture cannot be interpreted by itself. As St. Thomas used to say, "[I]t is the task of the good interpreter to look, not at the words, but at the meaning." According to Acts 8:30-31, Philip ran to the Ethiopian eunuch in his chariot, "and heard him reading Isaiah the prophet and said, 'Do you understand what you are reading?' He replied, 'How can I, unless someone instructs me?'"

This leads us to other questions: Who determines what the correct interpretation is? Who instructs us how to understand what we are reading? The Catholic answer is to point to the *Tradition* of the Church—the same tradition that produced the text and handed it down through the apostolic succession. If we don't let the Church determine the correct interpretation, we end up with multiple denominations which keep splitting into smaller and smaller segments, each one with their own interpretation of the Bible. It is not up to each individual Christian to determine which books should be included in Scripture and how they should be read. The Bible is a book that came from the very heart of the Church; the apostles authored and the Early Church authorized the New Testament. In other words, Scripture and Church have an intricate relationship: Scripture created the Church, and the Church created Scripture. It is the Church who "owns" Scripture; individuals do not. And the pope plays a pivotal role in all of this, a role Pope Benedict XVI describes as "the first preserver of Christian memory, the living Church across time."

Preserving "Christian memory" also entails to guard the Church against deviations and heresies. This may sound strange at first sight. Especially nowadays, many tend to see "heresy" in terms of a violation of "freedom of expression." In this latter assessment, there just are no heretical views—they are merely harmless, perhaps dissident, alternative views. In science, however, no one would ever defend such a position; for instance, saying that disinfection before surgery makes no sense is not just an alternative view but is definitely "anathema" in science. Something similar holds for heresy in religion—it is anathema. Sometimes a heresy is an untruth, but often it is a faulty, partial truth—not a total lie but a firmly held half-truth that needs to be contested. Truth is truth, even if we don't accept it; and untruth is untruth, even if we don't admit it. It is the Church's task to contest half-truths and untruths, for truth's sake (see 1.d and 3.c).

In the New Testament, the apostles were deeply imbued with the conviction that they must transmit the deposit of the Faith to posterity undefiled, and that any teaching at variance with their own would be a culpable offense that would warrant exclusion from the communion of the Church (1 Tim. 1:20; Titus 3:10). As the Catechism (748) puts it, "The Church has no other light than Christ's; according to a favorite image of the Church Fathers, the Church is like the moon, all its light reflected from the sun." From very early on, the New Testament tells us how the Christian community was forced to confront those people who obscured the light from the sun and persisted in teachings contrary to the Apostolic Faith.

St. Paul is very adamant that heresies do and will arise within the Church. In Acts 20: 29-30, his farewell to the Ephesian elders, he says,

> *I know that after my departure fierce wolves will come in among you, not sparing the flock; and from among your own selves will arise men speaking perverse things, to draw away the disciples after them.*

In the First Letter of St. John (2:19), it is stated that heresy always starts within the Christian family:

> *They went out from us, but they were not of us; for if they had been of us, they would have continued with us; but they went out, that it might be plain that they are not of us.*

The implication is clear: heresy begins within the circle of Christian truth and doctrine. That is where heresies have their roots, in spite of Jesus' deepest desire: "I have given them the glory you gave to me, that they may be one as we are one" (John 17:22). Violating this desire is also what the word "antichrist" suggests. We often take the term to mean someone who is against Christ, much like the attitude we see in Communism and atheism, where there is a blatant denial of God and Christ. But that is not the thought here. It is true that the eventual outcome of any antichrist is that he is against Christ, but the word really means "instead of Christ," a deceiver, a false Messiah. It is someone who comes in Christ's name, someone who declares that he or she is a Christian and is declaring the truth of Christianity. Yet, once we analyze that person's teaching, it turns out to be contrary to what God, in Christ, has said. All heretics tell us that we should go by their personal intuitions of Faith and their personal interpretations of Scripture. *Their* "truth" is supposed to be *the* truth for all of Christianity.

The constant threat of heresies is the reason why dogma stands tall in the Catholic Church. The Catechism (88-89) words it this way,

> *The Church's Magisterium exercises the authority it holds from Christ to the fullest extent when it defines dogmas, that is, when it proposes truths contained in divine Revelation or also when it proposes, in a definitive way, truths having a necessary connection with these.... Dogmas are lights along the path of faith; they illuminate it and make it secure.*

Gerard M. Verschuuren

6. Morality and Reason

Morality tells us which actions others owe us and which actions we owe others, as part of the "common good." Morality is about what "ought" to be done—by us, as a "duty," and towards us, as a "right"—otherwise a moral mistake would be made. Duties and rights go hand in hand, so they have a natural reciprocity: the duty of self-preservation comes with the right of self-preservation; the duty to seek the truth goes together with the right to seek it; the duty to work for justice is connected with the right to pursue it. In other words, "no duties" means "no rights," and "no rights" means "no duties." To give a few other examples: there is no duty to die, so there is no right to die; no duty to marry, so no right to marriage; no duty to have children, so no right to have children.

All of this is the domain of morality. The (philosophical) study of morality is usually called ethics, but morality itself is about our capacity to distinguish between right and wrong, and to know what is right or wrong. It is through morality that we have access to a world of duties and rights—that is, a world of morality beyond our control. Morality adds a very different dimension to social behavior: not everything that is thinkable or possible or reasonable— in rational terms and social terms—is also permissible in moral terms. So let us find out what faith and reason have to tell us about morality.

a. The Basis of Morality

What is morality based on? Where do the "oughts" of our duties come from? Why do we call moral actions right or wrong? Are they right or wrong by convention or by nature? Where do moral laws and moral values come from?

Let us find out first what does *not* qualify as a basis of morality, before we try to uncover its real basis. Unfortunately, there have been many attempts to trap morality into something non-moral—perhaps as something real but certainly not as moral. Perhaps reason can show us why those attempts are bound to fail.

Here is trap number one: morality comes from past experiences. Why is that hard to believe? Well, killing is morally wrong, but certainly not because we discovered so after we had killed some people or had seen some killings. That would mean we have to do something wrong before we can know what is right. A moral command comes before what it commands, not after. Morality may be corroborated by past experiences, but it is not created by such experiences, and it actually aims to prevent them. There is mounting evidence that babies as young as six months old already make moral judgments and can tell right from wrong. Their sense of fairness begins very young. Researchers have found that even if an experiment is unfairly rigged so that one child receives more rewards, they will ensure a reward is fairly split, whereas animals usually fight for the largest piece.

Babies also know the difference between "good guys" and "bad guys"—despite little or no previous exposure to such situations. Based on this natural feeling of right-and-wrong, they can later be taught something like the more specific "underwear rule" about "bad guys": they should not be touched by others on parts of the body usually covered by their underwear; and they should not touch others in those areas. Besides, children who were sexually abused at a very young age know "intuitively" they experienced something morally wrong. What we can learn from this is that moral values and moral laws are not discovered through empirical or experimental evidence, but instead are somehow "inborn" from early childhood on. More on being "inborn" later.

Then there is trap number two: morality comes from the animal world. That is also something hard to defend. Animals do not have morality and cannot have morality. They do have social behavior, but certainly not moral behavior regulated by a moral code. They just follow whatever "pops up" in their brains—and no one has the right to morally blame them. The relationship between predator and prey, for instance, has nothing to do with morality; if predators really had a conscience guided by a moral code of "Thou shalt not kill," their lives as predators would be pretty harsh.

As a consequence, animals never do awful things out of meanness or cruelty, for the simple reason that they have no morality—and thus no cruelty or meanness. When animals do seem to do awful things, it is only because we as human beings consider their actions "awful" according to our standards of morality. Yet, we will never arrange court sessions for grizzly bears that maul hikers, because we know bears are not morally responsible for their actions. Besides, if animals had moral rights, their fellow animals too would need to respect those "rights."

Then there is trap number three: morality comes from our genes. Why would it be hard to claim that our genes tell us what is morally right or wrong? First of all, those who believe that morality is rooted in their genes must face the possibility that this very belief then is also rooted in their genes—which makes it some kind of "boomerang" belief that undermines itself. Second, in the world of genes, there is only material stuff (DNA), but no immaterial truths and untruths—and hence, no intangible moral rights and moral wrongs either. DNA is physical "stuff" that can be long or short, light or heavy, but morals cannot be any of these—they have no mass, size, or color. So how could material genes ever create immaterial moral rules? Then there is a third reason why morality cannot be in the genes. If morality were in the genes, why would we need articulated moral rules to reinforce what "by nature" we would or would not desire to do anyway? As a matter of fact, if morality were encoded in the genes, a moral code would be completely redundant. Instead the opposite could be argued: morality has the power to overrule what our genes dictate—passions, emotions, and drives. Apparently, morality is at a level "above" the level of genes.

No wonder then that far too many people are willing to break a moral rule when they can get away with it. It is hard to believe they are going against their genes. When it comes to moral laws, everyone knows about them and yet everyone breaks them repeatedly. Genes do not seem to prevent this. Unlike the laws of nature, moral laws can in fact be ignored—but don't try to do so with the law of gravity. So we have here another flawed attempt of converting moral behavior into a non-moral phenomenon. The rules as to what is morally right and what is wrong do not and cannot come from genes. It is hard to see how non-moral causes such as evolution and DNA could ever produce a moral effect; they are of a completely different nature.

Then there is trap number four: morality is something acquired—through upbringing, training, disciplining, or education. No doubt, discipline is part of morality. People who are at the mercy of their lusts, drives, and passions may not do the good they ought to do, because they are not disciplined enough to resist their lusts. But that doesn't mean morality is nothing more than being educated, taught, and disciplined. Compare this with laws of nature, such as the law of gravity: these laws may have to be taught to us in a physics class or biology class, but that doesn't mean laws of nature are only a matter of training and teaching. True, it is partly through schooling that we know about them, but the laws themselves are not a product of schooling. In a similar way, parents may help us understand moral laws better and may help us be better prepared and disciplined to do what is morally right, but that doesn't make what is right and wrong a matter of upbringing. Even if it did, it would be a matter of their upbringing too—which then still raises the question where did it begin and how, so that we don't end up in an infinite regress argument.

Then there is trap number five: morality is a matter of intuition. This is a very common trap, yet very deceiving. At first sight, it may sound appealing that we know "intuitively" what is right or wrong, but the word "intuition" carries a strong subjective overtone—some may have it, some may not, and some are not "intuitive" at all. That opens it up to the attack that morality is not something real but only exists in a person's mind—famously expressed as "many heads, many minds." G. B. Shaw, for instance, spoke of "different tastes," as if there are many moralities. If morality were merely a matter of intuition or taste, no further rational discussion would be possible.

No wonder then that intuition is not a very reliable tool to find out what is morally right or wrong. It comes close to "gut feelings." However, "good" is not a matter of what *feels* good. Feelings can never be the standard for judging morality, for we would have to decide next who has the best "gut feelings" or the best "hunch feelings." It is actually the other way around: morality is the standard for judging feelings. Feelings of revenge, for instance, need to be curbed by morality. Everyone can claim that intuition told him or her what ought to be done, but that does not make such action morally right or wrong. If so, every defendant in court would be entitled to claim that they just followed their "gut feelings." It is the other way around: morality determines which intuitions are right or wrong. "It feels right" is not a very good argument to defend one's actions.

Then there is trap number six: morality is a matter of conscience. Just as intuition, so conscience may seem a good tool in itself to guide our moral behavior. No wonder it is often heralded as the ultimate source of moral good and evil. Ironically, even relativists, who deny that morality has any absolute authority, still hold on to at least one moral absolute that says, "Never disobey your own conscience." So they should then ask themselves the question as to where the absolute authority of a human conscience comes from. How can a person's personal conscience possibly be an infallible guideline for morality? We cannot validly justify that our act was morally right by claiming our conscience told us so. Were the Nazis "good" people because they followed their conscience? Both sides in a war believe in conscience and claim they are right—yet they contradict each other. Reason tells us that both cannot be right at the same time.

To call one's conscience infallible is at odds with the facts: pro-lifers follow their conscience, but so do abortion doctors. Are they both morally right? Only so, if morality were merely a matter of personal opinions and preferences. However, the consequence would be that we lower the standards of morality to our own personal standards, instead of having moral standards evaluate our personal standards. The idea that one's conscience *creates* moral law is as flawed as the idea that one's consciousness creates the laws of nature. Of course, there is more to a human conscience than this, but let's save that issue for later (see 7.c).

If morality does not come from any of the aforementioned sources, and if morality is truly something real, then the question arises: where do moral laws and moral values come from then? Reason tells us that "common sense" may be a good candidate. When someone denies the existence of the laws of nature, such as the law of gravity, all one can do is invoke the principle of common sense. Common sense tells us there is some kind of *physical* order in nature: stones that fall today will also fall tomorrow. We cannot prove this today, but we can confidently assume it.

Similarly, when someone denies the existence of moral laws and moral values, all one can do is invoke the principle of common sense again. Common sense tells us there is some kind of *moral* order in life: if murder is wrong today it will also be wrong tomorrow. This is true, in spite of the fact that some say there is no common morality that we share as humans. But these latter voices try to convince us that our moral laws are determined by whoever has the power to enforce them, rather than by what is actually good and right.

Common sense tells us there are things that all of us know we ought, or ought not, to do for the simple reason that we are human beings endowed with morality. There are moral values and moral laws that cannot be ignored—just like there are laws of nature that cannot be ignored. However, there is also a difference between the two: laws of nature cannot be violated, but moral laws certainly can. For instance, you can throw a heavy object upward, but that does not change the fact that the object will eventually fall. If I decide to ignore the law of gravity and jump off a cliff, my defiance will not cause gravity to cease working. Sure, we can ignore laws of nature but we cannot go against them. But when it comes to moral laws, we do have the capacity to violate them—for instance, we can violate the moral law that all human life is sacred. When we do so, however, that does not make murder morally right, but it does allow us to neglect or violate such a moral law by acting as if no such law exists. That is possible for the simple reason that there is human *freedom*.

Having said this, we pose the question again: where do our "oughts," our duties and our rights, our "moral laws" and our "moral values" come from? The answer is rather simple. Somehow, we just "know" what is morally right or wrong. We know what we do not want others to do to us, so we also know what we should not do to others—which is usually called the Golden Rule, "Do to others what you want to be done to yourself" (Tobit 4:15; Matthew 7:12; Luke 6:31). We use that rule constantly, especially to judge the actions of others (but not always to judge our own actions!).

The Golden Rule is a moral maxim or principle of altruism found in many human cultures and religions, suggesting it may be a common-sense issue related to a fundamental human nature. Much in the same way that we, without musical training, can judge certain tones to be off pitch, so we have moral "perceptions" that some actions are good and some bad, without having any explicit training about such kinds of actions. How is this possible? How can every human being know all of this?

Again, the basic answer is "common sense", something that comes with human nature and is shared by all of humanity. Thomas Aquinas mentions a very general rule: "Good should be done and pursued, and evil avoided." It is a principle that is more general than the Golden Rule, because it does not specify in detail what is good and what is wrong. So where do the details come from? True, there are some important disagreements between different cultures about what exactly is "good", but beneath all disagreements about lesser moral laws and values, there always lies an agreement about more basic ones. Peter Kreeft compares this with different languages: beneath the different words of different languages you find common concepts—and this is what makes translation from one language to another possible. In an analogous way, we find common moral laws beneath different social laws. Then he concludes, "We find similar morals, beneath different mores." As a matter of fact, there is not a great deal of difference between Christian morality, Jewish morality, Hindu morality, Muslim morality, Buddhist morality; although there's a great difference in these religions. C. S. Lewis tells us they all have some version of what he calls the "Tao," the natural moral law.

The first Christian philosopher, St. Justin Martyr, said something similar already around the year 150 while living in the turbulent, mostly pagan Roman Empire. He made some excellent observations:

> *Every race knows that such things as adultery, and fornication, and homicide are sinful. For example, though they all fornicate, they do not escape from the knowledge that they are acting unrighteously—with the exception of those possessed by an unclean spirit, those debased by wicked customs and sinful institutions, and those who have quenched their natural ideas. For we observe that such persons refuse to endure the same things they inflict on others. They also reproach each other for the evil acts that they commit.*

It is mostly through St. Thomas that this concept of moral communality has become known as the *natural law*. Its key idea is that moral laws are based on human nature—that is, on the way we *are*. As a consequence, morality is a function of human nature, so that reason can discover valid moral principles by looking at the nature of humanity and society. This means that what we ought to *do* is related to what we *are*. "Thou shalt not kill," for instance, is based on the real value of human life and the need to preserve it. "Thou shalt not commit adultery" is based on the real value of marriage and family, the value of mutual self-giving love, and children's need for trust and stability. We share these moral convictions to some degree with all of humanity.

Put differently, every culture in history has had some version of the Ten Commandments, including the Golden Rule. As the theologian Janet E. Smith puts it, "natural law holds that many of the most fundamental precepts of moral reasoning are obvious, that is easily known by all." This idea goes basically back to St. Paul who referred to pagans as people "who never heard of the Law but are led by reason to do what the Law commands" (Rom. 2:14).

b. The Natural Law

Natural law rests upon the claim that things have natures and essences that we can know through reason and that our actions can correspond to. All things possess a nature or essence; they flourish when they are acting and are treated in accord with that nature or essence—and they wither when they are not. There are many reasons for making this claim. One is the fact that all things act in a predictable fashion; when we learn the properties of oil and water, for example, we can predict certain things about their behavior. Natural law holds that we live in a universe of things that have a nature to them and that we shall get the best out of these things if we act in accord with the nature that is written into them. By acting rationally, man is acting in accord with his own nature and with a reality that is also ordered. When we act rationally, we act in accord with our own nature and reality and in accord with the nature and reality of other things. This holds also for morality.

This notion is taught not only by the Catholic Church but basically by all the world's major religions and nearly all pre-modern philosophies. Peter Kreeft again: it is the idea that the laws of morality are not rules that we invent but principles that we discover, like the laws of a science such as physiology; they are based on human nature, and human nature is essentially unchanging; and therefore the laws of morality are also essentially unchanging, just like the laws of physiology. Just as our physiological nature makes it necessary for us to eat certain foods and to breathe oxygen for our bodies to be healthy, so our moral nature makes certain moral rules and values necessary for our souls to be healthy. As G. K. Chesterton observed, you cannot free things "from the laws of their own nature. You may, if you like, free a tiger from his bars; but do not free him from his stripes."

Be aware, though, the natural law is a philosophical concept rather than a scientific one, which means there is no empirical or experimental evidence to cite. It is grounded in the metaphysics of human nature, including the "language of the body." So morality must be grounded in part on facts about human biology. One's morality is always dependent on one's anthropology, and therefore on one's metaphysics. As a consequence, you can't know what is good for man until you know what man is; and metaphysics always comes in, because what man is depends on what *is*. The natural law derives the essential principles of morality from unchanging human nature and its real, objective needs rather than from fluctuating subjective feelings and desires of individuals.

Therefore, St. Thomas argues that *reason* should be our

guide to morality. The word "natural" in natural law alludes both to human nature, in terms of which the content of morality gets defined, and to the fact that some moral knowledge is accessible to us naturally (as opposed to supernaturally)—through pure reason, that is (as opposed to Divine Revelation). The precepts of natural law are principles of human activity. Most philosophers agree that we do not need Revelation to figure out that some acts, such as murder, adultery, rape, and theft are wrong. Reason is capable of discovering that things have essences, natures, dispositions, and purposes, and that it is good to act in accord with those essences, natures, dispositions, and purposes.

Moral laws and values do have a certain foundation in reality: they are based on relationships between human beings and things. Where, for instance, does the moral value of loving one's parents come from? The answer is that the physical and mental constitution of human beings happens to be such that children ought to love their parents in order for them to prosper as human beings. Were our human constitution differently structured, we could perhaps have different morals. Because we can discover this without Divine Revelation, all of humanity has access to the truth of natural law. You don't have to be Catholic for this, although the idea itself is catholic!

The Catechism (1955) explains, "This law is called 'natural,' not in reference to the nature of irrational beings, but because reason which decrees it properly belongs to human nature." This text stresses that the natural law is not a law of biology, for it does not apply to "irrational beings" such as animals. But we do need a certain understanding of what human nature is—an understanding that is more than a biological understanding. David Hart rightly remarks that "we cannot talk intelligibly about natural law if we have not all first agreed upon what nature is and accepted in advance that there really is a necessary bond between what is and what should be."

Not surprisingly, some have accused St. Thomas of committing a fallacy here, an incorrect logical argument (see 1.b). The so-called "is-ought fallacy" was identified by the philosopher David Hume, and is sometimes called "Hume's Guillotine." It applies when we try to derive how things *ought* to be from the way things *are*. Hume says we cannot derive how things *ought* to be from the way things *are*. A conclusion that applies to morality cannot be deduced from propositions in which moral terms are entirely missing. Survival of the fittest, for instance, may be the way it *is* in nature, but we cannot infer from this that it *ought* to be that way in human society. Describing how the world *is* does not prescribe how it *ought* to be, so the argument's conclusion is a moral judgement that cannot be supported by its premises, for description cannot lead to prescription. It is not quite clear, though, how valid Hume's "principle" is. Some have even jokingly said that, because we can't derive an "ought" from an "is," we "ought" not to try. Indeed, the word "ought" may have various meanings.

Others have tried to get around this fallacy by defining moral terms in purely natural terms. But this leads to another fallacy, the so-called "naturalistic fallacy," which is the erroneous idea that what is natural (found in nature) can be defined as good in moral terms. In its simplest form, it says "X is found in nature; therefore X is natural; and therefore X is good." It creates another fallacy that erroneously equates a property such as "good" to a property such as "natural." We cannot argue from the premise "Taking revenge is natural" to the conclusion "Taking revenge is good." Being natural does not automatically make something good; seeking pleasure for pleasure's sake, for example, is not necessarily something that is morally good. When philosophers try to define "good" in terms of natural properties such as "pleasant" or "desirable" or "natural," they are committing the naturalistic fallacy. A natural concept cannot capture the essential property of a moral concept. A moral concept cannot be redefined in non-moral terms. When we define moral notions in non-moral terms, we betray their specifically moral aspect.

Is St. Thomas really committing such fallacies? The reason why he is not is the following. It is only immediately after his formulation of the first principle of natural law—"Good should be done and pursued, and evil avoided"—that Aquinas points to man's natural inclinations: man naturally inclines to self-preservation, to procreation, to sociability, and to truth about God. So we can only comply with the first principle of natural law by consulting our natural inclinations. Since we *do* have a natural tendency to act certain ways, we *ought* to act certain ways. It is precisely the first principle that prevents Aquinas from falling into naturalistic traps. It functions as a principle of practical reasoning in morality, similar to the way theoretical reasoning requires the principle of non-contradiction. Therefore, moral norms are not derived directly from nature, but from the moral command expressed in the first principle. In other words, nature itself is not the foundation of morals, but only plays a role where it informs us about our natural inclinations. So Aquinas does not argue from "is" to "ought," but consistently argues from "ought" to "ought," while "is" only plays an intermediary role.

Others have argued that in fact there is some deep connection between "ought" and "is," because nature cannot be seen as something independent of God—nature is God's creation. So if nature includes an inherent purpose or function, then that intrinsic purpose bridges the so-called is-ought gap. After all, if humans have a purpose grounded in their very nature as human beings, then they ought to fulfill that purpose. If you want to build a bridge that can withstand wind and traffic, you "ought" to follow the laws of nature. Since a clock is made to show the time, it is "supposed" to show the time for it to "be" a clock. This presupposes a *rational* (not naturalistic) conception of that which "is." Pope Benedict XVI recently confirmed that "the ought does flow from the is." What he meant is that once we get a sense of who God *is* and what a human being *is*—created in God's image and likeness—certain "oughts" do flow from what "is." Beneath the "ought" lies the "is"—namely, the natural order, which comes also with inclinations, dispositions, goals, and ends. So we are not dealing here with a simplistic version of the is-ought fallacy.

c. Moral Law Essentials

Because of his concept of natural law, Thomas Aquinas considers moral laws and principles *self-evident* (known through themselves). It is in that specific sense that the *United States Declaration of Independence* can state, "We hold these truths to be self-evident." When people claim they have certain unalienable rights, there is no evidence to support such a claim. When someone asks us why killing another human being is morally wrong, there is nothing we can point to as evidence—it is self-evident.

This does not mean, though, that moral laws are data-less "intuitions," for they can be known only by insight (*intellectus*) into data of human nature, human experience, human understanding, and the order of Creation. Through these rational "insights," imbedded in human nature, we discover eternal and absolute moral principles. However, Aquinas adds to this that "self-evidence" is relative, for what is not obvious to some will be self-evident to those who have more ample experience and a better understanding of other aspects of the matter. So we should expect our moral understanding to grow. This implies that the self-evidence Aquinas claims may not be fully present yet in each one of us.

This explains that there is also something like moral blindness, equivalent to color blindness. Although a blind person cannot see the trees outside, the trees are still there; the existence of the trees does not depend on whether the blind person perceives them or not. In a similar way a morally blind person cannot see the moral laws and values out there, yet they are there; their existence does not depend on whether a person with moral blindness can perceive them or not. Moral blindness can be caused by upbringing, culture, personality, and lust, which may temporarily obscure the self-evidence of moral values, principles, and laws.

Not only are moral laws self-evident, they are also *unconditional*. Most rules we are familiar with are conditional upon a certain goal: if you want Y, you must do X; if you do not want to attain that goal, the rule is useless. Not so with moral rules and laws. They are unconditional: just do X, for you *ought* to do X—no matter what, whether you like it or not, whether you feel it or not, whether others enforce it or not. Therefore, when it comes to morality, we cannot just pick whatever we want. We cannot just vote to decide whether we condone certain actions—such as slavery and abortion—or rather not. The legendary US President Abraham Lincoln put it well when he challenged the Nebraska bill of 1820 that would let residents vote to decide if slavery would be legal in their state: "God did not place good and evil before man, telling him to make his choice." There is no "pro-choice" in morality. Morality obliges us to go, unconditionally, for what is good and right. No more ifs; no more questions asked. Ironically, relativists are only pro-choice as long as your choice matches theirs.

In addition to being self-evident and unconditional, moral laws are also *objective*: they are a "given" independent of us and of any human authority. In other words, they are not invented but have to be discovered. In the words of the Catechism (1751), "Objective norms of morality express the rational order of good and evil." As a consequence, they are real—not just mental creations or a product of the mind. "Objective" means that something is real and true, regardless of whether or not we know it to be true. Something similar holds for laws of nature such as the law of gravity. This law has always been true, even before Isaac Newton discovered the law—it was a discovery, not an invention. Gravity is not a subjective experience, but an objective reality. Something similar holds for moral laws; we don't invent them but discover them; they are not merely a subjective experience but an objective reality.

In other words, if we were to create or invent new moral laws and new moral values, then they would no longer be moral laws or values, and they would no longer be anchored in reality. They would be just arbitrarily invented rules of the game—what is "right" in chess is not "right" in checkers. Hence, we would not feel obligated by them, or guilty when we transgressed them. As C. S. Lewis once put it, "The human mind has no more power of inventing a new value than of imagining a new primary color." We cannot creatively make hate good, or love evil. When we say justice "is" good, we are asserting something about reality, about what really *is*. The fact that people may disagree about specific moral laws does not make morality subjective. Disagreement about objective matters does not prove subjectivity; for if that were the case, every scientific disagreement would be a subjective issue.

As a side note, it might be prudent to refer more to moral *laws* than to moral values because it is probably more accepted to speak of "objective moral laws"—similar to "objective natural law"—than of "objective moral values," because spoken to modern ears, the idea of "objective values" is easily misunderstood as an unintelligible contradiction in terms. Many nowadays tend to associate "values" with the ever changing value of houses and stock, rather than something constant, absolute, and objective. Our secularized age has become crammed with "values"; corporations and universities are proud to tout their "values," but there is nothing "objective" about them. The idea behind this is that things in the world have the value I decide to give them. But if that's true, then the reverse must also be true. If I don't "value" something, it has no value. Besides, politicians often say certain policies go against their "values," but what they actually mean is those policies go against their political wishes. As Peter Kreeft astutely remarks, "God did not give Moses 'The Ten Values.'"

In addition to being self-evident and unconditional and objective, moral laws are also *universal*: they are the same for everyone everywhere. They are universally applicable to all of humanity, regardless of race, ethnicity, nationality, culture, religion, or political affiliation. Consequently, morality does not come with a specific race, ethnicity, nation, party, or church—it is a common property that belongs to all human beings. Morality is not connected with interest groups or with majority votes, but it is universal in nature and applies to anyone anywhere. The Catechism (1956) confirms this, "The natural law, present in the heart of each man and established by reason, is universal in its precepts and its authority extends to all men." Although the natural law is not universally obeyed, or even universally admitted, it is still universally binding and authoritative.

No wonder Thomas Aquinas made a clear distinction between, on the one hand, the universal "natural law" and, on the other hand, the local (legal, civil, or positive) laws made and upheld by governments. Interestingly enough, without the universality of the natural law, there would not have been any justification for the Nuremberg trials that took place after World War II—or for any other international court, for that matter. Seen from a purely legal point of view, it would not have been right, or even possible, to bring to trial and punish the Nazi perpetrators who had applied the civil laws that were created and implemented by a regime that had come to power through legal channels—for they were just "law-abiding" citizens following the law of the land. But seen from a natural law perspective, their "lawful" actions were in fact atrocities committed against humanity.

Those denying the universality of moral laws are basically relativists who privatize and politicize moral laws as if they were merely local civil laws. These moral relativists consider moral laws man-made, private, subjective, a matter of mere feeling—at best a matter of consensus or a majority vote or political power. According to moral relativism, each one of us is right when it comes to moral matters; according to moral absolutism, on the other hand, some of us may be wrong. Chesterton put it correctly, "Morality is always dreadfully complicated to a man who has lost all his principles." Principles mean moral absolutes—unchanging rocks beneath the changing waves of feelings and practices. Moral relativism, on the other hand, is a philosophy that denies such moral absolutes. This makes Peter Kreeft, in line with Aquinas, exclaim, "In fact, the moral language that everyone uses every day—language that praises, blames, counsels, or commands—would be strictly meaningless if relativism were true."

In addition to being self-evident and unconditional and objective and universal, moral laws are also *timeless*, and therefore unchangeable. Not only do they hold for anyone anywhere, but also at any time, past, present, and future. The Catechism (1958) says, "The natural law is immutable and permanent throughout the variations of history; it subsists under the flux of ideas and customs and supports their progress." Moral relativists would object to this idea;

they claim that moral values clearly have been subject to change during the course of human history. However, there is a mix-up here between moral *values* and moral *evaluations*. Moral evaluations are our personal feelings or discernments regarding moral values and laws at a certain point in time. Moral relativists think that, in making moral evaluations, we create moral values in accordance with these evaluations. So when evaluations change, the moral values and laws are said to change as well.

In response to this position of moral relativists, it should be emphasized that evaluations are merely a reflection of the way we discern absolute moral laws and values at a specific place and time. Whereas moral evaluations may be volatile and fluctuating, moral values and laws are timeless and unchangeable. That is the reason why we can disagree about certain moral evaluations, assuming some are true and others false. Think of the following comparison: our current understanding of physical or biological laws constantly needs revision each time we reach a better understanding of those laws in the way they really are. In the meantime, though, we assume there are timeless laws of nature, although we may not yet have fully captured them in our current understanding and in our contemporary evaluations. Something similar holds for moral laws.

We could illustrate this point a little further. A few centuries ago, slavery was not evaluated as morally wrong, but nowadays it is by most people. Had the slaveholders won the Civil War, so they say, we might see it today as an admirable institution. Did our moral values change? Our evaluations certainly did, but that does not mean moral values did too. Only some people in the past—heroes such as St. Cyprian, St. Gregory of Nyssa, St. John Chrysostom, St. Patrick, St. Anselm, St. Vincent de Paul, to name just a few—were able to discern the objective, intrinsic, and universal value of personal freedom and human rights (as opposed to slavery), whereas many of their contemporaries were blind for this value. That is the reason why Martin Luther King Jr. was right to call any unjust (legal) law "a code that is out of harmony with the moral law."

In addition to being self-evident and unconditional and objective and universal and timeless, moral laws are also *absolute*—which means they are without exceptions. Killing a human being is always morally wrong; stealing is always morally wrong; lying is always morally wrong—no matter who you are and where you are, regardless of your status in society, and regardless of any particular circumstances. The Catechism (1754) makes it very clear, "Circumstances of themselves cannot change the moral quality of acts themselves; they can make neither good nor right an action that is in itself evil."

Moral laws and values are also absolute in the sense that they cannot be validated by anything "relative." Take, for instance, the value of human life—a moral issue—which has often been based on the use of biological criteria, such as the extent of brain activity. This is a kind of quasi-moral argument that would go along the following lines: the more brain activity there is, the more value a human being has, and therefore, the more rights it has and the more protection it deserves. Others would rather choose viability as the main biological norm to determine the humanity of an unborn child—the more viable, the more human.

However, the biological criteria adduced here are relative, not absolute criteria, and thus become moving targets. So they do not make for moral but at best quasi-moral arguments.

Someone who showed us very clearly that relative criteria cannot make for absolute moral claims was again the legendary President Abraham Lincoln. He applied this to the contentious moral issue of slavery. His point was that all the answers slave holders might come up with to defend their "moral claims" use relative criteria: it is considered morally right to enslave people with a darker skin color or a lower intelligence. If that were so, someone with an even lighter skin or higher intelligence might show up and claim the "moral right" to enslave others, because those criteria are entirely relative. As Lincoln said, "By this rule, you are to be slave to the first man you meet, with a fairer skin than your own…. By this rule, you are to be slave to the first man you meet, with an intellect superior to your own." This is a serious warning for those who confuse absolute moral rules with non-moral, relative criteria.

A similar argument can be used for the moral value of human life. This value cannot be based on biological standards, since those are per definition relative, not absolute. In other words, the moral quality of human life cannot be quantified and measured on a scale. We cannot use relative standards of intelligence, viability, maturity, health, fitness, and the like to measure or judge the absolute moral value of human life, its human dignity, its human rights—and our human duties to respect it. The fact that there is biological development does not mean there is also a development in human dignity and human rights.

Consequently, there is no such thing as "growing in humanity." There certainly is growth of a biological body, but there is no growth of moral rights. Biological standards are of a quantitative nature and thus can be put on a scale, but moral standards are of a qualitative nature and cannot be rated or ranked. They are of an absolute nature.

So we must come to the conclusion that moral laws (the natural law) are universal (applicable to everyone everywhere), absolute (without exceptions), timeless (even if we do not know the underlying law yet), and objective (a given, independent of us and of any human authority). Just as "truths are true," even when we do not know yet they are true, so "rights are right," even though we may not realize yet they are morally right. The foundation for the latter claim comes from the natural law. As the Catechism (1959) puts it, "The natural law, the Creator's very good work, provides the solid foundation on which man can build the structure of moral rules to guide his choices." Reason apparently plays an important role in all of this.

Gerard M. Verschuuren

7. Morality and Faith

Morality can certainly be studied by reason. We found out that the natural law is discernable for everyone, even without Faith. So which connection could there be between morality and Faith? Is Faith perhaps able to explain where our morality ultimately comes from? Before we answer that question, let us make clear first why we cannot expect an explanation from science.

a. Faith, not Science

Sure, scientists have tried many times to anchor morality—our "moral nature"—in genes that we presumably received from the animal world during a process of evolution. Why is such an explanation doomed to fail? There are several reasons, some of which we mentioned earlier already (see 6.a).

Reason #1: As said before, reducing moral rules and laws to genetic instructions is almost impossible to defend. It is hard to believe that all those people who are willing to break a moral rule when they can get away with it are acting against their genes. Bad moral behavior can spread like wildfire, but genes don't spread that quickly. As a matter of fact, there are too many parents who ignore what some think is an "inborn" responsibility of parenting. There are too many spouses who violate the sixth commandment, "You shall not commit adultery." Too many folks violate also the fifth commandment, "You shall not kill." When it comes to moral laws, everyone knows about them and yet everyone breaks them again and again. Genes do not seem to prevent this.

Those who go against moral laws or ignore them may be steered by passions, but it is very unlikely that they are controlled by their genes. Instead the opposite could be argued: morality has the power to overrule what our genes dictate—passions, emotions, and drives. Perhaps genes contribute to us being moral beings, but they do not and cannot dictate specific moral laws, rules, and values. To use an analogy, genes may help create good or bad volleyball players, but that is not how the rules of the game are regulated. What is right or wrong in a moral sense is not determined by genes, for genes are material entities that cannot possibly make anything right or wrong in a moral sense. Genes may make us act a certain way, but whether such an act is morally right or wrong is a completely different issue—a moral issue, not a genetic one. There is no way that leads from "is" in the world of genes to "ought" in the world of morality. Preprogrammed behavior is what it is, but it doesn't qualify as morality.

Reason #2: We mentioned earlier that those who reduce moral rules and laws to genetic instructions should ask themselves why we need a moral code to do what we would do "by nature" anyway. A morality that is supposedly preprogrammed in our genes would make a moral code completely redundant. If morality can really be reduced to what we do "by nature," there would obviously be no need for a moral code as well. We would all act right by mere nature, so it would not even be possible to do something morally wrong. This makes us realize there must be a moral code beyond and above a genetic code. We do need a moral codes because God, according to St. Augustine, "wrote on the tables of law what men did not read in their hearts."

In contrast to a biological explanation of morality, one could very well argue that moral laws tell us to do what natural selection does *not* promote and what our genes do *not* make us do "by nature." If moral behavior were genetic, we would all act "right" by mere nature, so it would not even be possible to do something morally wrong. Of course, one could counter that some of us might have mutated genes that may direct them to do what is wrong. But if that were true, we would have no reason anymore to speak of right or wrong, for either way would be a preprogrammed outcome anyway that would release us from any moral responsibilities.

Reason #3: Reducing morality to a product "created" by natural selection must face the problem that morality is not survivor-friendly. Most moral laws do not have any survival value and therefore cannot be the target of natural selection. Ironically, the offenders of moral laws—the killers, the liars, the rapists, and the promiscuous—reproduce much better than their victims, which gives them an advantage in the struggle for survival. Apparently, morality and "survival of the fittest" do not go well together. Natural selection is about success at the *expense* of others; morality is about duties to the *benefit* of others. Natural selection eliminates the ones who cannot care for themselves; morality takes care of those who cannot care for themselves.

In other words, morality, or acting morally, is no good

friend to survival; it actually amounts very often to "genetic suicide." Whereas natural selection is based on self-preservation at the cost of others, morality is often self-sacrifice for the good of others. The notion of charity, for instance, is completely about giving for giving's sake, without expecting any benefits, let alone genetic benefits. Or take donating blood to strangers: it does not help relatives; it does not promote one's genes; it is not subject to natural selection. Francis Collins, the former Head of the *Human Genome Project* and currently Director of the *National Institutes of Health*, made very clear that morality goes against natural selection: "Evolution would tell me exactly the opposite: preserve your DNA. Who cares about the guy who's drowning?"

Reason #4: To claim that morality is "nothing but" a product of natural selection is actually a self-defeating activity. It is basically suicidal: the snake of this theory is eating its own tail, or rather its own head. If indeed we were to claim that morality is nothing but a "pack of genetic instructions," this very claim that we are making here would not be worth more than its molecular origin, and neither would we ourselves who are making such a statement. The claim that everything is a matter of genes would no longer be a rational claim but a genetic issue, so we could no longer even meaningfully claim that moral claims are genetic by nature. It would be the end of any truth claims.

Claims of "nothing-buttery" in matters of knowledge and morality just defeat and destroy themselves. They undermine their own truth claims by cutting off the very branch that the person who makes such claims is—or actually was—sitting on. This conclusion should put a science such as sociobiology in its proper place: it may be a fantastic specialty in the field of science, but there must be more to life than genetic instructions in charge of human behavior—unless sociobiology itself is a product of genetic instructions too. We're certainly not required to take the "survival of the fittest" law as a moral guideline—we are actually not allowed to.

Reason #5: Believing that morality is in the genes is a very shaky belief that undermines its own foundation and creates a paradox. Some people such as the biologist J. B. S. Haldane and the philosopher C. S. Lewis have worded this paradox along the following lines: if I believe that all my beliefs, including my moral beliefs, are the mere product of genes, then I have no reason to believe my belief is true—therefore, I have no reason to believe that my moral beliefs are the mere product of genes. Besides, as Francis J. Beckwith warns us, we have to face the following problem: "if your belief in the moral law can be attributed entirely to our genes tricking us into believing that there really is a moral law, why not extend that same analysis to all other beliefs that arise from your mind?" So we would end up with many more illusions fobbed on us by our genes—science and math, to name just a few. Do we really want to pay that price? This would amount to losing your mind—literally.

If we are looking for a key to understanding humans and their moral beliefs, this key will not be found in something material, such as genes, but in something spiritual, the mind. Morality comes from the immaterial mind, not from the material brain or genome. The brain is governed by laws of physics, chemistry, and biology, but thoughts and beliefs are not. It should not surprise us then that people have known the contents of their own minds from time immemorial without knowing anything about brains and genes. They knew also about morality without knowing anything about brains and genes. Claiming differently reduces the working of the mind to the materialism of the brain.

Reason #6: When reducing morality to genetics, we cannot have it both ways. First, evolutionary theory tells us that our moral behavior is inborn and that its reproductive success is based on our *believing* that morality is objective. And next it tells us that morality is not objective, in spite of the fact that all of us supposedly have an inborn belief that morality is objective. If we were really able to uncover the illusion of morality, morality would lose its evolutionary power immediately.

Thus we end up with a contradiction. The theory's success depends on our believing that morality is objective. It is because we desire to act in accord with this true belief that we presumably forego the pursuit of our own interests for the good of others, even when we can escape detection and punishment. If this theory is true, then the assumed objectivity of morality could only play its evolutionary role if we remained ignorant of the theory. Even if we happen to come in contact with the theory, we would still find ourselves pushed by a belief that is in contradiction with it. As a matter of fact, the evolutionary approach is not an explanation of morality; it's a denial of morality. It explains why we think moral truths exist when, in fact, they don't. That would be a troublesome outcome.

Reason #7: What biologists, especially sociobiologists, basically do is reducing morality to a mere issue of matter, more in specific of genes and their DNA molecules. This has materialism written all over it. Materialism claims the physical world is all there is. It emphatically proclaims, "Everything that exists is matter, and matter is all there is." But not everything is matter, not everything is material. The claim of materialism would at best be a dogmatic conviction, certainly not backed by science itself. Science on its own can never prove that matter is all there is, because it first limits itself to matter and then says there is nothing but matter. If materialism is true, we cannot even know that it is true.

Matter may indeed be everywhere, but it is certainly not all there is. If matter were all there is, then one should wonder what materialism itself is. Another piece of matter? So there must be more than matter. This leaves definitely room for nonmaterial things such as logic, mathematics, philosophy, and ultimately Faith. So why then not for morality as well? Morality is about what is right or wrong. In the world of matter, things are large or small, light or heavy, hard or soft, but never right or wrong. There are no "oughts" in the material world. There is so much in life that the thermometers and Geiger-tellers of materialism can never capture—things such as thoughts, values, beliefs, laws, experiences, hopes, dreams, and ideals. There is no way materialism can deal with these—other than denying them, but then it must deny itself as well.

In fact, morality is about something that is outside the scope of biology, actually beyond the reach of the natural sciences. Biology is by its nature blind to moral values, so it cannot possibly discern anything that is on its "blind spot." Therefore, science cannot monitor morality, but it is rather the other way around—morality ought to control science instead. Nazi-doctors such as Joseph Mengele show us what happens when morality does not control their scientific research. Albert Einstein was right when he spoke of "the moral foundations of science, but you cannot turn around and speak of the scientific foundations of morality." Morality can interrogate science, but science cannot question morality—it is beyond its reach.

Detaching the world from its Maker, as is done in science, creates a gap between "is" and "ought," or between "facts" and "values"—a gap that is almost impossible to cross. Science attempts to discover what *is* the case in a material sense; morality, on the other hand, is about what *ought* to be done in a moral sense. "Racial equality," for instance, is not a descriptive but prescriptive term; races are not equal in biological characteristics, yet their members do have the same moral rights. If morality is essentially prescriptive—telling us what should be the case, as opposed to what is the case—and if all evolutionary assessments of moral behavior are descriptive, then evolution and genetics cannot account for the most important thing that needs to be explained: the "oughts" of morality. Michael A. Simon summarized this well, "In order for a human trait to be explained biologically, it must first be 'biologized.'... The problem with such biological reduction is that it is likely to sacrifice precisely those features of human social behavior that give it a socially or philosophically distinctive character." So by "biologizing" morality, we inevitably lose its distinctive moral character.

Let's come to a conclusion as to why morality cannot be in the genes. Biology, including sociobiology, cannot have a monopolistic claim on human behavior, because biology will never be able to tell us a comprehensive, all-inclusive story about human life and human behavior, but at best a partial story. Biologists approach everything from a *biological* perspective only—the rest of the story must come from other fields such as physics, psychology, economy, philosophy, religion—and ethics, of course. Since moral laws and values add their own dimension and perspective to our world, there is not much hope for those numerous reductionist efforts of fully converting moral behavior into a non-moral phenomenon such as genetics and evolution— which keeps morality standing tall.

b. From Heaven

So where does our morality come from then, if it cannot come from our genes? The best, and arguably only, rational explanation would be that morality does not come from "below" but must come from Above. Only in a world with God can we derive "ought" from "is." If morality comes from God, then there can be no morality without God. This is actually the only way to explain why morality can be such a demanding issue—indeed demanding an absolute authority. This would be impossible if morality were only a matter of genes, or tradition, or majority votes, or political correctness. Do my genes, or any other natural factors, have the right to demand absolute obedience from me? Of course not! Does society or the government have the right to demand my absolute obedience? Certainly not! Does any person, including myself, have the right to demand my absolute obedience? None of the above! The only authority that can obligate me is someone infinitely superior to me; no one else has the right to demand my absolute obedience.

Interestingly enough, even an atheist such as the late French philosopher Jean-Paul Sartre realized that there can be no absolute and objective standards of right and wrong, if there is no eternal Heaven that would make moral laws and values objective and universal. As an atheist he had to conclude, though, that it is "extremely embarrassing that God does not exist, for there disappears with him all possibility of finding values in an intelligible heaven. There can no longer be any good *a priori*, since there is no infinite and perfect consciousness to think it." Because Sartre denies the existence of God, he realized very clearly that, by being an atheist, he also had to give up on morality. If there is no God, there cannot be evil either. As Thomas Aquinas famously said, "Good can exist without evil, whereas evil cannot exist without good."

The German philosopher Friedrich Nietzsche was another atheist to realize how devastating the decline of religion is to the morality of society, when he wrote, "God is dead; but as the human race is constituted, there will perhaps be caves for millenniums yet, in which people will show his shadow." Nietzsche is saying here that humanism and other "moral" ideologies shelter themselves in caves and venerate shadows of the God they once believed in; they are still holding on to something they cannot provide themselves, mere shadows of the past. These are "idols" constructed to preserve the essence of morality without the substance.

Nietzsche clearly understood that "the death of God" meant the destruction of all meaning and value in life. Once we think we can understand the world apart from God, God is dead in the way Latin is dead. Nietzsche saw in all clarity how in a world without divine and eternal laws, neither our dignity nor our morality would be able to survive in the long run. No wonder Jürgen Habermas, although a non-religious philosopher, expressed as his conviction that the ideas of freedom and social co-existence are based on the Jewish notion of justice and the Christian ethics of love. As he puts it, "Up to this very day there is no alternative to it." This does not mean, of course, that we must believe in God in order to live a moral life. As Nietzsche put it, we can still venerate "idols from the past."

Because of all of this, we must recognize that morality can ultimately come only from "Above." Moral laws and values reside in Heaven. That's where their universality and objectivity reside. We ought to do what we ought to do—for Heaven's sake! The *United States Declaration of Independence* is in tune with this when it declared that we are endowed by our Creator with certain unalienable Rights—not man-made but God-given rights, that is. When in 1948 the United Nations (UN) affirmed in its *Universal Declaration of Human Rights* that, "all human beings are born free and equal in dignity and rights," it must have assumed the same without explicitly mentioning it (the drafters famously left the term "right" vague in order to achieve passage). Without this assumption, all those rights would be sitting on quicksand, subject to the mercy of law makers and majority votes. But the Catholic philosopher Jacques Maritain expressed a profound truth when he said paradoxically, "We agree on these rights, on condition that no one asks us why." The only reason why we do have human rights is because God has endowed us with rights.

It is through the voice of God, in the natural law, that we know about right and wrong, about rights and duties. Without God, who is the author of human rights, we would have no right to claim any rights. If there were no God, we could not defend any of those rights we think we have the right to defend. Instead we would only have (legal) *entitlements*, or privileges, which the government provides us with, but no (moral) *rights*, which only God can provide. John F. Kennedy put it well in his Inaugural Address: "the rights of man come not from the generosity of the state, but from the hand of God." In response to Immanuel Kant, who said we should all start acting in a way that is moral "even if God does not exist," Pope Benedict XVI turned this around and argued that we should do the opposite and live a moral life "as if God existed." Without an eternal Heaven, there could be no absolute or objective standards of right and wrong. If these did not come from God, people could take them away anytime—which they certainly have tried many times.

When we live a life without God, when the eclipse of God has set in, when we lose sight of God and lead a life "as if there is no God," we may also lose the foundation of morality, because we no longer know *why* certain things are not permissible. Without morality, we would be mere animals again. Without moral laws and values, we could even lose our judicial laws, which have been protecting us so far to the extent they were rooted in the natural law. All of this will ultimately lead to the nihilism of no-law, no-authority, no-rationality, no-morality, and no-purpose to life. When Aleksandr Solzhenitsyn, in his 1983 Templeton Prize lecture, tried to locate the root of the evils of the 20th century—two world wars, three totalitarian regimes with death camps, and a Cold War—he discerned a profound truth: "Men have forgotten God." What does this lead to? The writer Fyodor Dostoyevsky had already given us the answer when he wrote in his novel *The Brothers Karamazov* that without God, all things are permissible.

The question remains, of course, from where humanists and other non-believers derive their motivation of doing good for other human beings. Why should whites care about blacks, or the rich about the poor, or the strong about the weak, if it were not for the *fact* that we are all children of the same God, made in his image and likeness? Of course, you can be moral without being Christian; you can be moral without knowing why you are a moral being. You certainly don't have to be a Christian to act morally or to know right from wrong, but Christianity may offer us the best explanation of why we should act morally and why certain things are intrinsically right or wrong.

When humanists "do" the same good things as Christians, perhaps one could say that they actually still live off of Judeo-Christian capital—without them being aware of it—venerating shadows of the past, in the words of Nietzsche. Sometimes they base their acts on the Golden Rule, presumably free of any ties from religion: do to others what you want to be done to yourself (Tobit 4:15; Matthew 7:12; Luke 6:31). But why would you follow this rule? The only reason left would be self-interest: helping only those who return the help; so in helping others, one helps oneself according to the old Roman motto *Do ut des*. But that is paganism, a worldview without God. And it hardly deserves the label "moral."

Yet, a worldview without God looks like a jigsaw puzzle

with some large and vital pieces missing—take away religion and it just doesn't look complete. So belief in God does not distort moral motivation, as many humanists think, but actually bolsters it, because morality ultimately needs Faith for its own foundation. It is only through faith and reason that we can bolster morality.

c. Moral Conscience

Not only does religious faith in God give us the best, and arguably only, explanation of where our morality comes from, but it also gives us the best explanation of what a "moral conscience" is. For some enigmatic reason, the authority of a person's conscience still ranks high in the polls. Conscience is now the highest court of appeal—it has been given ultimate "primacy," coming close to infallibility. As we said earlier (6.a), even moral relativists, who deny that morality has any absolute authority, still hold on to at least one moral absolute: "Never disobey your own conscience." Almost all people have something about conscience that they respect, even if their theory is that it's nothing. So you wonder how this view can be so popular. The main reason probably is that the slogan "Follow your conscience" has become a permit for pursuing one's personal preferences and desires.

What is wrong with this interpretation? Well, there is a lot of confusion and ambiguity lurking behind this view. Our conscience has often been compared with technical devices we are all familiar with: a compass, a global positioning system (GPS), a barometer, an alarm, a gas gauge in a car, and the list goes on and on. These analogies are right about one thing: our conscience is indeed some kind of monitoring device—it monitors what is good or bad, right or wrong. But what they mask is that these devices are merely tools that often may not work properly or may even fail entirely—and the same may be the case with our conscience.

A real compass, for instance, functions as a pointer to the magnetic north because the magnetized needle typically aligns itself with the lines of the Earth's magnetic field—that is, with something outside itself. But it should not be used in proximity to ferrous metal objects or electromagnetic fields as these can affect their accuracy. At sea, for example, a ship's compass must be corrected for errors, called deviation, caused by iron and steel in its structure and equipment. Something similar holds for any kind of gauge. The gas gauge in your car may no longer go down because it is broken, yet the tank may be almost empty. And your GPS system may not work when something obstructs the connection with the satellite high above your head.

In other words, a person's conscience may indeed function in ways analogous to a compass or GPS, but these "monitoring" tools have to be monitored themselves and be aligned to an outside source—and so does our conscience. Just as a compass needs to be aligned with the Earth's magnetic field and protected from surrounding interference, and a GPS system needs to be "aligned" to the right feed from satellites high in the sky, so needs a human conscience constant alignment. But keep in mind that, because our moral compass can sometimes fail, it does not follow there is no right direction at all. Just like with math, we can get our sums wrong, but just because we disagree on some of the calculations, it doesn't follow that there is no right answer. So the question then is: What is the "right math" in morality? What is the right feed for our conscience? How do we properly align it? What do we align it to? In short, how do we calibrate our conscience?

The Catholic Church would say human beings were created with a moral compass pointing to, not the magnetic North, but the "Above"—to a place where justice reigns and moral laws reside. So, our conscience is not a private "compass" that determines its own North Pole. It has to be aligned to the one and only real "North Pole Above"—otherwise we can easily go off track. So obviously, there is more to it than having a conscience and following one's conscience. When people say, "Never disobey your own conscience," they forget one can do things "in good conscience," but also "with a bad conscience." So a conscience on its own can be good as well as bad. Besides, many don't even know they have a moral compass—or they don't use it, or it is broken—so they just follow their genitals in sexual affairs, or their curiosity in biomedical research, or their personal desires in matters of life and death—no further questions asked. However, desires can't possibly be the source of morality, because it should be the other way around: morality judges our desires, not reversed. "Good" is not a matter of what *feels* good. Pleasure may be a natural property, but that doesn't make it a moral property.

Following your feelings—which some mask as "following your conscience" or "using your moral compass"—may sound nice, but more needs to be said. Someone's conscience, let alone someone's feeling, cannot have absolute authority in and of itself. A person's conscience does not speak on its own but it merely reflects the *natural law* bestowed on us by God (see 6.b). Our conscience does not create moral laws and values but merely receives them. That is the reason why we cannot take our conscience as an entirely private issue that we can form at our own discretion. One's moral judgment doesn't become true by the mere fact that it has its origin in conscience, because a conscience needs to be truthfully formed first so as to echo or reflect the natural law. To use an analogy again, a compass does not create its own magnetic field.

Therefore, a person's conscience is not the highest moral authority there is; it is subject to the supreme authority of the natural law, which comes directly from God. As the Catechism (1776) puts it, "in the depths of his conscience, man detects a law which he does not impose upon himself, but which holds him to obedience.... His conscience is man's most secret core and his sanctuary. There he is alone with God whose voice echoes in his depths." So when people follow their conscience, it is important they listen to God's voice, not their own. As said earlier (6.c), personal moral *evaluations* do not automatically or necessarily reflect universal moral *values*.

How come our conscience can possibly steer us the wrong way? Well, because our conscience is dependent upon human reason, it is also subject to all of the weaknesses to which human reason is prone, being damaged by Original Sin since the Fall in Paradise (see 1.b). Because of this tendency to error, we can no longer treat our conscience as an infallible guide to moral truth. Conscience, like any intellectual ability, can err because the human mind can reach different degrees of being mature, experienced, trained, healthy, sophisticated, imaginative, prudent, integrated with passion, etc. As a result of Original Sin, there is a permanent need for the correct formation or calibration of conscience. It is just a naïve understanding of conscience to think that following one's conscience is all there is to it. Archbishop Anthony Fisher of Sydney, Australia puts it this way: "Conscience is only right conscience when it accurately mediates and applies that natural law which participates in the divine law; it is erroneous when it does not."

d. Moral Blindness

We mentioned earlier (6.c) that there is something like moral blindness, comparable to color blindness. It is hard, if not impossible, to deny that moral blindness does exist when you consider all the moral evil in the world. One could even question whether every human being has the faculty of morality. There seems to be some evidence that certain people can be *a*-moral—never showing empathy, morals, guilt, shame, or remorse. They are a-moral like a robot is a-moral. Some psychiatrists label this as a disorder—as something that befell someone. It is hard to tell whether this is really a disorder beyond one's control, or rather a choice made earlier in life. On the other hand, there are certainly people who act in an *im*-moral way, in defiance of some moral obligations—for instance, by killing someone—but that is again a choice they make. And then there are people who choose to be *anti*-moral as a form of protest against something they resent, just as there are anarchists, atheists, and nihilists.

It is always possible to disqualify such choices by calling

them disorders, but it is equally possible to reject such explanations. The outcome ultimately depends on our concept of morality. If morality is considered extrinsic to being human, then a person can be a-moral. But if it is intrinsic to being human, there is no way for a person to be a-moral, except after *choosing* to be a-moral or immoral or anti-moral. Apparently, much can go wrong with a human conscience, but we are almost always dealing with decisions, moral or immoral. St. Augustine astutely remarked about his stealing pears from an orchard as a child, "I had no wish to enjoy what I tried to get by theft; all my enjoyment was in the theft itself and in the sin." This is an example of the perverse will that chooses evil for its own sake—a consequence of Original Sin in which the will rebels against reason and becomes a slave at the command of passions. Just as the good can be loved for its own sake, as something intrinsically desired, so evil can be willed for its own sake. That's when someone's moral sense becomes desensitized, making evil appear to be good.

Because, as the Catechism (1960) says, "The precepts of natural law are not perceived by everyone clearly and immediately," we may need "visionaries" who do see clearly what morality demands. We need such people to show us the disconnect that may exist between what we think is right and what is in fact right. It is not always right to obey our culture's values. Sometimes we need "visionaries" who have a trans-cultural standard, if you will, by which they can criticize the moral laws and values of an entire era or culture. Just as science needs geniuses like Newton and Einstein to discover scientific laws that no one else had seen before them, so morality also needs "geniuses" such as Moses, Prophets, and Saints to uncover moral laws that others were blind for. We certainly can see farther by standing on the shoulders of giants.

As Jesus would say, "You have heard that it was said ... But I say to you ..." What he actually tells us is, whether you "see" it or not, this is the way it ought to be in this world, as this is the way this world was created and designed by the Creator. Standing on the shoulders of Jesus, we can see so much more. Yet, some do not "see" certain moral values the way those values are, or they do see them but then violate them knowingly. But this should not give us any reason to lower our moral standards the way relativists would like us to do. Just as we should not lower standards in school teaching when some cannot make the mark, so should we not adjust moral standards to what everyone is able to handle or accept. Archbishop John Fisher would say, "If in our sinful world God's law seems unrealistic, the trouble is not with God's law but with the world!"

The fact that we can be morally blind—blinded by sin, upbringing, culture, character, personality, or passion—explains even more why we need help to correct a faulty conscience. Therefore, our conscience should be in a perpetual "dialogue with God." A "dialogue" with oneself, on the other hand, would only amount to a mere monologue that isolates and alienates us from God, our moral Lawgiver. We are supposed to follow the law, so we have no right to make ourselves the law-givers by becoming sovereign individuals in the place of God and his Church—that would be a form of idolatry. Peter Kreeft rightly makes the analogy, "The French Revolutionary slogan, 'the voice of the people is the voice of God,' is just as idolatrous, and proved to be just as totalitarian as 'the divine right of kings,' which it replaced." The only authority that can obligate us is someone infinitely superior to us, God—no one else has the right to demand our absolute obedience. Archbishop Fisher again, "A Catholic must be prepared to accept moral instruction from the Church and never appeal to conscience to make an exception for himself."

To use the image of an alarm again, our conscience is like an alarm that alerts us before we sin; when it goes off, we must not ignore it. When a red warning light in your car lights up, have the problem fixed—not by disconnecting the light but by fixing what causes it to light up. It is the same with our conscience: do not silence it. However, when the alarm does *not* go off, that doesn't mean there is an "all clear" sign, for we may have intentionally lowered its volume or ignored its upkeep. That is how we can intentionally manipulate or even damage our conscience. It requires "maintenance service" and needs to be "calibrated" repeatedly, often with help from the Church.

Pope Pius XI in his 1931 Encyclical said: "We have said recently that we are happy and proud to fight the good fight for the liberty of consciences, not ... for liberty of conscience." In other words, men have the right to follow their consciences without external interference. The conscience itself, however, is another issue; it is not free to ignore objective truth in making moral judgments. We cannot change freedom *of* conscience into freedom *from* conscience.

Nevertheless, freedom from conscience has become highly popular in our secularized society. A secularized society not only disregards moral laws and values but also wants them to be overridden if they conflict with its own utilitarian "values." Since a secularized society is supposed to be free from religion as well, morality has lost its grounding in God as a consequence. Fyodor Dostoyevsky could not have worded this problem better than he did in his novel *The Brothers Karamazov*:

> *It's God that's worrying me. That's the only thing that's worrying me. What if He doesn't exist? What if Rakitin's right—that it's an idea made up by men? Then, if He doesn't exist, man is the king of the earth, of the Universe. Magnificent! Only how is he going to be good without God? That's the question.*

The question is, indeed, how man is "going to be good without God." Again, we may still be able to be "good" without God, but then we have lost the very foundation of why we *ought* to be good. As we said earlier, not everything that is thinkable or possible or reasonable is also permissible. However, without faith in God, everything thinkable or possible or reasonable is in essence also permissible. That's basically the motto of a secularized society without God.

8. Science and Reason

The principle of "faith and reason" is very often narrowed down to the twosome of "faith and science," with science taking the place of reason. There is nothing wrong with such an adaptation as long as we realize that this makes for a *truncated* version of "faith and reason." But very often this truncated version does lead to rather serious consequences when it reduces "reason" to science's way of operating and reasoning, and thus causing "faith" to easily fall by the wayside (we will address this latter problem further in 9.a). But let us focus first on how "reason" is used in science.

When speaking of science, people often have very different things in mind. Most agree that physics and chemistry are "real" sciences. But what about psycho-analysis, to just mention one case of disagreement? Or take economics; it is very hard to find two economists who agree with each other on any economic issue. Even certain parts of the life sciences are questioned by some as to whether they deserve to be called science. Then there are some sciences that are hardly experimental—with astronomy on one side and paleontology at the other end.

Apparently, there is a great deal of disagreement as to what science stands for. Some say it is a systematic enterprise that builds and organizes knowledge in the form of testable explanations and predictions. What all sciences seem to have in common, though, is that they are about material things and issues that can be dissected, measured, counted, and quantified. In general, all sciences are empirical, but not necessarily experimental. They strive for empirical evidence—evidence acquired by means of the senses, particularly by observation and often also by experimentation. Let's leave it at that.

a. Inductive Reasoning

How do scientists develop scientific theories and hypotheses? The classical view is called inductivism, which is the traditional model of scientific method explained in the 17th century by Francis Bacon (not to be confused with Roger Bacon). According to the Baconian model, a scientist observes nature, then tentatively poses a modest axiom to generalize an observed pattern, then confirms it by repeated observations, next ventures a modestly broader axiom, and finally confirms this as well by adding more and more observations. This is called inductive reasoning.

In essence, inductivism is a way of building theories up through induction—that is, "from the bottom up," from case to case, from observation to observation. It is basically a form of "generalizing induction," which takes us from a general statement about *some* instances to a universal statement about *all* instances. One starts with singular statements about events or instances, and then by adding more and more instances, one comes closer and closer to a universal statement. After having seen many white swans, for instance, one concludes all swans are white. After having seen several times that iron expands by heating, one concludes that all iron does so. However, inductive reasoning is always provisional as we have seen, for it is never safe in a logical sense (see 1.b).

Besides, there is a more general problem with inductive reasoning. The fact that induction has worked in the past does not indicate that it will work in the future. For this reason, it is difficult to justify induction itself without using some form of inductive reasoning. Defending inductive reasoning based on the fact that it has worked well so far is itself a form of inductive reasoning, and therefore makes for a circular argument (see 1.b). In short, science understood as an inductive enterprise cannot be proven inductively by using empirical evidence, and thus science's way of inductive reasoning cannot be proven scientifically. Yet, scientists often do use inductive reasoning.

The classical "heroes" of induction and inductivism are Francis Bacon and John Stuart Mill. The former believed he had found a method stripped of all philosophical fancies. Mill actually went further and believed he could offer us an explicit set of clean and safe inductive rules which would help us in a "mechanical" way to seek and find causes—"from the bottom up," so to speak. The first of Mill's rules, for instance, tells us exactly how to find the cause of something. Its recipe is as follows: look for all the circumstances preceding some phenomenon (Y) and find out which circumstance in particular (X) occurs every time the phenomenon takes place. When we find that particular circumstance, we have demonstrated by induction that in the many cases studied, there is one particular circumstance which is the *cause* of the phenomenon in question in all the cases studied. Thus, we would end up with a universal statement saying that circumstance X is the cause of phenomenon Y in *all* cases. If a certain sickness, for instance, occurs in human beings who all carry a certain type of bacteria, we must assume that it is this kind of bacteria that causes the sickness.

However, some have argued there are many problems with a simplistic approach like this. To begin with, Mill's rules cannot be applied as crudely and mechanically as he suggested. After all, many things can go wrong when applying his rules. First of all, we have to be aware of the old saying "After this and yet not because of this." Sunrise may be after cockcrow, but it is not caused by cockcrow. In a similar way, the sickness in question may occur after a bacterial infection, but without being caused by it. Then there is the problem that the actual cause of the sickness may be completely different from the one we had come up with—for example, it could be a viral infection that only has a better chance of developing after a certain bacterial infection. And finally, there is the problem that there could be more than one cause involved. A poor immunity system, for example, may add to the chances of a bacterial or viral infection.

This leads us to a more general and more basic problem regarding generalizing induction. Through induction, we strive for "more and more cases of the same," but the question is: the same of what? The act of generalizing is based on the fact that objects and events are similar and look alike in certain respects—e.g. "being infectious," "being toxic," or "being genetic"—but this similarity is not visible until we know already what it is that "similar" cases have in common, which is only possible if we have the proper concepts available (see 1.a). Using concepts is somehow like cutting with a knife in the world around us: some are similar in a certain respect, others are not similar in that respect, so some entities should be separated, others taken together. We need to identify first what is relevant to our problem, because similarity cannot be established until it has been identified in a word, or actually in a concept. Therefore, we cannot mechanically infer from a few similar cases to all similar cases until their similarity has been conceptualized first. That sounds like a chicken-or-egg problem. Since things can be "alike" in many, many ways, we need a unifying concept of similarity first *before* we can classify and categorize things as being similar. Before we can "notice" a carnivore, for example, we need the "notion" of a carnivore to begin with. Without that notion, we cannot see that dogs and cats are "the same," but cows and horses are "different" from them.

In cases like these, the similarity stands or falls with concepts such as "carnivore," "infection," "toxicity," and "gene." Without cognition there is no re-cognition. Hence, there is always a conceptual leap involved. Take our case again of a sickness caused by bacterial infections. "Infection" is a similarity between these cases that no one could have "seen" before someone came up with the idea or hypothesis of a bacterial infection. Before Robert Koch and Louis Pasteur had published their experiments, no one would ever have thought human sickness could be caused by bacteria. Actually, the problem is that infinitely many factors may qualify as the potential cause of a certain phenomenon. Mill's rules of induction only work when we have before us *all* and *only* the facts relevant to the solution of our problem. But that is quite an assumption; most of the time we do not!

The following example may clarify this in a witty way. Imagine, you want to find out whether the headache you developed is caused by "gin on the rocks," or by "whisky on the rocks," or perhaps by "rum on the rocks." According to Mill's rules, you should extensively experiment with these three drinks, and then come to the conclusion that your headache is caused by ice cubes, because that is what all these drinks have in common. This conclusion seems quite reasonable, until you come to know of the more-embracing concept of "alcohol"—being a generic term for gin, whisky, and rum combined. Similarity is hard to be treated in a purely inductive way, for it requires a concept of what the underlying similarity is. Induction is based on "more and more cases of the same," but the question is always: the same of what?

b. Deductive Reasoning

In order to arrive at a new concept, a mental leap is needed that makes you see a particular similarity you could not see before. No kind of inductive rule can do this for you. Searching is a matter of imagination rather than calculation. In the search phase of scientific research there is more need of provisional ideas than of logical tools. This explains why no one saw the similarity between falling apples and orbiting planets before Isaac Newton had made the connection; and it took him a while too.

The problem we have here is probably best expressed by the good old philosopher Plato, although in a slightly different context, when he said: "How would you search for what is unknown to you?" Plato noticed a seeming paradox here: we are in search of something "unknown"—otherwise we would not need to search anymore—and yet it must be "known" at the same time—otherwise we would not know what to search for, or would not even know if we had found what we were searching for. This is the reason why we need concepts and hypotheses in science, as those can open our eyes for similarities we would not have been able to see without them. Concepts help us search; they act like searchlights.

Reasoning from observation to observation assumes that observations are clear-cut, preset elements underlying scientific knowledge and explanation. Well, this assumption must be seriously questioned. Karl Popper used to say that the command "Observe!" does not make any sense, since no one would know *what* to observe. His point is that scientific theories just do not and cannot spontaneously emerge from observation. We do not "have" observations—like we do have sensorial experiences—but we "make" observations by using our intellect. Inductivism makes it look like we can simply observe case after case and then see certain similarities. But that is hard to defend, as we found out.

Philosophical giants such as Aristotle and Aquinas would put it this way: all we know about the world comes through our senses, but this is then processed by the *intellect* that extracts from sensory experiences that which is intelligible. This is the reason why a camera cannot make observations. Cameras do not observe but they record. A surveillance camera, for instance, automatically records every single detail because it does not know what to observe in particular. It is for that reason that cameras cannot replace scientists—they may help them but cannot replace them.

The problem with any kind of images or pictures is that they do not show us observations until we give some *interpretation* to the things and events we see on the picture. It is thanks to our intellect that we can create mental concepts which transform "things" of the world into "objects" of knowledge, as we said earlier. Concepts are the "search lights" that change experiences into observations, thus enabling humans to see with their "mental eyes" what no physical eyes could ever see before. To be sure, all we know about the world does come through our physical senses, but this is then processed by the immaterial intellect that extracts from sensory experiences that which is intelligible in conceptual terms.

What could be concluded from this? It is highly unlikely that there are simple "rules of induction" by which hypotheses and theories can be mechanically generated from empirical data—let alone from so-called observations. Logic provides us with formal means that allow us to check an argument afterwards. The rules of logic are not rules of discovery but at best rules of validation. Logic does not allow us to detect statements before the event, but only to check them after the event and then provide them with a seal of approval, if possible. Hence, most philosophers would agree there is hardly any useful logic of discovery—and certainly not in an inductive way.

What would be the solution then, if we cannot build up theories by going from observation to observation in an inductive way? We could start at the other end, at a higher level where concepts, hypotheses, and theories reside. This makes most philosophers of science maintain that scientific hypotheses are "happy guesses," which are not derived or discovered but are invented first by some scientist. They guide us as to where and what to search. It is through deduction that we derive implications that can next be tested in the field or in the lab. Research is first of all a matter of asking the right questions—by means of new concepts, models, hypotheses, and theories. There is no such thing as seeing-in-a-neutral-way, or observing-without-expectation. The best way to search is to have an idea of what you are looking for; the idea may be wrong, but you cannot just search "blindly." The search phase thrives on ideas; without ideas in the search phase, science would be blind.

Examples of this approach can be found anywhere in the natural sciences. Take, for instance, the simple case of how William Harvey discovered the principle of a closed blood circulation. He came up with a novel idea, not discovered but invented. Harvey never saw the connecting blood capillaries needed for a closed circulation system. Instead Harvey came up with a concept, a hypothesis, and a model. We do not know what exactly gave him the idea of a closed blood circulation system. Was it the thought of an outlet needed for a pumped inflow, or rather Aristotle's idea of perfect circular motion, or perhaps the developing technology of pumps? Whatever it was that guided him, Harvey hypothesized two one-way circulations controlled by a heart pump—one between heart and lungs, and one between heart and the rest of the body. Obviously, not the capillaries showed him the circulation of blood—for he had no way of seeing them at the time—but it was the other way around: the very theory of a closed blood circulation would make the vessels visible when better microscopes became available. Harvey's new theory was initially one more of invention than discovery, but it was on its way to becoming a discovery.

In science, discoveries typically start as inventions—usually called hypotheses based on new concepts. However, not all inventions lead to discoveries. To use an analogy, the person who invented "Atlantis" did not discover Atlantis; it remains a legendary island until further notice. The same in science: most inventions do not make it to the stage of discoveries. Yet some scientists think they have made a discovery when all they have in mind is an invention, a hypothesis. However, a hypothesis is only an invention in the mind until it has been proven to be a discovery in reality. The Nobel laureate Peter Medawar's wise advice to a (young) scientist is that "the intensity of the conviction that a hypothesis is true has no bearing on whether it is true or not."

For this reason, a rigorous test is needed as to whether the hypothesis holds after we derive test implications from it. Karl Popper put it this way: "Every 'good' scientific theory ... *forbids* certain things to happen." This rule is based on a deductive, logically valid way of reasoning: if X is true then Y is true; well, Y is *not* true; therefore X *must* be false. Popper made falsifiability or refutability a requirement for scientific theories. Albert Einstein said something similar: "No amount of experimentation can ever prove me right; a single experiment can prove me wrong." Hence, scientists should always be ready to take "no" for an answer if falsifying evidence points that way (but there is more to it, of course). Falsification is basically a deductive way of reasoning: if we find one black swan, a previous inductive conclusion stating that all swans are white has been deductively and conclusively falsified.

Seen this way, scientific research is a process leading from hypotheses to test implications, followed by confirming or falsifying observations. Obviously, reason and intellect are essential for science. Observation is seen as a "theory-laden" (or "concept-laden") phenomenon that does not originate from "barren facts at the bottom" but from "reason and intellect at the top." From here it is only a small step to what has become known as the Duhem-Quine thesis, which states that hypotheses are not tested in isolation but always as part of whole bodies of interconnected theories. So there might be several reasons why we may encounter falsification, given the fact that there are many other assumptions involved. Pure reasoning, utterly free from any presuppositions, is arguably an illusion. To put it in more general terms, a science free from any assumptions simply does not exist.

Besides, we are talking here in rather idealistic terms, as if everything in science is done in a purely rational way. But reason is not the only "gold" that "blinks" in science. There are also "irrational" forces that drive science: media coverage, prestige, funding, competition, etc. Although science has always attracted many who have a real passion for the truth, nowadays science has become more of a career issue. Careers attract careerists. Scientists depend on a good reputation to receive ongoing support and funding, and a good reputation relies largely on the publication of high-profile scientific papers—"publish or perish." Clearly, this may sometimes motivate fame-hungry scientists to fabricate results. Since results are often difficult to reproduce accurately, this means that even if scientists do forge their data, they can expect to get away with it. Scientists may easily forget that they are made of the same crooked timber as the rest of humanity, which comes with incompetence, fraud, selfishness, immorality, and prejudice—all of which are the effect of Original Sin, of course.

c. The Problem of Causality

In this context, we should also discuss how scientists deal with the issue of causality in science. Scientists assume there is some kind of order in this Universe, based on the rule that says, "Like causes produce like effects." This is a vital, major rule in science. If there were no order in the Universe, it would make no sense to search for laws in physics, chemistry, the life sciences, or the social sciences. Only if there is "law and order" in nature are scientists able to explain and predict—which would be impossible in a world of disorder and irregularity. It is only because we "know" that like causes produce like effects that we are able to explain and predict in science.

The idea that like causes produce like effects is a universal principle. It is important not to confuse universal principles in metaphysics with general statements in science such as the general statement "All iron expands with heat." The latter are confirmed by testing more and more instances of iron under various temperature conditions; such cases are examples of generalization. In contrast, universal principles such as "All expanding of iron has a *cause*" are true, independently of any particular cases; their truth does not increase by testing more and more instances, because their truth does not depend on generalization but is based on a universal principle.

The issue of causality has been hotly debated in the philosophy of science. Let us skip that debate and just mention one particular aspect of it. Some scientists consider the real cause of something as a *sufficient* condition, in whose presence the effect is bound to occur. This usually leads to a series of conditions that, when taken together, are sufficient for the intended effect. But there is another, more common way of looking at causes in science—namely, as *necessary* conditions. Usually, scientists slim the cause of something down to *one* of the antecedent conditions, to the exclusion of other conditions. This means that scientists tend to select one, or at most a few, conditions as "the" cause of a certain phenomenon. In this view, causes are seen as "abnormal" conditions; they are not complete sets of causal factors, but factors that "make the difference." All the other conditions are then called "background conditions," which are not considered the focus of investigation.

Take, for instance, the causes of embryonic development. Scientists who call themselves geneticists usually take genetic factors as "the" cause of development, for it is these factors that create specific differences between organisms. This is not a denial of non-genetic factors, such as food or oxygen, which are also necessary conditions in development. However, in most cases these latter factors do not cause a genetic difference between organisms; therefore, geneticists consider them merely as background conditions. Every explanation comes with its own background conditions; they are the necessary conditions which can be left unspecified, left out for the sake of simplicity. In other words, scientific explanations are always piecemeal and selective.

But if that is true—that is, if a scientific explanation can be focused on a specific condition, while leaving background conditions untouched—then any phenomenon can be explained with reference to various causes. Because causal explanations can differ in their frame of reference, it is possible to look at certain phenomena from different angles and thus lead to different causes. Mating behavior, for instance, is a phenomenon-in-general which has several causes-in-specific. An ecologist may point to certain seasonal factors that cause particular physiological changes in the organism. The causes mentioned by an endocrinologist would probably be hormones, whereas a geneticist would more likely speak in terms of certain genes carrying the hereditary code for mating behavior. And last but not least, an evolutionist may look for causes located in a long evolutionary process. The question as to which causes are relevant just depends on the context a particular scientist is speaking of. In other words, each explanation depends on how you "look at it." That is one of the reasons why scientific explanations are never exhaustive—there is always "another way of looking at it."

No matter how divergent scientific explanations can be, what they all have in common is the assumption of "Like causes produce like effects." Causality is the solid basis of the scientific enterprise. However, this seemingly solid basis was eaten away by the "skeptic" approach of some philosophers, in particular the philosopher David Hume. He stressed that generalizing induction—that is, unrestricted generalization from some particular instances to all instances, by stating a universal law (see 8.a)—is basically illogical. His reason for stating this was that humans observe only sequences of sensory events, not something like cause and effect. According to Hume, we do not actually experience the necessary causal connection between events—we only observe a repeated conjunction between two events. Therefore, Hume argued that the "mechanism" of causality is merely a kind of illusion produced by habit or custom. We simply imagine causality. In his own words, "From causes which appear similar we *expect* similar effects."

This stand made Hume one of the first skeptic philosophers, who questioned the very idea of causality— actually of objective truth in general. He argued that all connections we observe in life are nothing but constant conjunctions in our minds based on generalizing induction. Therefore, our perceptions of them never give us insight into the modus operandi of the connection. So he declared causal connections to be mere "metaphysical" inventions, based on an illusion. As a consequence, causal connections in themselves are ultimately subjective phenomena on Hume's view.

Many have criticized Hume's analysis ever since. First of all, his analysis would erase the important scientific distinction between causality and correlation; they would both be reduced to a series of mere subjective associations, conjunctions, or generalizations. In contrast, scientists always want to make sure that causality is not just a matter of correlation; there certainly is, for instance, a correlation between wind velocity and windmill activity, but it is the wind that causes windmill activity, not the other way around. Hume was right, we do not see causation in the same way in which we see colors and shapes and motion. But that does not mean we don't *experience* causation at all. To reduce causation to a habitual connection in the mind does not do justice to our actual experience. When we hear the cock crow before dawn every morning, it never occurs to us that the cock's crowing is causing the sun to rise. Apparently, we do not equate causation with correlation. That's why we always question correlations as to whether they are based on causal relations.

Another problem of Hume's approach is his dubious assumption that cause and effect are rooted in a relationship between *events*. Instead, causality is based on the identity of acting *things*. The actions an entity can take are determined by what that entity is. On this latter view, when one billiard ball strikes another, it sends it rolling because of the nature of the balls and their surroundings, not just antecedent events. When we know that billiard balls are solid and when we see one ball moving towards another, then certain effects are quite impossible. The moving ball cannot, for example, just pass through the second ball and come out the other side continuing at the same speed; nor can the first ball stop at exactly the same place as the second ball; nor can one of the balls suddenly vanish, and so on and so forth. The qualities of the balls determine the kind of effect that the impulse of the first ball will have on the second.

Third, although we do know the world through sensations or sense impressions, many would counter these are just the means that give us access to reality. There is a way things are, independent of how they may be apprehended.

The philosopher John Haldane put it this way, "One only knows about cats and dogs through sensations, but they are not themselves sensations, any more than the players in a televised football game are color patterns on a flat screen." Knowledge does rest on sensation, but this does not mean it is confined to it.

If we were to follow Hume's philosophy, we would end up with what the late physicist and historian of science Fr. Stanley Jaki calls "bricks without mortar." Jaki says about Hume's sensations, "the bricks he used for construction were sensory impressions. Merely stacking bricks together never produces an edifice, let alone an edifice that is supposed to be the reasoned edifice of knowledge." In other words, we need a different philosophy—one that does not treat the "law of causality" as a general statement that requires more and more cases to become validated in an inductive way, but rather as a universal principle that is true independently of any particular cases because it is rooted in the identity of things. It is St. Thomas again who offers us this remedy. In the words of Stanley Jaki, "for Aquinas it is natural for man to be in a cognitive unity with nature"—whereas Hume leaves us in a cognitive desert.

In other words, science cannot explain *causality* itself but must assume it for its explanations. It is not an intra- but extra-scientific notion; it is in fact a proto-scientific notion that must come first before science can even get off the ground. It is a philosophical notion, not a scientific notion. It is a "prerequisite" for scientific knowledge, actually for any kind of knowledge. It is not an *a priori* form of thought but a *given* in reality, "engraved" in the structure of the Universe. It is a given that enables intelligibility, allowing us to grasp reality by using reason and intellect.

No wonder then, science can never prove there is order in this Universe, but instead must *assume* it as a universal principle before it can prove anything else. When John Stuart Mill said, "It is a law that every event depends on some law," he never wondered where that law itself then came from (other than from himself). As Dimitri Mendeleev, who discovered the Periodic Table of Elements, put it, "It is the function of science to discover the existence of a general reign of order in nature and to find the causes governing this order."

Even the deductive tool of falsification, which we mentioned before, is essentially based on this very assumption of order, for the fact that scientific evidence can refute a scientific hypothesis is only possible if there is in fact causality, order, and lawfulness in this Universe to begin with. Interestingly enough, the word "cosmos" in Greek means "order." Science can explain things by using laws, but it certainly cannot explain the very existence of those laws. Without "law and order" in nature, there simply could not be any falsifying evidence. When we do find falsifying evidence, we do not take such a finding as proof that the Universe is not orderly, but instead as an indication that there is something wrong with the specific order we had conjectured up in our minds.

Apparently, falsification itself is based on order and cannot be falsified by disorder. Hence, counter-evidence does allow us to falsify theories, but not the principle of falsification itself. In utter amazement, Albert Einstein once wrote in one of his letters, "But surely, a priori, one should expect the world to be chaotic, not to be grasped by thought in any way." Einstein was enough of a philosopher to realize the importance of a given order, one of the main pillars of science. Indeed, there is a vital link between order and causality. It is obvious, science needs reason to reach results. But there must also be "something" in reality that makes this order in the Universe possible. Perhaps this "something" found in reality could open the door for Faith.

Gerard M. Verschuuren

9. Science and Faith

Given the impressive track record science has developed in the course of four centuries, we might get the false impression science can practically explain everything. This impression might make us wonder if there would still be any space left for faith and religion. The answer to this question depends on how we assess science. Recently, many people have come to glorify science as the only legitimate way of finding truth. Limiting reason to science, and limiting truth to scientifically verified facts might easily close the door for any facts and truths about God, about morality, or about the meaning of life.

Once reason is limited to scientific reasoning, then reason knows nothing about God, can settle nothing about morals, and knows nothing of life's meaning. In fact, the reduction of reason to science has left multitudes of people without any religious, moral, or spiritual truths and beliefs. No wonder Pope Benedict XVI was adamant when he rejected the tendency to "exclude the question of God" from reason.

a. Against Scientism

To equate reasoning with scientific reasoning and to identify reason with the way scientists use reason is a position commonly called *scientism*. Supporters of scientism claim that science provides the one and only valid way of finding truth. They pretend that all our questions have a scientific answer phrased in terms of particles, quantities, and equations. They maintain that there is no other point of view than the "scientific" world-view. They believe there is no corner of the Universe, no dimension of reality, no feature of human existence beyond science's reach. In other words, they have a dogmatic, unshakable belief in the omni-competence of science. It is a creed that makes for a semi-religion, based on a strong "faith" in the power of science. In that sense, scientism may sound very compelling, but reason gives us many reasons why we should challenge what scientism claims.

A first reason for questioning the viewpoint of scientism is a very simple objection: those who defend scientism seem to be unaware of the fact that scientism itself does not follow its own rule. How could science ever prove all by itself that science is the only way of finding truth? There is no experiment that could do the trick. Science cannot pull itself up by its own bootstraps—any more than an electric generator is able to run on its own power. One cannot talk *about* science without stepping *outside* science. Well, that is exactly what scientism does: it steps outside science to claim that there is nothing outside science and that there is no other point of view—which does not seem to be a very scientific move. Whatever you neglect you cannot just reject.

Consequently, the truth of the statement "no statements are true unless they can be proven scientifically" cannot itself be proven scientifically. It is not a scientific discovery but at best a philosophical or metaphysical viewpoint—and a poor one at that. It declares everything outside science as a despicable form of metaphysics, in defiance of the fact that all those who reject metaphysics are in fact committing their own version of metaphysics. Scientism rejects any religious faith and replaces it with its own "faith." This makes scientism a totalitarian ideology, for it allows no room for anything but itself.

A second reason for rejecting scientism is that a method as successful as the one that science provides does not disqualify any other methods. A blood test, for instance, is an excellent method to assess a person's health. But there are many other reliable methods, such as X-rays, MRIs, etc., depending on what we are trying to assess. But a blood test on its own cannot be used to prove that a blood test is the best and only method there is. Yet, that is somehow similar to what scientism does; it steps outside science and then claims, in an unscientific way, that science has the only legitimate method that offers us the only reliable view on the world. First scientism declares one particular method, science, as far superior and then claims that this disqualifies any other methods. It makes for megalomania and turns science into a know-all and cure-all.

The late University of California at Berkeley philosopher of science Paul Feyerabend, for instance, comes to the opposite conclusion when he says that "science should be taught as one view among many and not as the one and only road to truth and reality." Even the "positivistic" philosopher Gilbert Ryle expressed a similar view: "[T]he nuclear physicist, the theologian, the historian, the lyric poet and the man in the street produce very different, yet compatible and even complementary pictures of one and the same 'world.'" Science provides only one of these views.

The astonishing successes of science have not been gained by answering every kind of question, but precisely by refusing to do so. One could even agree with the late Nobel Laureate and biologist Konrad Lorenz that a scientist "knows more and more about less and less and finally knows everything about nothing."

A third argument against scientism is that scientific knowledge does not even qualify as a superior form of knowledge; it may be more easily testable than other kinds, but it is also very restricted and therefore requires additional forms of knowledge. Mathematical knowledge, for instance, is the most secure form of knowledge but it is basically about nothing. Other kinds of knowledge may arguably be more significant but that also makes them less secure. Consider the analogy used by the philosopher Edward Feser: A metal detector is a perfect tool to locate metals, but that does not mean there is nothing more to this world than metals.

Those who protest that this analogy is no good, on the grounds that metal detectors detect only part of reality while physics detects the whole of it are simply begging the question again, for whether physics really does describe the whole of reality is precisely what is at issue. An instrument can only detect what it is designed to detect. And that is exactly where scientism goes wrong: instead of letting reality determine which techniques are appropriate for which parts of reality, scientism lets its favorite technique dictate what is considered "real" in life—in denial of the fact that science has purchased success at the cost of limiting its ambition.

To best characterize this restricted attitude, an image used by the late psychologist Abraham Maslow might be helpful: If you only have a hammer, every problem begins to look like a nail. So instead of idolizing our "scientific hammer," we should acknowledge that not everything is a "nail." Admittedly, it is true that if science does not go to its limits, it is a failure, but it is equally true that, as soon as science oversteps its limits, it becomes arrogant—a know-it-all. There is no way we can prove that the scientific method is the only way to prove anything, for we cannot use the scientific method to prove that the scientific method is the only way to prove anything. Using the scientific method to assess the scientific method is a form of circular reasoning (see 1.b). The late philosopher Ralph Barton Perry expressed this as follows: "A certain type of method is accredited by its applicability to a certain type of fact; and this type of fact, in turn, is accredited by its lending itself to a certain type of method."

A fourth argument against scientism is that science is about material things, yet it requires immaterial things such as logic and mathematics to do its job. G. K. Chesterton liked to ask his readers, "Why should not good logic be as misleading as bad logic? They are both movements in the brain of a bewildered ape?" Logic and mathematics are not physical and therefore not testable by the natural sciences—and yet they cannot be rejected by science. In fact, science heavily relies on logic and mathematics to interpret the data that scientific observation and experimentation provide. Logic and reason are perfect examples of the kinds of immaterial phenomena that we all know exist, but naturalistic science cannot measure, analyze, or account for. Yet, these immaterial things are true and demonstrable, even though they are beyond scientific observation.

Ironically, scientism itself is one of those immaterial things. First, scientists decide to limit themselves to what is material and can be dissected, counted, measured, and quantified. From then on, everything that cannot be dissected, measured, counted, or quantified is off-limits for science. But then scientism kicks in and says that there is nothing else in this world than what is material and can be dissected, measured, counted, or quantified. However, this verdict itself is not material and cannot be dissected, counted, measured, or quantified. So it becomes like a boomerang that destroys its own claims.

A fifth reason for rejecting scientism is that no science, not even physics, is able to declare itself a superior form of knowledge. Nevertheless, some scientists have argued, for example, that physics always has the last word in observation, for the observers themselves are physical. But why not say then that psychology always has the last word, because these observers are interesting psychological objects as well? Neither statement makes sense; observers are neither physical nor psychological, but they can indeed be studied from a physical, biological, psychological, or even statistical viewpoint—which is an entirely different matter.

Often scientism results from hyper-specialized training in a narrow field of science coupled with a lack of exposure to other disciplines and methods, in spite of the fact that the findings of science are always partial and fragmentary. There is no science of "all there is." Someday physics may have its much looked-for "Grand Unified Theory" (GUT), but that is not the same as a "Grand Unified Theory of Everything." A theory of *everything* would also have to explain why some people have faith in that theory and some do not. Limiting oneself exclusively to a particular viewpoint such as physics is in itself at best a metaphysical decision. However, to quote Shakespeare, "There are more things in heaven and earth, Horatio, than are dreamt of in your philosophy." One cannot give science the metaphysical power it does not possess.

A sixth argument against scientism is of a historical nature. The first legendary pioneers of science in England were very much aware of the fact that there is more to life than science. When the *Royal Society of London* was founded in 1660, its members explicitly demarcated their area of investigation and realized very clearly that they were going to leave many other domains untouched. In its charter, King Charles II assigned to the fellows of the Society the privilege of enjoying intelligence and knowledge, but with the following important stipulation: "provided in matters of things philosophical, mathematical, and mechanical."

That's how the "division of the estate" was executed; it was this "partition" that led to a division of labor between the natural sciences and other fields of human interest. By accepting a separation, science bought its own territory, but certainly at the expense of inclusiveness; the rest of the "estate" was reserved for others to manage. On the one hand, it gave to scientists all that could "methodically" be solved by dissecting, counting, and measuring. On the other hand, these scientists agreed to keep their hands off of all other domains—education, legislation, justice, ethics, philosophy, and certainly religion.

In spite of all the above objections, scientism is still very much alive, albeit mostly hidden underground. The Dutch physicist Hendrik Casimir—the Casimir effect of quantum-mechanical attraction was named after him—once said, "We have made science our God." Indeed, science has become a semi-religion of which the scientists are the priests. It is a "new faith," replacing religious faith. Science is supposed to explain *everything* but in a much better way than God once did, at least so in the opinion of many scientists. They think they can explain the world now without invoking God. In this line of thought, Stephen Hawking gladly exclaimed, "our goal is a complete understanding of the events around us and of our own existence" (notice that last word). Scientism likes to broadcast, "It's all about science." Well, science may be everywhere nowadays, but science is certainly not all there is. The Encyclical *Fides et Ratio* (88) puts it this way:

> *Another threat to be reckoned with is scientism. This is the philosophical notion which refuses to admit the validity of forms of knowledge other than those of the positive sciences; and it relegates religious, theological, ethical and aesthetic knowledge to the realm of mere fantasy.*

So we must come to the conclusion that there is more to reason than scientific reasoning. Though science is based on reason, it is a truncated version of reason—yet often glorified and sometimes even deified (see 1.c). However, science inevitably breaks down as soon as it reaches its limits. It is confined to secondary causes, to things that can be dissected, counted, measured, and quantified. Everything else is beyond its scope. Even its own presuppositions are beyond its scope. Without the assumption that there is an objectively real world, science would not be possible. Without the assumption that the world is comprehensible, science would not be possible. Without the assumption that our sense perception is reliable, science would not be possible. Without the assumption that our rationality is reliable, science would not be possible. Without the assumption that there is order and uniformity in nature, science would not be possible. Without the assumption that mathematics, logic, and reason are valid tools, science would not be possible. Science is something you need to believe in before you can practice it.

b. Faith as the Cradle of Science

Whereas reason reduced to science blocks religious faith, reason in its fullest sense actually leads us to religious faith. It makes us pose many serious questions: How could there be secondary causes in science without a Primary Cause? How could nature be intelligible if it were not created by an intelligent Creator? How could there be order in this world if there were no orderly Creator? How could there be scientific laws in nature if there were no rational Lawgiver? How could there be design in nature, if there were no intelligent Designer? How could there be human minds, if the Universe were mindless?

We have a choice here when answering these rhetorical questions: we either accept that there is *no* explanation at all for these observations in nature (which is basically irrational)—or we look for a *rational* explanation of all of this. The only rational explanation seems to be that there is indeed an intelligent, rational, orderly, and lawgiving Creator God who made this Universe the way it is. In this case, belief in a Creator God is like "connecting the dots"—although some may connect the dots differently, and others may connect different dots. Belief in God makes the world so much more understandable. C. S. Lewis beautifully summarized this, "I believe in Christianity as I believe that the sun has risen: not only because I see it, but because by it I see everything else."

So we end up with a rather perplexing conclusion: we actually need Faith to explain why reason as used in science does in fact work. Why do we need Faith for this? It is Faith that can explain why there is an almost perfect harmony of thought and being, of rationality and reality. There seems to be some mysterious conformity between the rationality of our minds and the rationality found in the world around us. Somehow the mind seems to be able to capture nature the way it *is*. Hence, there must be an objective source and foundation for knowledge, reason, and rationality, even so and particularly so in science. That source and foundation can be found in Faith—Faith in a personal and rational God who makes the harmony between rationality and reality possible and understandable. One could even make the case that denying or neglecting the existence of God would undermine rationality and thus would eat away the very foundation of science. This gave the late astrophysicist Sir James Jeans reason to say, "[T]he Universe begins to look more like a great thought than a great machine."

One can even find evidence of a Creator God in what some scientists call "anthropic coincidences," which are features that happen to be—just coincidently—exactly what is required for the emergence of life to be possible in this Universe. The laws of science, as we know them at present, contain many fundamental numbers, like the size of the electric charge of the electron and the ratio of the masses of the proton and the electron. Science has shown us that the conditions for life in the Universe can only occur when these universal fundamental physical constants lie within a very narrow range. Therefore, if any of several fundamental constants were only slightly different, the Universe would most likely not be favorable to the establishment and development of matter, astronomical structures, elemental diversity, or life as we understand it. The idea that our Universe is uniquely "fine-tuned" to give rise to life, and even human life, has become better known as the *anthropic principle*, which made some say that the Universe was made specifically for us. No matter how we take this principle—there are many different versions of it—the fact remains that the odds against a Universe like ours appear to be enormous.

Now that the laws of nature as discovered by science receive more and more attention, and now that it has been found they form a single magnificent edifice of great subtlety, harmony, and beauty, Stephen Barr finds reason to declare, "[T]he question of a cosmic designer seems no longer irrelevant, but inescapable." One could certainly take this as "empirical evidence" for the existence of a Creator God. Even Albert Einstein had to acknowledge, "Everyone who is seriously involved in the pursuit of science becomes convinced that a Spirit is manifest in the laws of the Universe—a Spirit vastly superior to that of man." One could also make the case that denying or neglecting the existence of God undermines rationality and thus eats away the very foundation of science itself.

Even though many modern scientists are self-declared agnostics or atheists, a growing number of them is beginning to see the Faith dimension behind reason and science. One of them is the late nuclear physicist and Nobel Laureate Werner Heisenberg who once said: "The first drink from the cup of natural science makes atheistic... But at the bottom of the cup, God is waiting." Interestingly enough, Pope Pius XII had said already in 1951 that "true science discovers God in an ever-increasing degree—as though God were waiting behind every door opened by science." In other words, the unseen can be found in and behind what is seen, even behind what is seen in science. Reason allows us to argue from what is seen to what is unseen.

And then there is Max Planck, who revolutionized physics with his quantum theory. It was his observation that "the greatest naturalists of all times, men like Kepler, Newton, Leibniz, were inspired by profound religiosity." And then he goes on, "For the believer, God is the *beginning*, for the scientist He is the *end* of all reflections." Interestingly enough, Aquinas had said something similar much earlier: "All our knowledge has its origin in sensation. But God is most remote from sensation. So he is not known to us first, but last." Elsewhere Planck says,

> *All matter originates and exists only by virtue of a force which brings the particles of the atom to vibration. I must assume behind this force the existence of a conscious and intelligent mind. This mind is the matrix of all matter.*

The physicist Paul Davies once summarized this well:

> *People take it for granted that the physical world is both ordered and intelligible. The underlying order in nature—the laws of physics—are simply accepted as given, as brute facts. Nobody asks where they came from; at least they do not do so in polite company. However, even the most atheistic scientist accepts as an act of faith that the Universe is not absurd, that there is a rational*

> basis to physical existence manifested as law-like order in nature that is at least partly comprehensible to us. So science can proceed only if the scientist adopts an essentially theological worldview.

Apparently, science in itself is not the problem for religious faith. Reality tells us that there are atheistic scientists as well as religious scientists. Atheistic scientists are no better scientists than religious scientists, nor vice-versa. They both are dedicated scientists who believe in the power of the scientific method. But they differ in one thing: the latter keep an open mind and believe also in the power of religious faith, whereas the former close their mind for anything that cannot be dissected, counted, measured, or quantified. In either case, though, it is not science itself to decide who is right. Such a decision is a matter of "faith." Therefore, it is not science that "kills God or religious faith," but rather particular scientists who do so in a very unscientific way.

Interestingly enough, the history of science shows us that many scientists, through their belief in God, in fact found reason to investigate nature. The achievements of Nicolaus Copernicus, for example, were actually based on his religious belief that nothing was easier for God than to have the earth move, if he so wished. And Johannes Kepler's Christian belief told him God would not tolerate the inaccuracy of circular models of planetary movements in astronomy, so he knew he had to replace circular orbits with elliptical ones. More recently, Fr. George Lemaître spoke about the God of the Big Bang as the "One Who gave us the mind to understand him and to recognize a glimpse of his glory in our Universe which he has so wonderfully adjusted to the mental power with which he has endowed us." Johannes Kepler summarized all of this beautifully,

"The chief aim of all investigations of the external world should be to discover the rational order and harmony which has been imposed on it by God." If the Creator can do whatever he likes, there is only one way to find out what God has actually done: interrogate nature by observation and experiment.

All of this is a matter of "faith and reason" in its original, Catholic sense. One could actually go much further and make the case that science could not have come forth without a belief in God. It is essential to the Judeo-Christian view that the Universe is the creation of a rational Intellect that is capable of being rationally interrogated by all human beings, including the scientists among them. In contrast, nature remains an enigma as long as it is ruled by whimsical deities, chaotic powers, or our own philosophical decrees and regulations. The physicist Fr. Stanley L. Jaki used the phrase "stillbirths of science" in reference to the ancient cultures of Egypt, China, India, Babylon, Greece, and Arabia. Their cyclical worldviews—a "cosmic treadmill" in Jaki's words—prevented the breakthrough of science as a self-sustaining discipline. Jaki claimed that science—as a universal discipline where one discovery leads to another, and through which laws of physics and systems of laws were established—was born of Christianity. In Jaki's own words,

> *Within the biblical world view it was ultimately possible to assume that the heavens and the earth are ruled by the same laws. But it was not possible to do this within the world vision that dominated all other ancient cultures. In all of them the heavens were divine.*

Although Aristotle, for example, did make a few significant discoveries, his classical Greek culture was unable to maintain and nurture further development. The Ancient Greek world conceived of the Universe as a huge organism dominated by a pantheon of deities, and destined to go through endless cycles of birth, death, and rebirth. Aristotle taught that all things had a soul, so he thought that all motion is directed toward what the soul most desires. It was this animistic view of physics that led Aristotle to conclude that if two bodies were dropped from the same height on earth, the one with twice the weight of the other one would fall twice as fast because it had twice the nature and twice the desire to seek its place.

The pagan culture Aristotle lived in obviously had taken its toll. If the world is controlled by the whim of animistic or pantheistic pagan powers, then there would be no real laws of nature to discover. The rejection of the ancient ideas of an eternal, cycling, pantheistic, animistic world had to be refuted before real science could emerge in Christian Europe. Christianity tells us that nature is to be investigated not worshipped. Stanley Jaki again:

> *Within the Greek ambiance it was impossible, in fact it would have been a sacrilege, to assume that the motion of the moon and the fall of an apple were governed by the same law. It was, however, possible for Newton, because he was the beneficiary of the age-old Christian faith.*

Something similar can be said about other non-Christian civilizations. When the first Jesuits went to China, they were amazed at the Asians' lack of progress in their understanding of the world and the heavens. These cultures did contribute talent and ingenuity, but scientific enterprise came to a standstill. In the Muslim world, as another example, leading Muslim mystics such as al-Ashari and al-Ghazzali held that reference to laws of nature was a blasphemy against Allah's omnipotence. Laws of nature would limit "Allah's freedom to act" whenever he wishes to act. Even the non-religious philosopher Bertrand Russell was convinced that Islamic "science," while admirable in many technical ways, was mainly important as a preserver of ancient knowledge and transmitter to medieval Europe. One could add to this that if Muslims did make some scientific discoveries, it was because they had been influenced already by the Christian perception of the world, centuries before Mohammed came along in the 6-7th century AD. And they are still surrounded by Judeo-Christian achievements in science.

c. The Catholic Roots of Science

In light of this, one might argue that all scientists keep living off Judeo-Christian capital, whether they like to admit it or not. They borrow from Christianity what they themselves cannot provide. There is more and more evidence that Christianity furnished the conceptual framework in which science could flourish, so it would be dangerous for scientists to cut off the roots they came from. Just as the Catholic Church patronized the arts, so did she vigorously support scientific research—perhaps not explicitly from the very beginning, but at least from the late Middle Ages on.

Many nowadays still have the false impression that the Middle Ages were "dark" ages that did not have any scientific activities. Nowadays it is common to distinguish the "Dark Ages" (ca 500 – ca 1000) from the "Middle Ages" (ca 1000 – ca 1500). The "Dark Ages" were certainly not "dark" because of the Catholic Church, but rather because of invading vandals. The only reason any science at all made it through these "dark" ages was because of the Catholic Church hiding all her textbooks from the rampaging and pillaging Huns, Vandals, Visigoths, and Vikings. Had it not been for the Catholic Church, all schools of learning would have died during these "Dark Ages."

During the Middle Ages, the positive influence of the Catholic Church would benefit the sciences even more. It is actually amazing how someone like the astronomer Carl Sagan, in one of his books, makes it look as if nothing happened in the natural sciences between 415 AD and 1543 AD. That can only be historical ignorance. It is becoming more and more evident, and has been accepted by a growing contingent of historians, that science was born in the Catholic cradle of the Middle Ages. Just look at following list of some of its pioneer crafters. As early as the 7th century, the English Benedictine monk Bede studied the sea's tidal currents. At the end of the first millennium, Pope Sylvester II had already used advanced instruments of astronomical observation, driven by a passion for understanding the order of the Universe. He also endorsed and promoted study of arithmetic, mathematics, and astronomy. All of these would be important tools for the advances of science.

During the Middle Ages, monasteries of that era were also very active in the study of medicine. As early as 633, the Council of Toledo required the establishment of a school in every diocese, teaching every branch of knowledge, including medicine. Then, around 800, King Charlemagne decreed that each monastery and Cathedral chapter establish a school, and in these schools medicine was commonly taught. It was at one such school that the later Pope Sylvester II taught medicine. Clergy were active at the School of Salerno, the oldest medical school in Western Europe. Famous physicians and medical researchers included the Abbot of Monte Cassino, Bertharius, the Abbot of Reichenau, Walafrid Strabo, and the Bishop of Rennes, Marbodus of Angers. Hildegard of Bingen (1098-1179), a Doctor of the Church, is among the most distinguished of Medieval Catholic women scientists. Hildegard wrote a text on the natural sciences [*Physica*], as well as a text on "Causes and Cures" [*Causae et Curae*].

During this time period, Bishop Robert Grosseteste introduced the scientific method, including the concept of falsification, while the Franciscan friar Roger Bacon established concepts such as hypothesis, experimentation, and verification. In other words, the scientific project, even the scientific method itself, was and is an invention of these Catholic pioneers. Had it not been for the Catholic Church, the Scientific Revolution would most likely never have happened. After all, science did not take root in South America, Africa, the Middle East, or Asia—it took place in Christian Europe. It was during the Middle Ages that the first universities arose. The Middle Ages in Europe were of course Catholic, so these first universities of the world were Catholic universities. They were the hotbed for a period of great technological and scientific advancements, as well as achievements in nearly all other fields.

And more was coming. It is in fact revealing that the "scientific revolution" in the 17th century coincided with the period when Christian belief was at its strongest. It was in God that these scientists found reason to investigate nature and trust their own scientific reasoning. The founder of quantum physics, Max Planck, put it well: "It was not by accident that the greatest thinkers of all ages were deeply religious souls." People who come to mind are Johannes Kepler, Isaac Newton, Blaise Pascal, and later, Fr. Gregor Mendel, Louis Pasteur, Fr. George Lemaître, and so many others. As shown before, science was born in the cradle of the Catholic Church, and could not be born anywhere else—not in China (with its sophisticated society), not in India (with its philosophical schools), not in Arabia (with its advanced mathematics), not in Japan (with its dedicated craftsmen and technologies), but on Judeo-Christian soil.

In the Catholic mindset, the Universe is the creation of a rational Intellect capable of being rationally interrogated. A rational God has made a Universe that we can rely on with our rational minds, made in likeness of God's mind. A created world, by definition, is not divine in itself; it is other than God, and in that very otherness, scientists find their freedom to investigate. Nature is to be investigated not worshipped. The Book of Wisdom (11:20) praises God, "You have arranged all things by measure and number and weight." Hence the only way to find out what the Creator has actually done is to go out and look—which opens the door for scientific exploration. It actually requires the "humility" of scientists to wait for and subject themselves to the outcome of their experiments.

No wonder many scientists have thanked the Catholic Church for this belief. The 20th century physicist Pierre Duhem had to come to the conclusion that "the mechanics and physics of which modern times are justifiably proud [came] from doctrines professed in the heart of the medieval schools." When the mathematician and philosopher Alfred North Whitehead told his Harvard audience in 1925 that modern science was a product of Christianity, they reacted surprised, out of mere ignorance. The nuclear physicist J. Robert Oppenheimer—not a Christian himself—had to acknowledge, "Christianity was needed to give birth to modern science." Philosopher Alvin Plantinga supports this claim: "Modern science was conceived, and born, and flourished in the matrix of Christian theism." Obviously, Christianity furnished the conceptual framework in which science could flourish. Even someone like the physicist Thomas Kuhn, who coined the term "paradigm shift," had to say about Europe— without identifying its Judeo-Christian core, though—"No other place and time has supported that very special community from with scientific productivity comes."

After the Middle Ages, the Catholic Church got even more involved with the sciences, especially through the work of Jesuits. The historian Jonathan Wright mentions the breadth of Jesuit involvement in the sciences. He says about them:

> *[The Jesuits] contributed to the development of pendulum clocks, pantographs, barometers, reflecting telescopes and microscopes, to scientific fields as various as magnetism, optics and electricity. They observed, in some cases before anyone else, the colored bands on Jupiter's surface, the Andromeda nebula and Saturn's rings. They theorized about the circulation of the blood (independently of Harvey), the theoretical possibility of flight, the way the moon effected the tides, and the wave-like nature of light. Star maps of the southern hemisphere, symbolic logic, flood-control measures on the Po and Adige rivers, introducing plus and minus signs into Italian mathematics—all were typical Jesuit achievements, and scientists as influential as Fermat, Huygens, Leibniz and Newton were not alone in counting Jesuits among*

their most prized correspondents.

In the centuries to follow, things would be moving ahead quickly, but still with the continuous support of the Catholic Church. In the words of Bishop Robert Barron of Los Angeles,

> *The great founders of modern science—Copernicus, Galileo, Tycho Brache, Descartes, Pascal, etc.—were formed in church-sponsored universities where they learned their mathematics, astronomy, and physics. Moreover, in those same universities, all of the founders would have imbibed the two fundamentally theological assumptions that made the modern sciences possible, namely, that the world is not divine—and hence can be experimented upon rather than worshiped—and that the world is imbued with intelligibility—and hence can be understood....*
>
> *May I mention just a handful of the literally thousands of Catholic clerics who have made significant contributions to the sciences? Do you know about Fr. Jean Picard, a priest of the seventeenth century, who was the first person to determine the size of the earth to a reasonable degree of accuracy? Do you know about Fr. Giovanni Battista Riccioli, a seventeenth century Jesuit astronomer and the first person to measure the rate of acceleration of a free-falling body? Do you know about Fr. George Searle, a Paulist priest of the early twentieth century who discovered six galaxies? Do you know about Fr. Benedetto Castelli, a Benedictine monk and scientist of the sixteenth century, who was a very good friend and supporter of Galileo? Do you know about Fr. Francesco Grimaldi, a Jesuit priest who discovered the diffraction of light? Do you know about Fr. George Coyne, a contemporary Jesuit priest and astrophysicist, who for many years ran the Vatican Observatory outside of Tucson? Perhaps you know about Fr. Gregor Mendel, the Augustinian monk who virtually invented modern genetics, and about Fr. Teilhard de Chardin, a twentieth century Jesuit priest who wrote extensively on paleontology, and about Fr. Georges Lemaître, the formulator of the Big Bang theory of cosmic origins.*

To sum up this discussion, the creation of the university,

the commitment to reason and rational argument, and the overall spirit of inquiry that characterized medieval intellectual life and culminated in Aquinas' philosophy amounted to what the historian Edward Grant calls "a gift from the Latin Middle Ages to the modern world." The modern world glories in its science which has allowed us to see to the very edge of the Universe, to the beginnings of time, and even to the invisible world that may be the very boundary marker between physics and metaphysics. It is this very gift Thomas Aquinas has given us that may in fact never be widely acknowledged. The evolutionary anthropologist and science writer Loren Eiseley summarizes this well:

> *It is surely one of the curious paradoxes of history that science, which professionally has little to do with faith, owes its origins to an act of faith that the Universe can be rationally interpreted, and that science today is sustained by that assumption.*

When, in 1936, Pope Pius XI re-established the *Pontifical Academy of Sciences* (originally founded in 1603) in order to support serious scientific study within the Catholic Church, he said in his *Motu Proprio,*

> *Science, when it is real cognition, is never in contrast with the truth of the Christian faith. Indeed, as is well known to those who study the history of science, it must be recognized that the Roman Pontiffs and the Catholic Church have always fostered the research of the learned in the experimental field.*

More than 75 years later, in 2013, Pope Francis would take a similar stand in his Apostolic Exhortation *Evangelii Gaudium*:

> *The Church has no wish to hold back the marvelous progress of science. On the contrary, she rejoices and even delights in acknowledging the enormous potential that God has given to the*

> *human mind. Whenever the sciences—rigorously focused on their specific field of inquiry—arrive at a conclusion which reason cannot refute, faith does not contradict it.*

Apparently "religion and science" complement each other as much as faith and reason do. There is no basis for putting these two in a position of conflict against each other. One cannot be without the other. On the one hand, science could never silence religion, for there's no scientific proof that science is the only way to prove things. There is actually more to life than science alone. One cannot just think, one also needs to believe. On the other hand, religion could never silence science, for there is no religious proof that religion is the only way to prove things. There is more to life than faith alone. One cannot just believe, one also needs to think. This insight has been expressed in many ways. As Albert Einstein, a scientific authority, once said, "Science without religion is lame, religion without science is blind." Or as Pope John Paul II, a religious authority, put it, "Science can purify religion from error and superstition. Religion can purify science from idolatry and false absolutes."

Another way of saying this is that there are two "books"—a "Book of Scripture" and a "Book of Nature." The origin of this distinction can be found in these words of St. Augustine: "It is the divine page that you must listen to; it is the book of the Universe that you must observe." This conviction was a belief shared in the past by many other Christian thinkers: from early Apologists and Fathers to St. Basil; from St. Gregory of Nyssa to St. Augustine, from St. Albert the Great to St. Thomas Aquinas, from Roger Bacon to William of Ockham.

How do we read these two "books"? Science knows how to read the "Book of Nature," whereas the Church knows how to read the "Book of Scripture." These two books complement each other, for they have the same Author—a match made in Heaven, so to speak. To set them up against each other creates a false dichotomy. Cardinal Baronius worded it well at the time of Galileo, "The Bible teaches us how to go to heaven, not how the heavens go." In order to find out more about God, we need to read the "Book of Scripture"; to find out more about the Universe, we need to read the "Book of Nature." Scientific, natural truths come from the book of Nature, and religious, supernatural truths come from the Book of Scripture. But they can never be in conflict with each other (see 3.c).

Pope Benedict XVI used the same image when he advised us to see "nature as a book whose author is God in the same way that Scripture has God as its author." But there is a caveat: we should never read the Book of Scripture as if it were the Book of Nature, or vice-versa. Scientific discoveries and research have helped us enormously to get a better and better reading of the Book of Nature. But reading the Book of Scripture does not tell us how the heavens go, nor does reading of the Book of Nature tell us how to go to Heaven. As it turns out, science in itself is incomplete, and religion on its own is insufficient. That's why we need both books together—that is, faith *and* reason, religion *and* science.

In other words, putting the Big Bang against Creation, or evolution against Creation, or randomness against Providence boils down to reading the "Book of Nature" as if it were the "Book of Scripture"—or the other way around.

Doing so creates conflicts that should not be. These two books do not compete with each other, nor can they replace each other. In the words of *Fides et Ratio* (34), "It is the one and the same God who establishes and guarantees the intelligibility and reasonableness of the natural order of things upon which scientists confidently depend." Science needs reason to get results, but it also needs Faith to get started. And religion requires Faith, but it needs science to stay anchored in reality. Thomas Aquinas could not have said it more clearly, "The faith is made ridiculous to the unbeliever when a simple-minded believer asserts as an article of faith that which is demonstrably false." (De Potentia Dei, Q. 4, Art. 1, Ad. 8).

In short, Faith provides answers to questions that would otherwise be unanswerable, and science provides answers to questions Faith alone could never solve. We need them both, without becoming "schizophrenic." Seeing the world from both the perspective of science and the perspective of religion is something the English theoretical physicist and Anglican priest John Polkinghorne describes as seeing the world with "two eyes instead of one." He explains: "Seeing the world with two eyes—having binocular vision—enables me to understand more than I could with either eye on its own."

Gerard M. Verschuuren

10. Index

A

agnosticism 61-64, 72
analogy... 6, 19-20, 54-55, 70, 118, 120, 124, 127, 129, 131-134, 144-145, 222, 237, 240, 252, 266
Anselm 59, 83, 104-106, 148, 217
anthropic coincidences 272
anthropic principle 273
anthropomorphism.. 16-17
apologetics 114, 118
Aquinas 8, 45, 52, 72, 96, 110, 128, 129, 137-139, 156, 157, 160, 176, 178, 203, 209-211, 214, 215, 230, 249, 259, 274, 284, 285, 287
argument
  by analogy 19
  deductive ... 18, 19, 23, 27, 32, 248, 252, 253, 260
  from contingency... 107-109
  from motion.............107
  inductive ... 18-20, 23, 244, 245, 248, 250, 252, 259
  ontological 105, 106
  arguments for the existence of God 53, 106
Aristotle 7, 8, 43, 93, 95, 249, 251, 276, 277
atheism 53, 62, 64, 112, 193
atonement............148-150
Augros, Michael ... 22, 28, 125, 133, 138
Augustine 50, 82-86, 118, 145, 180, 182, 223, 239, 285
Ayala, Francisco 137

B

Bacon, Francis ...244, 245
Bacon, Roger ... 244, 280, 285
Barr, Stephen M 51, 76, 108, 131, 273
Barron, Robert......55, 283
Barth, Karl 59, 65
Beckwith, Francis J. ...225
Benedict XVI ... 6, 63, 82, 149, 165, 191, 210, 232, 263, 286
Bernard of Clairvaux .. 167
Bochenski, Joseph........43
Book of Genesis .. 49, 138, 160, 161
Book of Nature ...285-286

Book of Scripture 285-286
born-again 184

C

Calvin, John 174, 178, 180, 181
canon of the Bible 190
Carlin, David 35
Casimir, Hendrik 270
causality 113, 133, 254-261
Chesterton, G. K. ... 37, 41, 70, 100, 159, 187, 206, 215, 267
circular reasoning . 21, 22, 26, 267
Collins, Francis 224
concept ... 5, 10-15, 20, 45, 70, 75, 76, 111, 114, 143, 144, 170, 182, 190, 204, 206, 209, 210, 239, 246, 247-253, 278, 280, 282
condition
    background 255-256
    sufficient vs. necessary
    255
conscience ... 63, 171, 197, 200-201, 234-241
contingent 45, 48, 108-111, 127, 130, 137-138, 174, 279
Copernicus, Nicolaus .. 94, 275, 283
correspondence theory
.... 93-95

D

Darwin, Charles 16, 25-26

Davies, Paul 274
Dawkins, Richard ... 44, 67
death . 30, 42, 50, 136, 148, 160, 161, 170, 186, 230, 233, 236, 277
deism 151
Descartes, René 28, 43, 104, 283
determinism 24, 25
dogma 29, 78, 117, 143, 144, 147, 184-187, 193
Dostoyevsky, Fyodor . 233, 242
double truth 88-91, 100
Duhem, Pierre 281
Duhem-Quine thesis .. 253

E

Einstein, Albert 95, 123, 228, 239, 252, 260, 261, 273, 285
Eiseley, Loren 284
Enlightenment 30, 151
Epicurus 135
evil . 77, 101, 118-121, 135-138, 139, 149, 155, 158-162, 165, 176, 177, 200, 203, 204, 209, 212, 213, 217, 230, 238, 239
    moral 136, 161, 238
    physical 136, 139, 161

F

faith 5, 6, 8, 29-31, 39-116, 221-242, 263-288
Fall ... 148, 158, 160-163,

170, 186, 237
fallacy 22, 208-210
   naturalistic......208-210, 267
falsification 37, 98, 252, 253, 260, 280
Feser, Edward 266
Feyerabend, Paul 265
Feynman, Richard 67
fideism 58-61, 64, 67-68, 74, 81-4, 101
Fisher, Anthony .. 238-241
Five Ways 106, 110, 111, 114
Flew, Anthony 53
fore-knowledge 128, 129, 182, 183
Franklin, Benjamin 67
free will .. 130, 134-5, 158, 174, 179, 180, 182
Freud, Sigmund 32

G

Gödel, Kurt..................106
Golden Rule 203, 205, 233
Gould, Stephen Jay 25, 26
grace ... 89, 114, 156, 171, 173-184, 189
Grant, Edward............ 284
Groeschel, Benedict 164
Grosseteste, Robert.... 280
Guardini, Romano 114,115

H

Habermas, Jürgen 231
Haldane, J. B. S.....27, 225

Haldane, John 259
Harris, Sam.............66, 67
Hart, David Bentley..... 47, 208
Hawking, Stephen 270
Heisenberg, Werner ...274
Hell 177, 178, 182
heresy 78, 143, 168, 169, 191, 192
Herodotus.....................33
Hildegard of Bingen .. 280
Hippolytus 134, 144
Hume, David ... 135, 208, 256-259
Huxley, Julian 62

I

Ignatius of Loyola........175
immortality... 117, 161, 163
Incarnation 85-86, 117, 141, 143, 147, 148, 151, 163-165
infinite regress.22, 46, 47, 109, 110, 199
intellect .. 5, 9-16, 28, 37, 52, 56, 60, 73, 74, 80, 82, 88, 93, 94, 96, 97, 105, 127, 141, 184, 218, 249, 250, 253, 260, 276, 281
intelligence 9-16, 81, 141, 218, 269
irrationalism............31-32

J

Jaki, Stanley 259, 276-277
Jeans, James...............272

John Paul II .6, 8, 38, 50, 74, 82, 101, 119, 120, 142, 285
Justin Martyr 119, 204

K

Kant, Immanuel 28, 32, 43, 68, 105, 106, 232
Kennedy, John F. ...18, 232
Kepler, Johannes 274, 275, 281
King, Martin Luther 217
Kreeft, Peter 6, 34, 47, 73, 203, 206, 214, 215, 240
Kuhn, Thomas 282
Kuitert, Harry 65

L

Leibniz, Gottfried ..28, 43, 274, 282
Lemaître, George .... .80, 275, 281, 283
Leo XIII 77
Lewis, C. S. ... 26, 37, 124, 133, 159, 177, 204, 213, 225, 272
Lincoln, Abraham 212, 218
Luther, Martin.59, 60, 91, 174, 188, 189

M

Maritain, Jacques 231
Maslow, Abraham 267
materialism 27, 41, 63, 75-78, 99, 125, 126, 158, 226, 227
McInerny, Ralph 110
Medawar, Peter 252
Mendeleev, Dimitri 260
Merleau-Ponty, Maurice 95
Mill, John Stuart 245-248, 260
monotheism ...69, 71, 144, 145
moral blindness .. 211, 238
morality 36, 99, 103, 160, 195-242, 263
mysteries .. 5, 85, 86, 101, 117, 141, 143

N

natural law 204-210, 213-215, 219, 221, 232, 237-239
naturalism . 26, 75-78, 158
naturalistic fallacy 208-209
Newton, Isaac 12, 212, 239, 248, 274, 277, 281, 282
Nielsen, Kai 112
Nietzsche, Friedrich ..230, 231, 233
nihilism 36, 232

O

omnipotence ... 132, 133, 135, 137, 148, 155, 173, 174, 278
omnipresence 122
omniscience . 122, 127, 130

Oppenheimer, J. Robert 282
Original Sin 158, 159-164, 237-239, 254

P

Padre Pio 156
Pascal, Blaise .. 32, 43, 53, 55, 59, 114, 115, 281, 283
Paul, the Apostle .40, 118, 142, 153, 178 (see also St. Paul)
Perry, Ralph Barton ... 267
Pius XI 241, 284
Pius XII 274
Planck, Max 274, 281
Plantinga, Alvin.. 106, 282
Plato 43, 248
Polkinghorne, John C. 58, 80, 113, 287
Popper, Karl 24, 37, 249, 252
positivism 32
preambles to faith 119
predestination 143, 177, 178, 180, 182
premise .13, 17-19, 21, 23-25, 28, 35, 79, 105, 106, 113, 208, 209
Primary Cause 45-50, 54, 90, 108, 110, 111, 113, 121-134, 138, 174, 271
proofs for God's existence 102-112
Protagoras 33

Providence 90, 91, 118, 143, 151-158, 166, 178, 286

R

Rahner, Karl 171
randomness .90, 126, 156-158, 286
rationalism..27-32, 63, 72, 74-78, 81, 99, 101
rationality 6, 8-10, 16, 17, 27, 31, 32, 34-36, 58, 79-82, 98, 101, 103, 149, 232, 271-273
reality ... 9, 29, 32, 41, 47, 63, 77, 79-81, 93-100, 104, 105, 113, 114, 123, 184, 205, 207, 212, 213, 252, 258-261, 264-266, 272, 275, 287
reason 5-39, 48, 50, 56-72, 73-116, 117-193, 195-220, 243-262
redemption 149, 150, 165, 168, 172, 173, 177, 180
reductio ad absurdum .23, 24, 105
Reformation 188
relativism 32-36, 38, 97-101, 215
Revelation 30, 53, 56, 65, 74, 77, 78, 82, 84, 89, 91-93, 102, 111, 114, 117, 118, 120, 139, 142, 146, 163, 166, 170, 185, 186, 193, 207

rights vs. entitlements 232
Rorty, Richard M. 34
Russell, Bertrand . 30, 278
Ryle, Gilbert 37, 265

S

Sagan, Carl 66, 279
salvation 56, 135, 143, 147, 149, 156, 158, 163, 167, 169-184, 186, 187
Sartre, Jean-Paul 132, 133, 230
Sayers, Dorothy........... 187
Schall, James V. 179
scientism 63, 99, 158, 263-270
Shaw, George Bernard .67, 200
signal 11, 13-15
Simon, Michael A. 228
skepticism .32, 36-38, 61, 97, 101
Smith, Janet E. 205
sociobiology .34, 98, 225, 229
Sola Scriptura............ 188
Solzhenitsyn, Aleksandr 232
St. Paul ...54, 58, 102, 143, 172, 179, 184, 188, 192, 205 (see also Paul, the Apostle)
suffering 56, 139, 143, 149, 155, 158, 160-170
superstition 41, 49, 50, 285
Sylvester II 279, 280

symbol 14, 15

T

theism 53, 62, 151, 282
theodicy 118
Thomas Aquinas......... *See* Aquinas
Tillich, Paul................... 44
time . 17, 46, 49, 108, 123-125, 128, 131, 157, 165, 180, 216, 282, 284
transcendence .39, 43, 60, 167
Trinity ...86, 117, 141, 143-146, 148, 190
truth ... 27-29, 33-38, 50, 54, 56, 58, 62, 63, 66, 68-70, 73, 74, 76-79, 82-86, 88-115, 119, 128, 141-143, 146, 150, 185, 186, 191-193, 195, 209, 210, 219, 224, 226, 237, 241, 253, 254, 257, 263-265, 284, 286
Twain, Mark 44, 67

V

values vs. evaluations 216, 237

W

Whitehead, Alfred North 43, 282
Wilson, E. O. 67
Wright, Jonathan 282

Endorsements

"This book is not a moment too soon. One of the signs of our times has to be the displacement of both faith and reason by a tyranny of the emotive. Truth is no longer found at the intersection of faith and reason but is now located in vague, individual sentiment. The way out of this cultural morass is for clear minds and holy hearts to lead the way. Gerard Verschuuren has proven himself to be such a guide in this important book."

— Fr. Joseph M. Gile, S.T.D., Dean of Graduate Studies and Adult and Continuing Education, Newman University, Wichita, KS.

"If you are searching for a Catholic book on the link between philosophy and theology that you can actually understand, look no further. Faith and Reason is a clearly written exposition and defense of man's ability to know God and his creation. Gerard Verschuuren sets forth a truly Catholic appreciation of our place in the Universe: man is a free, rational creature with an eternal destiny. His reasoning power allows him to understand who he is, who God is and to discover that the embrace of God by the act of faith is the fulfillment of our being and of every true and good desire in the human heart."

— Fr. Gerald E. Murray, J.C.D., Pastor of Holy Family Church in New York City, NY. Commentator for religion on EWTN and Fox News.

Gerard M. Verschuuren

About the Author

Gerard M. Verschuuren is a human geneticist who also earned a doctorate in the philosophy of science. He studied and worked at universities in Europe and the United States. Currently semi-retired, he spends most of his time as a writer, speaker, and consultant on the interface of science and religion, faith and reason.

Some of his most recent books are:

- *At the Dawn of Humanity – The First Humans.* (Kettering, OH: Angelico Press, Fall 2018).
- *Darwin's Philosophical Legacy—The Good and the Not-So-Good.* (Lanham, MD: Lexington Books, 2012).
- *God and Evolution?—Science Meets Faith.* (Boston, MA: Pauline Books, 2012).
- *What Makes You Tick?—A New Paradigm for Neuroscience.* (Antioch, CA: Solas Press, 2012).
- *The Destiny of the Universe—In Pursuit of the Great Unknown.* (St. Paul, MN: Paragon House, 2014).
- *It's All in the Genes!—Really?* (Charlestown, SC: CreateSpace, 2014).
- *Five Anti-Catholic Myths—Slavery, Crusades, Inquisition, Galileo, and Holocaust.* (Kettering, OH: Angelico Press, 2015).

- *Life's Journey—A Guide from Conception to Growing Up, Growing Old, and Natural Death.* (Kettering, OH: Angelico Press, 2016).
- *Religion under Siege: The Eclipse of God* (St. Louis, MO: En Route Books and Media, 2017).
- *St. Thomas and Modern Science—A Match Made in Heaven.* (Kettering, OH: Angelico Press, 2016).
- *Matters of Life & Death—A Catholic Guide to the Moral Dilemmas of Our Time.* (Kettering, OH: Angelico Press, 2017).
- *The First Christians*: Keeping the Faith in Times of Trouble (St. Louis, MO: En Route Books and Media, 2017).
- *The Myth of an Anti-Science Church—Galileo, Darwin, Teilhard, Hawking, Dawkins.* (Kettering, OH: Angelico Press, Spring 2018).

For more info:

http://en.wikipedia.org/wiki/Gerard_Verschuuren.

He can be contacted at www.where-do-we-come-from.com.

www.ingramcontent.com/pod-product-compliance
Lightning Source LLC
Chambersburg PA
CBHW060657100426
42735CB00040B/2907